AUTHENTIC READING ASSESSMENT:

●●●●●●●●●●●●●●●

PRACTICES AND POSSIBILITIES

Sheila W. Valencia
University of Washington

Elfrieda H. Hiebert
University of Colorado–Boulder

Peter P. Afflerbach
University of Maryland/
National Reading Research Center

Editors

International Reading Association
Newark, Delaware 19714, United States

The International Reading Association attempts, through its publications, to provide a forum for a wide spectrum of opinions on reading. This policy permits divergent viewpoints without assuming the endorsement of the Association.

Director of Publications Joan M. Irwin
Managing Editor Anne Fullerton
Associate Editor Romayne McElhaney
Assistant Editor Amy Trefsger
Editorial Assistant Janet Parrack
Production Department Manager Iona Sauscermen
Graphic Design Coordinator Boni Nash
Design Consultant Larry Husfelt
Desktop Publishing Supervisor Wendy Mazur
Desktop Publishing Anette Schütz-Ruff
                       Cheryl Strum
                       Richard James
Proofing Florence Pratt
            David Roberts

Cover and interior photos by Laima Druskis
Copyright 1994 by the
International Reading Association, Inc.

Library of Congress Cataloging in Publication Data

Authentic reading assessment: practices and possibilities/Sheila W. Valencia, Elfrieda H. Hiebert, Peter P. Afflerbach, editors
    p.   cm.
    Includes bibliographical references (p.) and index.
    1. Reading—United States—Ability testing—Case studies. 2. Educational tests and measurements—United States—Case studies. 3. Portfolios in education—United States—Case studies. I. Valencia, Sheila W. II. Hiebert, Elfrieda H. III. Afflerbach, Peter P.
LB1050.46.A96   1994   93-11920
428.4'076—dc20   CIP
ISBN 0-87207-765-9

Contents

Foreword

EVEN CASUAL OBSERVERS OF the education landscape recognize the enormous amount of attention currently being given to nontraditional forms of educational assessment. Few education-related publications fail to include an article extolling the virtues of what has become known as "authentic" assessment. While the term has great semantic appeal (after all, why use something artificial when we can have the real thing?), its definition remains nebulous. "Authentic" has almost come to mean "anything that isn't multiple choice," unfortunately encompassing many forms of rather traditional assessment. In their enthusiasm for assessment reform, many proponents seem to have missed the critical point: authenticity in an assessment resides *not* in its response format, but in its content, the underlying constructs it taps, and the correspondence among the assessment, the instruction from which it samples, and the purposes for which the assessment will be used.

Despite the now several years of promises that authenticity is around the corner, there persists a significant void in documented, concrete descriptions of program implementations. Reports from even highly funded and heavily promoted projects continue to be heavy on hype and short on results. This volume takes us a meaningful step forward. The editors uncovered a broad spectrum of projects—in terms of geography, scope, conceptual framework, purposes, politics, funding, and locus of initiative—and, by doing so, help clarify what authentic assessment means and how it can be manifested in classrooms, schools, districts, and states or provinces.

The projects described are all evolving and, as is true of most "works in progress," are full of promise but not yet of concrete outcomes. The authors candidly discuss problems as well as possibilities, failures as well as successes. This sort of evaluation is critical at the early stages of any reform movement. The inclusion of insightful, thoughtful, and provocative reactions of commentators on each chapter further encourages reflection and professional dialogue regarding areas for improvement and avenues for future research.

This dialogue highlights several common threads that run through these projects and offer insight into the strengths and weaknesses of authentic assessment as it is being implemented:

- *Commitment.* Several chapters overflow with the deep commitment of program pioneers, whose personal drive to make a difference is a clear theme of the volume.

- *Context dependence.* Readers will quickly see the enormous effect of locale on each project's acceptance. Probably none of these programs is "exportable" in its current form to other classrooms, schools, or districts.

- *Pilots.* The district-level projects are reported as essentially small-scale pilots. This is a necessary step: mandating such significant and far-reaching assessments on a large-scale basis before the "debugging" process of piloting is unwise and ascientific—if not educational malpractice. Large-scale assessments too often force massive, sudden upheavals without first laying more localized groundwork. Before we plunge into large-scale implementation of assessments, we must test the procedures; we must also investigate and attempt to resolve unaddressed concerns in the areas of score consistency, content generalizability, disparate impact, instructional validity, and, yes, cost effectiveness.

- *Support.* Almost all of these projects have heavy teacher-training components. Although this is certainly desirable, the necessity for such support tells a deeply troubling story about the status of formal training in assessment philosophies and methods. This "incidental in-servicing," while critical to each project's success, cannot overcome years of inattentiveness in formal teacher-training programs to the intimate, inextricable connection between instruction and assessment. Neither can procedures such as teacher-made or -adapted tests, observation, grading, and "performance evaluation" entirely replace commercial or externally mandated tests—if such replacement is determined to be desirable—without first providing preservice and in-service teachers with serious and sustained training in sound assessment practices.

- *Hopes versus results.* While anecdotes and testaments contained herein are numerous and full of promise, substantive documentation of effects on children's cognitive or affective development is still lacking. Research in these areas is much needed, for such results will provide the only compelling justification for these projects.

Readers approaching this book for solutions need read no further: it contains none. Those looking to sample the current state of the art, however, will find the book alternately stimulating, enervating, informative, incomplete, inspiring, and depressing. The chapters, individually and as a whole, add some badly needed meat to the skeleton of authentic assessment. I heartily wish you well in your journey through the practical—and, yes, authentic—issues of implementing meaningful assessment in the "real worlds" depicted in this volume.

It is challenging to tell one's own story; it is especially difficult to do so while the story is still unfolding. To the authors—and to the editors who convinced them to share their evolving stories—we owe a debt of gratitude. All serious students of educational assessment will be rewarded by the willingness of these professionals to offer us their important, authentic works in progress.

Michael D. Beck
Beck Educational and Testing Associates, Inc.
Pleasantville, New York

Contributors

Peter P. Afflerbach
University of Maryland/National
Reading Research Center
College Park, Maryland

Kathryn H. Au
Kamehameha Schools
Honolulu, Hawaii

Teri Bembridge
St. Vital School Division No. 6
Winnipeg, Manitoba, Canada

Robert C. Calfee
Stanford University
Stanford, California

Brian Cambourne
University of Wollongong
Wollongong, New South Wales,
Australia

Gertrude V. Collier
Maryland State Department of
Education
Baltimore, Maryland

Pasquale J. DeVito
Rhode Island Department of
Education
Providence, Rhode Island

Mary W. Garcia
Arizona Department of Education
Phoenix, Arizona

Jan Hancock
University of Western
Sydney–Macarthur
Campbelltown, New South Wales,
Australia

Jane Hansen
University of New Hampshire
Durham, New Hampshire

Elfrieda H. Hiebert
University of Colorado–Boulder
Boulder, Colorado

Barbara A. Kapinus
Council of Chief State School
Officers
Washington, D.C.

Hannah Kruglanski
Maryland State Department of
Education
Baltimore, Maryland

Susan Skawinski Lima
Rhode Island Department of
Education
Providence, Rhode Island

Marjorie Y. Lipson
University of Vermont
Burlington, Vermont

Robert J. Marzano
Mid-Continental Regional
Education Laboratory (MCREL)
Aurora, Colorado

P. David Pearson
University of Illinois at Urbana–
Champaign
Champaign, Illinois

Charles W. Peters
Oakland Schools
Waterford, Michigan

John J. Pikulski
University of Delaware
Newark, Delaware

Nancy A. Place
Bellevue Public Schools
Bellevue, Washington

Ileana Seda
Instituto Tecnológico de Estudios
Superiores de Monterrey
Monterrey, N.L., Mexico

Mary Ann Snider
Rhode Island Department of
Education
Providence, Rhode Island

Jan Turbill
University of Wollongong
Wollongong, New South Wales,
Australia

Sheila W. Valencia
University of Washington
Seattle, Washington

Kathy Verville
Arizona Department of Education
Phoenix, Arizona

Barbara Weiss
California Department of
Education
Sacramento, California

Karen K. Wixson
The University of Michigan
Ann Arbor, Michigan

Kenneth P. Wolf
University of Colorado at Denver
Denver, Colorado

Introduction

ASSESSMENT IS ONE OF THE MOST IMPORTANT AND PRESSING ISSUES facing the literacy community. At every turn, we are hearing and telling others that we must reform assessment if we are going to help students become thoughtful, critical, responsive, and effective readers and writers. Although the current movement for reform is fairly new, interest and motivation within it are high; educators are anxious to find ways to overcome problems associated with traditional assessment practices. Dozens of new assessment initiatives have been implemented in the past several years. Many of these are the result of grassroots efforts at the state/province, school district, or classroom level that have not been shared outside the community in which they were developed. This lack of communication limits the degree to which the assessments can benefit from experiences of others working on similar initiatives; it may result in duplication of effort and, ultimately, little progress in the field as a whole. When communication about these projects does occur, it frequently takes the form of informal conversation about surface features and logistics, rather than the deep, focused discussion that should accompany and enhance new assessment efforts.

For assessment to be effective and feasible, we need descriptions and perspectives: we need to know what the assessment looks like, how it was constructed, the conceptual framework for its development, and its intended purpose. We need to be able to step back to take a critical look at our assessment reform efforts. Without reflection and an understanding of assumptions and processes, we may not design assessments that accomplish their intended goals. It is as necessary to ask "Did the assessment accomplish its intended aim?" as "What does this assessment look like?" *Authentic Reading Assessment: Practices and Possibilities* examines both questions. Its purpose is to share information about new assessment efforts and to foster communication and dialogue about both the products and the processes of development. In Part One we elaborate on various definitions of and perspectives on authentic reading assessment. This section provides a framework and vocabulary for understanding authentic assessment initiatives. Parts two to four describe nine assessment programs that were selected from more than 50 projects in the United States, Canada, and Australia to represent a balance of different types of assessments, geographic regions, and levels at which the information gained from the assessments is used and reported.

We recognize that there are different audiences for different types of information about reading assessment. However, we feel it is important that each audience gains an understanding of the perspectives and methods of the others. Parts two to four of *Authentic Reading Assessment* are intended to highlight the needs of various audiences. Part Two, edited by Sheila Valencia, focuses on the classroom with particular emphasis on how information gathered during instruction is used for assessment and decision-making that contribute to student learning. The classroom assessment projects described do not formally address accountability issues or the reporting of information to other audiences. Part Three, edited by Elfrieda Hiebert, presents assessment projects that have been implemented at the classroom level and used to report to other audiences. The chapters in this section represent examples of ongoing classroom assessments designed to yield information that can be used for programmatic and systemwide student evaluation. Part Four, edited by Peter Afflerbach, addresses large-scale assessment. It includes reports on three reading assessment programs in which large numbers of students take new types of literacy tests or engage in literacy tasks in a fairly standard situation. The chapters in this section have implications for classroom, school, and district personnel, as well as for state/provincial assessment and curriculum leaders. Not only will the form of new large-scale assessments influence curricula and instruction, but the experiences of implementing and conducting these projects will serve as a guide to administrators and classroom teachers as they struggle with their own assessment development, evaluation and scoring, and reporting of information.

The book closes with Part Five's summary of the trends in authentic reading assessment and suggestions regarding future issues. Here we address the accomplishments of *and* the problems facing new assessments so that, as a profession, we will be more likely to contribute to their successful development and implementaion.

The chapters in this volume focus on reading assessment, although in most of the projects, students generate written work as well. We have chosen to highlight the aspects of these cases that focus on constructing meaning from text in written or oral form. Literacy professionals have been making great progress in teaching and assessing writing, but we are still struggling with assessment of reading and the reading process. Therefore, in this volume we focus on reading assessment and integrated reading-writing assessment.

The authors of each chapter have worked directly on the assessment they describe. Their work here is intended to provide readers with a description of each project, including its purpose, conceptual framework, development, and format. Since goals, instruction, and assessment intersect in complex ways and should be tailored to each school, community, or state/province, readers should not expect the chapters to include all the information they would need to replicate the project. Instead, these case studies have been written to provide sufficient information to enable readers to identify projects similar to their own or to inspire them to think about directions for the future.

In addition, the volume offers insights on the projects from two perspectives. The chapter authors offer one—the thoughts and reflections of each project's designers and implementers—and the second comes in the commentaries that follow each chapter. In these, a "chapter respondent" who has dealt with similar issues in the design and implementation of other assessment efforts provides critical analysis, clarification, and insight about each project. These responses are intended to foster discussion by highlighting important aspects and merits of each project as well as raising issues that need to be addressed. Clearly, for successful reform of assessment, such dialogue is critical. We hope this book will encourage you to enter into the exchange.

SWV

EHH

PPA

PART ONE

UNDERSTANDING AUTHENTIC READING ASSESSMENT

CHAPTER 1

Elfrieda H. *Hiebert*
Sheila W. *Valencia*
Peter P. *Afflerbach*

DEFINITIONS

AND

PERSPECTIVES

For TEACHERS, THE TERM "AUTHENTIC ASSESSMENT" does not represent a new concept. Assessment strategies such as informal reading inventories, classroom tests, teacher observations, and evaluation of students' written work have a history longer than that of standardized measures. Teachers have always viewed their ongoing interactions with children as occasions for assessing students' learning processes, abilities, and accomplishments. Sometimes these occasions are documented in written notes—about students' participation in a writing conference, their interactions during literature circle discussions, or their scores on a comprehension quiz, for example. At other times, teachers' notes are mental—they observe responses of particular students and file this information away in memory. Taxpayers, legislators, parents, district administrators, and even students rarely have been privy to the results of these sorts of assessment that happen daily in thousands of classrooms. To these groups, students' accomplishments are represented by scores on standardized tests. Because of the emphasis on accountability and achievement, test scores have gained more and more credence as the sole indicators of students' accomplishments.

Recently, however, numerous reports have documented the negative consequences of overreliance on traditional norm-referenced tests (Andelin & Staff, 1992; Cannell, 1988; Darling-Hammond & Wise, 1985; Linn, Graue, & Sanders, 1990; Smith, 1991). First, there is growing awareness that these types of tests do not capture the higher level literacy abilities needed for participation in the communities and workplaces of the 21st century. Standardized tests have not evolved with our research-based understanding of the reading process, and they are poorly aligned with classroom instruction that reflects this research and promotes the development of higher level thinking and complex literacies. Second, standardized tests have an inappropriate influence on curriculum, instruction, and learning. Teachers look to the content or actual items of tests as concrete indications of what they should teach (Koretz, 1991; Shepard, 1990), and some textbook series have included tests that simulate standardized tests (Pearson & Valencia, 1987; Stallman & Pearson, 1990; Valencia & Pearson, 1987). The net result has been a narrowing of curricula and fragmentation of teaching and learning (Linn, 1985). Third, the overreliance on standardized tests has caused many teachers and students to feel they are passive recipients and targets of assessment rather than active participants and partners in the process. They may receive the results of assessment when these are no longer timely or relevant; results frequently are not meaningful for teachers seeking information on the effectiveness of their instruction or for students seeking feedback on their progress. Finally, dependency on standardized tests has led many policymakers and teachers to discount assessment carried out in the classroom and to rely on a single indicator of accomplishment rather then multiple indicators. The more complex, situated classroom assessments have not been granted the credibility of norm-referenced measures.

As questions about the value of traditional standardized tests have surfaced, attention has turned increasingly to other vehicles for assessment, such as collections of student work, projects, and students' written responses to texts they encounter naturally in class. Policymakers, measurement specialists, and educators alike have taken seriously the need for better assessment and, as a result, we now find ourselves in the midst of a movement to develop what has become known as authentic assessment. Simply stated, authentic assessment efforts try to address the concerns that have been raised about standardized testing. New efforts focus on the assessment of higher level literacy abilities using authentic, or "real life," literacy tasks and actual classroom artifacts and projects as part of the total picture of students' accomplishments. They emphasize the active engagement of teachers and students in the assessment process while acknowledging the different needs of policymakers, the community, and school personnel.

Concepts and Terms

There seem to be as many definitions of authentic assessment as there are people interested in it. Interest surveys, observational checklists, interviews, conference forms, think-aloud protocols, literature logs, observations and analyses of records from projects, cooperative group activities, writing folders...the list of authentic assessment activities is a long one. At first, teachers and reading supervisors may be tempted to jump in and simply implement the assessment activities that sound most interesting. However, unless goals and purposes are kept foremost in educators' minds, authentic assessment will probably have an end no different from standardized tests: the assessment techniques, rather than the philosophy or rationale, will drive the system. The reasons behind the desire to reform assessment must be paramount in designing and implementing authentic assessment systems. One fundamental criticism of standardized tests lies primarily with concern that their context and content fail to capture "authentic" uses of literacy. An activity in which students work individually to select from several choices the right answer to a question based on a passage of several paragraphs has little relation to students' developing use of literacy in schools, communities, and workplaces. In more authentic contexts, literacy involves such things as reading and responding to newspaper articles or editorials, escaping through a novel, finding out about the people of another culture, or using information from a bus schedule or equipment manual. The aim of authentic assessment is to assess many different kinds of literacy abilities in contexts that closely resemble the actual situations in which those abilities are used.

Goals

Attempts to define authentic assessment, then, must begin with an exploration of goals. Attention to our own goals for the children we teach and to district and state frameworks and desired outcomes should precede the creation of measures—and in the more comprehensive and better funded projects (such as the United States' National Assessment of Educational Progress, or NAEP) that has happened. Because teachers' time is scarce and immediate demands for classroom-based assessment are often pressing, defining goals for student learning at school and district levels is sometimes hurried. Without clear definition of goals, however, assessment will be ambiguous in both nature and purpose, and its use may be misguided. Only after goals have been established and clarified can attention turn to the appropriate tasks and contexts for gathering information.

Establishing goals and benchmarks for goals is not an easy task. Different philosophies are represented in the literacy community (see, for example, Edelsky, 1990; McKenna, Robinson, & Miller, 1990), and debates continue about the role of word identification, teaching materials, and instructional strategies. A collaborative effort of the International Reading Association, National Council of Teachers of English, and the Center for the Study of Reading was initiated in 1992 with the aim of setting guidelines for English language arts standards in U.S. schools. While these guidelines are not yet available, examinations of various state reading and writing frameworks, documents such as the *Framework of the 1992 National Assessment of Educational Progress*, and district curriculum guides and textbook-adoption programs suggest substantial agreement among those who teach children to read. At the core of their efforts is a focus on making meaning—including aesthetic and efferent responses—of different kinds of texts in a variety of contexts.

Definitions

Definitions and interpretations of terms used in authentic assessment are probably as numerous as the projects dedicated to developing them. This new vocabulary has generated considerable confusion; explicit definitions of several terms and clarification of others will be useful.

General terms used to describe new assessment practices are the first to consider. One such term is apparent in the title of this volume: authentic assessment. This term is especially appropriate to signify assessment activities that represent literacy behavior of the community and workplace, and that reflect the actual learning and instructional activities of the classroom and out-of-school worlds. While "authentic" may have lost some of its potency through overuse, it is preferable to "alternative," which is sometimes used. The word "alternative" immediately raises the question "Alternative to what?" and sets up an implicit tension and dichotomy that may not be productive.

A second common term, especially among those with backgrounds in measurement and evaluation, is "performance assessment." In performance assessment, students are required to demonstrate their level of competence or knowledge by creating a product or a response. The use of the term began in assessment of content areas such as science, in which students have problems to solve, some of them hands-on (Shavelson, Baxter, & Pine, 1992). Similarly, new methods of writing assessment require performance—the writing of compositions—which is quite different from standardized writing tests in which students are required to recognize features of existing writing. In reading assessment, students have always been asked to read texts, but performance assessment uses longer passages and often requires students to write ideas rather than to select the best of several responses.

Both "authentic assessment" and "performance assessment" are general terms that encompass a wide range of procedures and formats. By "procedures" we mean the processes by which the assessment is administered. These procedures fall along a continuum from more to less traditional. Some may involve a traditional sort of "on-demand" assessment task, for example, in which all students are given a standard set of directions and time limits for completion; the details of these test "rules," however, may be fairly untraditional. Students completing a writing assessment may be provided with a choice of topics or be permitted to choose their own topic, but they might be given specific guidelines about how long they have to write (one hour or three days, perhaps), when they are to work (February 10–12, for example), and the resources they may use (dictionaries, peer conferences, and so on). In reading, they may be given two passages to read on a particular day and have two days to work on their responses. In other instances, students may be given several weeks to produce a project. These types of tasks are typical of large-scale assessments such as those used on the national level (the New Standards Project [Resnick & Resnick, 1992] or the NAEP, for example) or state level in which large numbers of students are assessed and results are often aggregated for reporting to other audiences. Although the content and tasks in this sort of assessment may have changed dramatically, the procedures are simply an extension of the on-demand nature of traditional multiple-choice tests.

In contrast, other authentic assessment efforts use less traditional procedures, relying on ongoing collections of students' work and artifacts. Portfolios, for instance, use the work students produce naturally in daily classroom activities as evidence of students' capabilities. With portfolios, the duration of the assessment is longer, the procedures less standard, and the product less predictable than with on-demand tasks. The terms classroom- or teacher-based assessment also have been used to describe this general type of assessment procedure (Calfee & Hiebert, 1988, 1991). As will become clear from the chapters in this volume, combinations of on-demand and classroom-based assessments are common.

There is also a continuum of different types of student products that can be used in authentic assessment. This ranges from relatively simple student-constructed responses—"fill in the blanks," for example—to much more complex, comprehensive bodies of work collected over time—such as portfolios or research projects. So at one end of this response-format continuum we find short-answer responses (single words or simple sentences) and short paragraphs; these represent a change from asking students to recognize a correct response to asking them to produce their own response.

Further along the continuum are more extended responses (essays, longer writing samples) that often require students to spend several days engaged in planning and carrying out the task. Other types of extended assessment include projects, demonstrations, and experiments, which may require a presentation. According to Resnick and Resnick (1992), projects that represent work done over longer periods than is typically the case with the artifacts in portfolios or the tasks that characterize on-demand assessment should be used as one of the indicators of student accomplishment. Few districts, provinces, or states have implemented this sort of project assessment, but it is likely that this will change as the results of assessment efforts are shared among educators. Assessment of projects easily can be envisioned at the classroom level and, indeed, is already part of many classrooms. Collections of student-authored books or videotapes of plays written and produced by a class exemplify the kinds of projects that happen in classrooms around the world and that could become part of the assessment of students' learning.

At the other end of the response-format continuum are portfolios, which are *collections* of artifacts of students' learning experiences assembled over time (Valencia, 1990). These artifacts represent students' performances in the worlds of classroom and home. One of the distinguishing characteristics of portfolios is student involvement. Most proponents of portfolio assessment suggest that students should play a key role in assembling their portfolios and in evaluating their own work and progress over time. A second characteristic is that portfolios permit evaluation and reflection of both the processes and products of learning because they include early drafts of student work and evidence of learning in its beginning stages. Finally, assessment of work collected over time shifts the focus from a snapshot of student capabilities at a particular moment to an emphasis on growth and progress.

Both procedures and formats for authentic assessment are influenced by the audience for whom information is being gathered, the age and number of students involved, and the literacy goals targeted. There are many more assessment options available today than in the past. It is important to understand which of these, alone or in combination, will best serve a particular set of needs.

The Challenges of Authentic Assessment

Authentic assessment presents many opportunities to literacy educators: the opportunity to assess many different dimensions of literacy, the potential to use classroom-based information, the capacity to involve students in their own evaluation, and the use of multiple measures of students' abilities. At the same time, authentic assessment presents a number of critical challenges. Educators are being asked to assist in the assessment of dimensions of literacy that rarely have been assessed. In addition, the contexts and tasks for assessment—such as observing classroom events or evaluating extended writing—differ from the timed, multiple-choice format of standardized tests and therefore present new puzzles to be solved. Some of these issues are still largely untouched. But, in one way or another, all the projects described in this volume deal with several recurring issues. A review of the solutions devised by the developers of the case studies and the problems that remain is presented in the last chapter; the issues are raised here so readers will have a sense of the challenges the developers faced.

A first challenge involves the tension between assessments that support instruction and those that inform policymakers. As Cole (1988) asserts, teachers need information about specific children so that interaction, instruction, and experiences can be adapted accordingly, while policymakers are concerned with the accomplishments of groups of children. While the differences in the needs of teachers and policymakers should not obscure their shared interest in students' attainment of critical literacy goals, the fact remains that the needs of both groups cannot necessarily be filled by precisely the same instruments.

Using parallel systems of gathering information for instruction and for policy creates a dilemma. The instruments administered for policy purposes typically are given heavier emphasis than the measures gathered by teachers. If the information that teachers gather is not used or valued by anyone other than themselves, teachers are likely to devalue their participation and discount their observations. While it is doubtful that teachers' systems can fulfill all assessment needs, information from classrooms is a critical part of representing accomplishments in higher level literacy abilities and students' proficiencies across time and various contexts. Some of the compromises in approaches to assessment that are necessary may not please both groups equally. The give and take between the groups is apparent in the case studies of this volume.

Another challenge that surrounds reading assessment is how best to capture students' interpretations and responses to text. When the task is exclusively one of responding to existing interpretations, as is the case with standardized silent reading tests, students' ability to generate their own ideas is not valued or measured. Total reliance on open-ended formats, however, may not be the answer because of the demands on written expression of such tasks (Garcia & Pearson, 1991). As readers examine the case studies in this volume they should keep in mind ways of obtaining multiple indicators that will give a more complete picture of students' reading processes and achievements.

The issue of collaboration versus individual performance presents still another challenge. In the typical testing context, children work by themselves. Collaboration among children is regarded as contaminating the results—or, as it is conveyed to children, cheating. In most real-world contexts, however, interpretations of text are discussed and negotiated—a newspaper editorial or report is debated among a group of friends, employees speculate about the implications of a company memo, or a citizen gives the rationale behind his or her interpretation of a form to a taxation agent. The inclusion of assessment tasks in which students can collaborate and cooperate in ways similar to the literacy-related events of community and workplace has been advocated by various research groups (see, for example, Palincsar & Brown, 1986; Slavin, 1983). One approach to this challenge taken in several performance assessments—including those described in chapters 8 and 10 of this volume—has been to integrate components in the assessment that make it more like a typical instructional event or life experience. On the other hand, assessment that includes collaborative activities must address new issues such as evaluation of oral processes, reporting of individual and group scores, and the impact of group interaction on individual interpretation. Providing occasions to discuss the topic prior to reading or to share and listen to interpretations with peers represents a significant departure from the isolated event of a standardized test. However, most performance assessments continue to be based on individual responses.

Another challenge concerns specification of tasks. Issues of text difficulty and text type have been overlooked in many authentic assessment efforts, especially those that fall into the category of portfolio assessment. For example, in *The Primary Language Record* (Barrs, Ellis, Tester, & Thomas, 1988), evaluations can be done on familiar or unknown texts selected by student or teacher. Since low-achieving students often select text that is too difficult or too easy for them (Anderson, Higgins, & Wurster, 1985), evaluations of students' reading that are based almost solely on samples of that reading disregard the issue of automaticity and fluency with increasingly difficult text. Research has suggested that readability formulas may be inappropriate for judging the difficulty of text (Brennan, Bridge, & Winograd, 1986), but it remains clear that some texts are more difficult for students than others (see, for example, Applebee, Langer, & Mullis, 1988). Current methods of attending to genres and text complexity in authentic assessment and possibilities for future directions can be seen in the case studies.

These issues demonstrate the challenges of authentic assessment that confront teachers, teacher educators, measurement and evaluation specialists, and staff in state/provincial and national agencies. Underlying all of them is a fundamental question: Is authentic assessment necessarily better than traditional testing? The intention to design better means of assessing students does not necessarily translate into the successful development of those means. Linn, Baker, and Dunbar (1991) proposed criteria for the evaluation of authentic assessment, many of which are different from the validity and reliability procedures used to evaluate standardized tests. For example, they propose asking "Do the texts and tasks of an assessment truly require higher levels of cognitive complexity?" and "Is the assessment representative of meaningful literacy use?" Other criteria—such as generalizability and fairness—raise issues that have confronted test developers for generations. Does the assessment truly represent the use of literacy in contexts other than that of the assessment? Have precautions been taken to ensure that students' proficiency is fairly evaluated and scored?

Authentic assessment should not be equated with a lack of standards. To the contrary, in authentic assessment the standards are those that truly matter in community and workplace settings. Like the criterion-referenced assessment movement of the 1970s, authentic assessment means that all students can strive to attain these high standards. Unlike the criterion-referenced movement of the 1970s, however, the standards to which all students progress pertain to critical uses of literacy in communities, not to trivial and decontextualized tasks.

Contributing to Progress

Interest in authentic assessment is high. Literacy professionals have an important contribution to make to the design and implementation of these promising new approaches. Numerous challenges remain to be addressed, some of which have been outlined here and some of which have not yet been identified. These issues should not be viewed as roadblocks but as opportunities. They present us with a chance to represent the critical goals of literacy learning more clearly and to move instruction away from a narrow view of literacy dominated by short-paragraph, multiple-choice tests. Educators need to forge ahead and meet these challenges. The reports in this volume represent such efforts by educators working with a new set of questions and possibilities. The underlying reason for their hard work is to represent higher level literacy abilities accurately and completely. As this goal becomes paramount in assessment, the emphasis on developing these abilities in the daily school lives of millions of students will increase as well.

References

Andelin, J.& Staff. (1992). *Testing in American schools: Asking the right questions.* Washington, DC: Congress of the United States, Office of Technology Assessment.

Anderson, R.C., Higgins, D., & Wurster, S.R. (1985). Differences in the free-reading books selected by high, average, and low achievers. *The Reading Teacher, 39,* 326-330.

Applebee, A.N., Langer, J., & Mullis, I.V.S. (1988). *Who reads best? Factors related to reading achievement in grades 3, 7, and 11.* Princeton, NJ: Educational Testing Service.

Barrs, M., Ellis, S., Tester, H., & Thomas, A. (1988). *The primary language record: Handbook for teachers.* Portsmouth, NH: Heinemann.

Brennan, A., Bridge, C., & Winograd, P. (1986). The effects of structural variation on children's recall of basal reader stories. *Reading Research Quarterly, 21,* 91-104.

Calfee, R.C., & Hiebert, E.H. (1988). The teacher's role in using assessment to improve learning. In C.V. Bunderson (Ed.), *Assessment in the service of learning* (pp. 45-61). Princeton, NJ: Educational Testing Service.

Calfee, R.C., & Hiebert, E.H. (1991). Classroom assessment of reading. In R. Barr, M.L. Kamil, P.B. Mosenthal, & P.D. Pearson

(Eds.), *Handbook of reading research: Volume II* (pp. 281-309). White Plains, NY: Longman.

Cannell, J.J. (1988). Nationally normed elementary achievement testing in America's public schools: How all 50 states are above the national average. *Educational Measurement: Issues and Practice,* 7(2), 5-9.

Cole, N.S. (1988). A realist's appraisal of the prospects for unifying instruction and assessment. In C.V. Bunderson (Ed.), *Assessment in the service of learning* (pp. 103-117). Princeton, NJ: Educational Testing Service.

Darling-Hammond, L., & Wise, A.E. (1985). Beyond standardization: State standards and school improvement. *Elementary School Journal,* 85, 315-336.

Edelsky, C. (1990). Whose agenda is this anyway? A response to McKenna, Robinson, and Miller. *Educational Researcher,* 19(8), 7-11.

Garcia, G.E., & Pearson, P.D. (1991). The role of assessment in a diverse society. In E.H. Hiebert (Ed.), *Literacy for a diverse society: Perspectives, practices, and policies* (pp. 253-278). New York: Teachers College Press.

Koretz, D. (1991, April). *The effects of high-stakes testing on achievement: Preliminary findings about generalization across tests.* Paper presented at the annual meeting of the American Educational Research Association, Chicago, IL.

Linn, R.L. (1985). Standards and expectations: The role of testing (summary). In *Proceedings of a National Forum on Educational Reform* (pp. 88-95). New York: College Board.

Linn, R.L., Baker, E.L., & Dunbar, S.B. (1991). Complex, performance-based assessment: Expectations and validation criteria. *Educational Researcher,* 20(8), 5-21.

Linn, R.L., Graue, M.E., & Sanders, N.M. (1990). Comparing state and district results to national norms: The validity of the claims that "everyone is above average." *Educational Measurement: Issues and Practice,* 9(3), 5-14.

McKenna, M., Robinson, R., & Miller, J. (1990). Whole language and the need for open inquiry: A rejoinder to Edelsky. *Educational Researcher,* 19(8), 12-13.

Palincsar, A.S., & Brown, A. (1986). Interactive teaching to promote independent learning from text. *The Reading Teacher,* 39, 771-777.

Pearson, P.D., & Valencia, S.W. (1987). Assessment, accountability, and professional prerogative. In J.E. Readence & R.S. Baldwin (Eds.), *Research in literacy: Merging perspectives* (pp. 3-16). Rochester, NY: National Reading Conference.

Resnick, L.B., & Resnick, D.L. (1992). Assessing the thinking curriculum: New tools for educational reform. In B.R. Gifford & M.C. O'Connor (Eds.), *Future assessments: Changing views of aptitude, achievement, and instruction* (pp. 37-75). Boston, MA: Kluwer.

Shavelson, R.J., Baxter, G.P., & Pine, J. (1992). Performance assessments: Political rhetoric and measurement reality. *Educational Researcher, 21*(4), 2-27.

Shepard, L.A. (1990). Inflated test score gains: Is the problem old norms or teaching the test? *Educational Measurement: Issues and Practice, 9*(3), 15-22.

Slavin, R.E. (1983). *Cooperative learning*. White Plains, NY: Longman.

Smith, M.L. (1991). Put to the test: The effects of external testing on teachers. *Educational Researcher, 20*(5), 8-11.

Stallman, A.C., & Pearson, P.D. (1990). Formal measures of early literacy. In L.M. Morrow & J.K. Smith (Eds.), *Assessment for instruction in early literacy* (pp. 7-44). Englewood Cliffs, NJ: Prentice Hall.

Valencia, S.W. (1990). A portfolio approach to classroom reading assessment: The whys, whats, and hows. *The Reading Teacher, 43,* 338-340.

Valencia, S.W., & Pearson, P.D. (1987). Reading assessment: Time for a change. *The Reading Teacher, 40,* 726-732.

PART TWO

Sheila W. Valencia
Editor

AUTHENTIC ASSESSMENT IN CLASSROOMS

O VERVIEW   One of the most prominent messages of the authentic assessment movement is that classroom-based assessment is powerful and important. Whether the assessment audience is the nation, state or province, school district, or classroom, the contribution of classroom-based assessment is now being acknowledged. Situating assessment in the classroom, closest to instruction and to the learner, validates the notion that what students actually do in classrooms is a critical source of assessment information. Furthermore, classroom assessment places both teachers and students in positions of power: they are responsible for evaluation, and they are considered the primary consumers as well as producers of information that can be used for decision-making, self-reflection, and goal setting.

The chapters in this section offer three perspectives on classroom-based assessment and its impact on teaching and learning. Each case study focuses on a slightly different aspect of assessment; one chapter highlights students, another teachers, and another, a classroom assessment tool. In the first chapter, Hansen focuses on students' ownership of their learning and on the power of portfolios to help students discover their potential by including artifacts produced both in and out of school. Hancock, Turbill, and Cambourne introduce a staff-development process for helping teachers closely evaluate their own teaching and their students' learning through a careful examination of classroom instruction. Snider, Lima, and DeVito present one state's efforts to encourge teachers to explore portfolios as a means of understanding students and making instructional decisions.

Although very different in purpose and structure, these case studies also have several common themes. First, the priority in each of these projects is to look closely at the child and the classroom context as a source of assessment information and as the basis for instructional decisions. Because reporting to others for accountability or policy reasons is not of concern in these cases, the format and structure of the projects are remarkably different from the assessment projects presented in parts two and three of this volume—and, indeed, from many of the new assessment projects being developed on the national level in the United States. Self-evaluation and self-directed learning, teaching, and decision-making about assessment are emphasized here. The consequences of such assessment projects are restricted to the classroom; there is little, if any, attention to issues such as norms, criteria for performance, comparability, reliability, or reporting to those outside the classroom.

Second, each project uses the unique curriculum of individual classrooms as the basis for observing students and teachers. To varying degrees, they all rely on the teacher and the student to evaluate performance, rather than the judgment or criteria of others. All three cases focus on particular children and teachers in projects that ask each individual to evaluate his or her own learning and teaching processes.

Third, each project can be viewed as a professional-development effort. In all three, teachers worked with others—collaborators from outside the classroom or a group of colleagues—to develop their assessment projects. Each project emphasizes the importance of the process of thinking about authentic assessment rather than the actual product or instrument. The teachers in all three cases were provided with time and support to think about and work through difficult ideas.

The case studies in this section examine classroom assessment through multiple lenses, and in doing so, they suggest there are several different approaches that might be fruitful. Each perspective deserves consideration by educators who are trying to figure out the role of classroom assessment within the broader authentic assessment picture.

CHAPTER 2

Jane Hansen

LITERACY PORTFOLIOS: WINDOWS ON POTENTIAL

THE MANCHESTER LITERACY PORTFOLIOS PROJECT (1990-1996), now taking place in K-12 classrooms in Manchester, New Hampshire, began with seven inner-city teachers' desire to create classrooms in which their students would exert initiative. As the project evolved, more specific purposes came to the forefront. As of this writing, those of us involved with the project believe the ideal classroom is a place where students bring together their school and nonschool lives. The teachers have as much interest in and are as knowledgeable about their students' lives outside school as their performance in English class. School and nonschool lives merge for these students, and they find themselves working toward resolution of their concerns and celebration of their joys within the school day and beyond.

Classrooms in Manchester have become places where students realize their potential. As they become involved in tasks that are relevant to them, they strive to accomplish something. Less often do they slouch, arms folded, eyes half closed. These classrooms are workshops in which students and teachers use reading, writing, and other facets of literacy to carry out their plans. During the school day, students work on self-designed assignments they have created to move them toward goals they have set for themselves. Their journeys place them in positions where they can use literacy to their advantage. When they acknowledge that literacy is the vehicle by which they can best accomplish their goals, they see the necessity for specific plans to develop their ability to read, experiment, respond to others, share, request help, and write.

For these students and their teachers, evaluation is primarily an act performed by the students. Students learn to evaluate their present, past, and future; the teachers' task is to help students see the merits and areas for possible growth in what they are doing, the strengths in what they can already do, and the limitless possibilities that lie ahead. These classrooms are places where students are surprised by what they and their classmates can do.

The place of literacy portfolios is central in the creation of such classrooms. Students select items for their literacy portfolios that portray them as they want others to see them. Each item is chosen to guide each student to begin the lifelong process of answering the questions "Who am I?" and "Who do I want to be?" Students' written reflections about the items they select are often more significant than the items themselves. For example, if a student included a drawing without a written reflection about it, a reader of the portfolio would not know if it was a response to a book, a celebration of the first time the student had colored sky to meet the horizon, or a gift from a reading buddy who recently moved. This is important because the portfolios are meant to be enjoyed by others. Through their sharing of the items included, students become acquainted with one another, and teachers get to know their students in ways they did not in their previous years of teaching.

Students gain a notion of their evolving selves (literacy portfolios are never complete) by analyzing their present interests and accomplishments compared with those of previous years (literacy portfolios often contain items that are several years old). When they can document their experiences as learners, they can look ahead. They set goals. For the Manchester teachers, it has been revolutionary to learn that their students have agendas (Harris, 1992). Now they expect them to have goals and to make plans. The students' plans become the curriculum. In a sense, the literacy portfolios are not related to the curriculum—they are the curriculum. If they were removed, the core of the curriculum would be gone.

The Organizational Scheme

Several features of the literacy portfolios project set the stage on which the story unfolds. The site of the project is the inner city of Manchester, which, with a population of 100,000, is New Hampshire's largest city. The schools are Central High, where the dropout rate is approximately one-third, a junior high that feeds into Central, and three elementary schools that feed the junior high. In one of the elementary schools, 70 percent of the students' parents regularly use alcohol or drugs, according to the school psychologist. Another school has the highest percentage (79) of students receiving free or reduced-price lunches through funding from federal aid programs of any school in the state.

There are seven teachers in the first two years of our project: a high school English teacher, a junior high English teacher, two sixth grade teachers of self-contained classrooms, an elementary resource room teacher who has a pullout program, a first grade teacher, and a kindergarten teacher. The directors of reading and writing for the school district also participate. Five professors and doctoral students from the University of New Hampshire (UNH) are paired with the two secondary teachers, one sixth grade teacher, the special education teacher, and the first grade teacher. One other professor also participates; he interviews the project teachers and other teachers in their buildings. All of those involved want to learn how to view these inner-city students as resources rather than problems (Goldberg, 1992) and how to help the students view themselves as contributors.

Each university researcher spends two days a week in his or her teacher's classroom to collect fieldnotes and interact with the students. My partner is the sixth grade teacher, and each day when I leave her classroom I give her my fieldnotes to read. Before I return, she not only reads my notes but writes a response to me. At our weekly meeting she shares with me the many classroom events that I have missed, we discuss the significance of my fieldnotes, and we share any questions we have about the portfolios.

Our full research team meets twice a month. The nine Manchester educators and six UNH educators convene to share portfolios and classroom data: students' words about their literacy portfolios, their evaluations of themselves and their work, and their thoughts about their reading and writing. At every meeting we each share our own portfolios or copies of a one-page report about something interesting that we have heard a student say or write since our last meeting. We believe our own writing is crucial. Initially we were afraid to share our writing, but eventually we got over that hurdle (or at least adjusted to the fear) and the payoffs began. Because we know we will write twice a month, we now look for things to write about. We search, research, and search some more; we find data. Sometimes we create situations in which students talk or write about their portfolios, themselves, and their reading and writing.

Our data show surprises—the bursts that give unexpected evidence of what students can do. Not only are we surprised, but so are the students. The teachers try to create an atmosphere in which students and teachers push their boundaries. This revelation of potential is what we see as the goal of evaluation (National Commission on Testing and Public Policy, 1990).

Finding Answers

At one of our research team meetings, Jody Coughlin, the junior high teacher, told about Leslie, a girl in one of her classes who wrote interesting answers to several questions Jody had posed about their portfolios. The first question was "Choose one item from your portfolio and write an explanation of what it shows about you as a person." Leslie wrote, "This certificate is from a day camp that I've gone to for the past two years. This certificate says, 'Most likely to go into Alexander's [a large department store] looking like a freak.' It shows how my personality has changed." In response to the next question—"What does this information about you have to do with you as a reader or writer?"—Leslie wrote, "Since I went to this camp, I've lightened up a lot and sat back and finally, after 11 years, started to enjoy life. Ever since this happened I've been able to write poems with more feeling than I used to." To "What would you like to learn next in order to become a better reader or writer?" Leslie answered, "I'd like to learn how to write short stories instead of really long ones that seem to go on and on...." When asked "What will you do to accomplish this goal?" Leslie answered, "I'll probably start a story as a poem and make it into a short story...."

And in response to the final question—"When you accomplish this goal, how might you show it in your portfolio?"—Leslie wrote, "I will probably put one of the short stories in my portfolio, or I would put something in that I accomplished because of this."

Leslie's evaluation of herself and her work shows the three main findings of our portfolio project thus far:

1. Items produced outside school (what we call "nonschool items") give insight into students' uses of literacy and how they value these uses in school and beyond.

2. Students' reflections on why they include items give insight into the value they attribute to literacy.

3. Students' goals can place literacy portfolios in the center of the curriculum because classroom learning and students' writing and reading emanate from their individual goals; in order to give students class time to work toward their goals, teachers often have to restructure their classrooms.

The Importance of Nonschool Items

At the beginning of the project, we did not know what our portfolios would look like. With the many possibilities that exist for portfolios (see, for example, Graves & Sunstein, 1992), we knew we would not find an established type that would suit all our needs; we would have to create our own sort of portfolio. We soon learned that if the portfolios were going to represent students' literacy, we would have to permit the students to include nonschool items. Their literacy is not school property. Students are also literate outside school (Vogel & Zancanella, 1991) and the print they see and use in their homes and community counts.

By encouraging students to include nonschool items in their portfolios along with material created in school, we showed them that we valued their out-of-school lives (Pellegrini, 1991). We started, brick by brick, to take down the wall that often separates school from students' real worlds. When students drop out of school it is sometimes because they see their assignments as irrelevant. If their schoolwork were linked to the concerns and joys of their lives, they would find school a worthwhile place to be. They would have no reason to leave.

Distaste for school begins in the elementary years for some students. Karen Harris (see Harris, 1993), the resource room teacher, wrote about a girl who had just come to her school. The student's cumulative record folder was three inches thick. Written in large letters across the top sheet was one word: "Illiterate." The administration immediately referred the girl to Karen for diagnosis.

Karen, an experienced teacher, was not accustomed to this label, even for students who were regularly referred to her. Because she had decided to learn how to evaluate without administering tests, Karen interviewed the girl. In the process, she learned about an after-school activity the girl enjoyed with a friend. They read fan magazines about popular music and conducted mock interviews with stars: one would play the part of a rock star and the other would conduct the interview, and then they would switch roles. Then they wrote up the interviews and printed their own rock star magazine. Illiterate? Karen was amazed. She decided to tell the girl what she knew: "In the information that your old school sent, they wrote that you can't read or write. But you can. Why did they write that?"

"Because in that school I never read or wrote. All the stuff they gave me to do was so stupid. I didn't do a thing they told me to do."

Nonschool literacy counts. Students need to know that we are interested in what they do when they are off campus. We need to ask them to bring in samples of their nonschool literacy. They need not leave their real selves on the doorstep when they enter school. Too many students cross their arms and sulk when the work of school strikes them as inconsequential (Gilmore, 1991). It is better if students write rock star interviews in school than if they do nothing.

With Leslie, the junior high girl whose portfolio questions I presented earlier, we see the importance of a nonschool item. The certificate from camp showed something important about who she is, has been, and is becoming. She has "lightened up." Evidently at some previous time, she would not have had the nerve to walk into Alexander's looking like a freak. Leslie's literacy is tied to what kind of person she is. Literacy is big. It is self-discovery and self-definition; it is much more than reading and writing (Gee, 1988).

The high school students in the project realize the complexity of self. Some of them use their portfolios to show their various sides. One boy put in a copy of the speech he gave at his eighth grade graduation to "show his responsible side." Then he put in a book he never read. "I carried this book around with me...and kept moving the bookmark further toward the back. Eventually, I just made up the book report. This shows my irresponsible side."

When students view their literacy portfolios as places to show who they are, portfolios are not display cases for "best" work. Showing only one's finest accomplishments represents an entirely different purpose from addressing the question "Who am I?" This question honors diversity and creates an environment in which everyone learns not only who he or she is but also who everyone else is. They learn to respect complex people who have positive and negative sides.

Parents appreciate the inclusion of diverse items, including artifacts from home. When the sixth grade students take home their portfolios along with their report cards, they arrange a time to show the portfolio formally to a family member. Then, the family member fills in a "What Do You Think of My Portfolio?" sheet, which already has the comments and signatures of several classmates with whom the bearer shared his or her portfolio before taking it home. The parents' comments often show their increased understanding of their children based on seeing what was included in the portfolios from both home and school and on hearing the reasons various items were significant.

The students' goals sometimes dovetail with their parents'. For example, one resource room student's mother was taking a writing course, which gave her the opportunity to work on compositions at the same time as her child. Such instances, in which we saw home and school coming together, prompted us to include parents in our project. Parents now become parent-researchers who create their own portfolios; share them with their child at home, in their child's classroom, and at research team meetings; and bring one-page accounts of their portfolio experiences to team meetings.

The Importance of Written Reflections

When Helen shared her portfolio with a group of her sixth grade friends, the reason she gave for inclusion of one item, a sheet from the memo pad of her father's business, surprised me. She read her written reflection about it to the group: "My brother designed these. I have items in my portfolio about other people. Every item isn't about me only. My portfolio shows that

I'm the kind of person who cares about other people. Some people only have items about themselves."

Immediately Nathan said, "Yes, some people are snobs. There's this woman who lives in my building...."

Monique added, "I don't want my portfolio to look like I'm a snob."

These three students caused me to reconsider my own portfolio. Maybe it could show me as someone who cares about others. This was not the first time during the project that the students and other researchers had done something that made me take a new look at myself.

When we began the project I had a three-pocket portfolio. One pocket showed me as a person, another showed me as a professor, and the third as a reader-writer. The categories were a help but also a hindrance. Often I did not know which category an item fit into. During the spring of the first year, some of the sixth graders put items in chronological order rather than in categories. I thought about their organization for my portfolio. Then, Jane Kearns, the Manchester director of writing, shared her portfolio at our end-of-the-year resource team meeting. She had no categories; her portfolio showed her as a seamless person. She had also written reflections about each item. She made a statement about those reflections that impressed me: "The writing of reflections was probably more important than the choosing of the items themselves. When I wrote, I learned about the significance of each item."

I changed my portfolio. I now have no categories and I have a one-page evaluation of the significance of each artifact. For all of us, our portfolios are and always will be ever-changing documents of our literacy. They represent our unfolding natures. I find that I regularly rewrite my reflections as I continue to explore the significance of my items.

The teachers use their portfolios for this sort of self-reflection and also as instructional tools. Most of the teachers introduced the notion of portfolios to their students by sharing their own portfolios—both the items they included and the written reflections that explained the value of various artifacts. As the students started to choose their nonschool and school items, the teachers asked them to articulate the reasons for their choices.

A common school artifact for students and teachers to include is a book. The reasons for including a book vary, of course. One first grader included *The Hungry Thing*, a book about a boy with a speech problem. Why did he put this book in his portfolio? "Because the boy in the book has trouble talking and so do I." Literacy is personal and exists for real reasons that remain hidden until we ask the questions (Hansen, 1987). I was surprised when Leslie explained her present comfort with her poetry: "I lightened up a lot...." Her explanation of why she is now able to write well adds significant information to the inclusion of one of her poems in her portfolio. Items do not stand alone.

By the end of the first year, students at all grade levels (and the adults) had become better able to explain the significance of the items (Hansen, 1992). Self-evaluation had become an important aspect of the portfolios (Ballard, 1992). In June 1991, I asked Brenda Ross, the first grade teacher, "Why were portfolios a good thing to do this year?" She answered, "I'd be able to predict what they'd choose to put in, but I would have chosen incorrectly. The kids showed me they truly could self-evaluate."

The Importance of Students' Goals

Self-evaluation leads to the establishment of goals. That is what evaluation is for. We evaluate in order to find out what we have learned so we will know what to study next. People who self-evaluate constantly ask themselves, "Where am I going? Am I getting there? Am I getting somewhere? Am I enjoying the trip? Is this worthwhile? Do I approve of the way I'm spending my time?" The influence that goals can have on students' movement toward success with more difficult tasks became evident to me one day when I sat in on a small group of sixth graders while they shared their portfolios. Monique's evaluation of her reading prompted her to set a new goal during the session. After she shared a book from the Baby Sitter's Club series, she said she had it in her portfolio because "I collect them."

I asked, "What would you like to learn next in order to become a better reader?" She said she would like to learn to read bigger words—a rather common sixth grade goal, I've learned.

Then I asked, "What will you do to accomplish this goal?"

She sat there. I could sense her mind working. Finally she said she knew all the words in the Baby Sitter Club books, so she would have to read something more difficult. She named one book she could try. With the setting of her goal, Monique started to take a new look at herself. In order to learn, she must move out of familiar territory.

Similarly, Leslie will move into uncertain terrain when she tries to become a better writer of short stories. Her close look at herself helped her realize what to do to move forward. She will start with something she can write well—a poem—and use it to help her begin a short story.

When students have some choice in the path they take, many of them have more desire to learn than when they must follow plans prescribed by a teacher (Newkirk, 1991). They appreciate being in classrooms where the decisions about what they will do are largely theirs (Samway et al., 1991). Inner-city students use strong voices in their lives outside school and often face adult situations; their in-school lives should also give them a great deal of responsibility (Taylor & Dorsey-Gaines, 1988). This can be a challenging path. A handful of the students in the high school teacher's classes had become so disillusioned by school that they were not able to set goals and plan for in-school growth. In this school, students enroll for single-semester classes; more than one semester is necessary for students to develop a strong enough sense of self to make plans for a future. I cannot be sure, but I believe that if these students remained with one group for an entire year, they would become engulfed by the class-room culture and would be able to set goals for their own growth.

Most of the high school students, however, did begin to think of ways to expand their literacy. They learned to trust their own decisions more than to trust suggestions from the teacher. This is as it should be. For example, one high school student wrote, "By making a portfolio I found, even though my teachers often tell me this, that I am too much a one-dimensional reader, and that I should broaden my horizons to more than sports. I may have trouble doing so, but I am willing to try."

The Impact on the Classroom Climate

Self-evaluation pushes students forward, which pleases us adults. But to the high school students, the greatest benefit of creating portfolios is "getting to know the other students in the class." In their other classes, these students sit in rows in silence throughout an entire semester, without even learning one another's names. They want to know their peers.

In all the classrooms, the sharing of portfolios has had a major impact. As students share their items they become aware of one another's potential. They begin to value the diversity of the group, support one another, and look to their peers for help. As they learn the areas of expertise and interests of their classmates, they can use others' talents to help them achieve their own goals. The climate of the classroom changes. Accomplishing something becomes the thing to do. The students realize that their teacher and classmates assume they have plans for themselves. These hopeful students can initiate school tasks that will improve their literacy.

References

Ballard, L. (1992). Portfolios and self-assessment. *English Journal*, 81(2), 46-48.

Gee, J.P. (1988). Discourse systems and Aspirin bottles: On literacy. *Journal of Education*, 170(1), 27-40.

Gilmore, P. (1991). "Gimme room": School resistance, attitude, and access to literacy. In C. Mitchell & K. Weiler (Eds.), *Rewriting literacy: Culture and the discourse of the other* (pp. 57-73). New York: Bergin & Garvey.

Goldberg, M.F. (1992). Portrait of Shirley Brice Heath. *Educational Leadership*, 49(7), 80-82.

Graves, D., & Sunstein, B. (Eds.). (1992). *Portfolio portraits*. Portsmouth, NH: Heinemann.

Hansen, J. (1987). *When writers read*. Portsmouth, NH: Heinemann.

Hansen, J. (1992). Literacy portfolios: Helping students know themselves. *Educational Leadership*, 49(8), 66-68.

Harris, K. (1992, November). *Resource room students set their own goals*. Paper presented at the meeting of the New England Reading Association, Manchester, NH.

Harris, K. (1993). Interviews to supplement tests. In *Researchers reflect: Writings from the Manchester portfolio project, 1990–92* (p. 72). Durham, NH: University of New Hampshire, Writing Lab.

National Commission on Testing and Public Policy. (1990). *From gatekeeper to gateway: Transforming testing in America*. Chestnut Hill,

MA: National Commission on Testing and Public Policy, Boston College.

Newkirk, T. (1991). The middle class and the problem of pleasure. In N. Atwell (Ed.), *Workshop 3: The politics of process* (pp. 63-72). Portsmouth, NH: Heinemann.

Pellegrini, A.D. (1991, November). A critique of the concept of at-risk as applied to emergent literacy. *Language Arts, 68*(5), 380-385.

Samway, K.D., Whang, G., Cade, C., Gamil, M., Lubandina, M.A., & Phommachanh, K. (1991). Reading the skeleton, the heart, and the brain of a book: Students' perspectives on literature study circles. *The Reading Teacher, 45*(3), 196-205.

Taylor, D., & Dorsey-Gaines, C. (1988). *Growing up literate: Learning from inner-city families*. Portsmouth, NH: Heinemann.

Vogel, M., & Zancanella, D. (1991). The story world of adolescents in and out of the classroom. *English Journal, 80*(6), 54-60.

Robert J. Marzano

COMMENTARY ON *Literacy Portfolios: Windows on Potential*

JANE HANSEN'S CHAPTER is an excellent description and example of many of the current trends in portfolio use. While I recognize the risk of drawing conclusions not intended by the author, it seems that Hansen suggests two main functions that literacy portfolios can serve: (1) as a self-evaluation tool for students; and (2) as a vehicle with which students might learn about themselves and ultimately discover their own potential. Although it is not highlighted in the chapter, one would assume that Hansen's project also focuses on the use of portfolios as an assessment tool since she states that within the study, students, teachers, administrators, and university researchers created literacy portfolios as part of their efforts to assess, reflect on, and plan their growth.

To accomplish these goals, Hansen asserts that portfolios must have a number of features. Portfolios should:

- include nonschool items and school items;
- be used as the focal point of the curriculum because they focus on personal goals;
- be different from student to student;
- not be display cases for "best work" but include whatever is meaningful to students.

Like all developing technologies at any point in time, the portfolio movement has both positive and questionable aspects. I will discuss both briefly in terms of Hansen's model.

Positive Aspects

One of the most powerful aspects of the model presented in this chapter is its emphasis on the personal goals of students. Research and theory by specialists in motivation (for example, McCombs, 1991; Schunk, 1990) strongly suggest that human beings operate at their highest and most effective levels of performance if they are in the process of working toward goals that are meaningful to them. Some theorists even assert that individuals must be "passionate" about the goal they are attempting to accomplish if their latent skills and abilities are to surface. In other words, if an individual is not actively engaged in attempting to accomplish a meaningful goal—one about which he or she is passionate—then it is virtually impossible to assess his or her skills and abilities.

Unfortunately, goals about which students are "passionate" and traditional school practices appear incompatible. Specifically, Nichols (1983) has illustrated that the goals presented to students within a traditional classroom setting are most commonly unrelated to those for which students have intrinsic motivation. It is probably not an exaggeration to say that most students are passionate about goals that are at best not addressed and at worst not achievable within a traditional school setting. This inherently contradictory situation renders invalid almost all traditionally based attempts at assessment. That is, if one believes the current research and theory on motivation, assessment that truly is "authentic" can be conducted only within the context of students passionately seeking meaningful goals, because it is only within such a context that students' true strengths and weaknesses are displayed.

Hansen's conceptualization of a literacy portfolio focuses on student-selected goals. Students also are free to identify those artifacts that signify or symbolize progress toward these goals. Extending Hansen's model a bit based on the theory and research in motivation, one can conclude that students should be encouraged to identify goals that truly "turn them on." These goals should then become the centerpiece of the curriculum for each student; activities within the traditional content areas would be linked to them, like spokes to the hub of a wheel. Such an approach could legitimately be called a "learner-centered" instructional system.

Questions and Concerns

The most questionable aspect of Hansen's model and, indeed, of the general direction of the entire portfolio movement is the extent to which it satisfies one of the basic functions of effective assessment —namely, to provide feedback.

It was with the dawn of the theory of cybernetics in the middle part of this century that psychologists began to understand the importance of feedback as a basic principle of human behavior. Gregory Bateson, the well-known anthropologist, is reported to have said that cybernetics is "the biggest bite out of the fruit tree of knowledge that mankind has taken in the last 2000 years" (Brand, 1974, p. 28). However, it was the psychologist William Glasser (1981) who first described how cybernetic theory related to human behavior in school.

Basically, human beings are goal-seeking mechanisms—cybernetic systems. At any time we are trying to accomplish some goal—whether it be a low-level subsistence goal such as obtaining food or a high-level self-actualization goal like developing a new understanding of some intriguing concept. From this perspective, cybernetic theory is right in line with Hansen's model of portfolio use—goal setting should be an integral part of assessment since it is an integral part of human behavior. However, to accomplish goals cybernetic systems require specific and accurate feedback. That is, to accomplish a goal, human beings need information about what they are doing right and what they are doing wrong. Herein lies the problem with the models proposed by Hansen and others—they do not facilitate feedback that is specific and accurate. This is particularly troublesome for goals that require basic skill development and knowledge acquisition. The research of Adams (1991) and others clearly indicates that literacy goals require a certain amount of skill development and knowledge acquisition.

One can conclude, then, that literacy assessment must involve some specific and accurate feedback relative to skills and knowledge that constitute literacy. Unfortunately, a portfolio that is primarily an open-ended repository of self-selected artifacts and information does not perform such a function. This is not to say that the models proposed by Hansen and others should be abandoned or even altered; it is to say that they cannot be used as the sole method of assessment. Portfolio assessment should be augmented by other formal and informal methods of assessment that have a stronger feedback function. Many of these methods can be found in traditional forms of literacy assessment.

The use of traditional forms of assessment is, of course, not very popular at present. This, I fear, is due to the lure of some of the rhetoric about "seamless," "authentic" assessment curing all or most of the ills of education. While the emphasis on such a powerful new format for gathering evaluative information is certainly a necessary change, it does not imply, as some believe, that traditional forms of assessment are obsolete.

As is the case with all complex human phenomena, there is no one single answer to the issue of literacy assessment. The challenge for modern-day educators is to take the best of what current research and theory have to offer and integrate it with the best of what has been successful and useful in the past. Hansen's model of portfolio use should be an exciting addition to a teacher's array of assessment techniques.

References

Adams, M.J. (1991). *Beginning to read: Thinking and learning about print.* Cambridge, MA: MIT Press.

Brand, S. (1974). *Cybernetic frontiers.* New York: Random House.

Glasser, W. (1981). *Stations of the mind.* New York: HarperCollins.

McCombs, B.L. (1991). Motivation and lifelong learning. *Educational Psychologist, 26*(2), 117-128.

Nichols, J.G. (1983). Conceptions of ability and achievement motivation: A theory and its implications for education. In S.G. Paris, G.M. Olson, & H.W. Stevenson (Eds.), *Learning and motivation in the classroom* (pp. 211-238). Hillsdale, NJ: Erlbaum.

Schunk, D. H. (1990). Goal setting and self-efficacy during self-regulated learning. *Educational Psychologist, 25*(1), 71-86.

CHAPTER 3

Jan Hancock
Jan Turbill
Brian Cambourne

ASSESSMENT AND EVALUATION OF LITERACY LEARNING

OUR TEAM OF AUSTRALIAN LIT-
ERACY EDUCATORS was faced with a challenge: to construct
a fresh vision, a redefinition, of the practice of assessment and evaluation of literacy learning within classroom contexts. At the heart of this project was our
belief that assessment and evaluation both need to be
viewed as ongoing and cyclic processes intricately
interwoven with teaching and learning. Our specific
goal was to implement a staff-development procedure
that would help teachers develop a coherent approach
to evaluation in the language arts and, perhaps, in the
whole curriculum. Brian Cambourne, one of the coresearchers, highlighted the nature of the project during the opening meeting of the research team in March
1991: "The evaluation processes promoted in the staff-
development procedure will be responsive, ongoing,
and naturalistic," he said. "They will also be doable
within classrooms and in all school contexts and will

meet not only the needs of the school, but also those of the teachers, students, and parents."

This chapter reports on our efforts to implement a new form of assessment known as "responsive evaluation" and to explore a process for implementation we called "teacher as coresearcher." The project involved a diverse group of educators, all of whom were philosophically committed to a whole language theory of literacy education but were faced with the problem of making classroom evaluation consistent with this holistic philosophy. Although the details may vary from place to place, the problems and issues we face in Australia are similar to those faced by all educators who are serious about implementing a holisitic philosophy.

Background

Our research team was composed of a wide range of educators: 30 teachers from 7 schools, some of whom had been researching assessment and evaluation issues for a number of years and all of whom had volunteered to participate; 2 principals; a district curriculum consultant; a district superintendent; and 4 university-based teacher educators.

We knew we would have to confront several critical issues facing educators in New South Wales. Teachers had begun to express concern about the mismatch between their beliefs and practices in teaching literacy and the existing beliefs and practices in assessing literacy. This issue concerned what we called "congruence"—that is, the degree of "fit" between the philosophy of language and learning that guides instruction and the theory that governs the application of evaluation procedures. Prior to the 1960s this was not an issue—beliefs about language, learning, teaching practice, and evaluation all fit together snugly. At that time, it was believed that language was learned from part to whole, and teaching was decontextualized. Similarly, this view was found in the fragmented evaluation practices of standardized and teacher-made tests that evaluated learners as either right or wrong and focused on products rather than processes.

We realized, however, that with the adoption of the holisitic theory of whole language, the fit was no longer snug. Learning and teaching now take place in more natural settings; we recognized that we needed to place assessment in the same framework. It was apparent that a measurement-based model of assessment and evaluation was no longer appropriate. Our beliefs about learning had shifted; we now believed that language was learned from whole to part in naturalistic ways. Consequently, we needed an evaluation model that drew information from the classroom context, emphasizing what each student could do and had attempted to do and the processes he or she used during learning. The challenge for us was how to implement this model in classrooms.

The second issue we faced was the advent of outcome-based syllabi. For the first time, Australian teachers were required to conduct their assessment and evaluation measures from within a specific set of desired learning outcomes. The new syllabus for New South Wales for language arts in kindergarten through grade six was being developed and was scheduled to be in place in 1992. The proposed learning outcomes were sequentially arranged and categorized according to proficiency levels specified in a set of mandatory curriculum documents that covered "key learning areas."

Although we accepted that clearly articulated learning outcomes were needed, we realized that the issue of how teachers actually guided students to achieve these goals needed to be approached with care.

Explicitly stated learning outcomes could be used to a student's advantage as broad templates against which to compare student development and as a vehicle for reflection on individual learner's needs; alternatively, they could be used as a mold into which each student's developmental path could be relentlessly forced. We did not want to see this occur.

Description of the Project

These conditions in New South Wales gave us a clear focus for our work. We needed to conduct research that would bring about professional development in those teachers who participated. The research project needed to develop a framework for thinking about assessment and evaluation congruent with the beliefs of a whole language philosophy. We knew that the first step would be clarifying our own understanding of assessment. We also decided to explore the potential of responsive evaluation in concert with a research methodology known as teachers as coresearchers (TACOR).

Shared Meaning

Because group members came from such diverse backgrounds, we found it necessary to decide on "shared meanings"—first for the terms "assessment" and "evaluation," and second for some common standards of effective assessment and evaluation practice. We agreed that for our purposes "assessment" meant the gathering of data and "evaluation" was the making of judgments about or the interpretation of these data. We also recognized that the concepts represented by these two terms were interdependent.

The issue of what constituted effective assessment and evaluation was not as easy to determine. After much reading, discussion, and heated debate, we agreed on four criteria as the basis for beginning our project:

1. Assessment and evaluation must result in optimal learning for all involved.
2. Assessment and evaluation must inform, support, and justify teacher decision-making.
3. Assessment and evaluation practices must reflect the theories of language learning and literacy that guide our teaching.
4. Findings that result from our assessment and evaluation practices must be accurate, valid, reliable, and perceived to be rigorous by all who use them.

With these definitions and assumptions clarified, we were ready to consider the implementation of our research on evaluation within a whole language philosophy.

Responsive Evaluation

We began with an exploration of responsive evaluation. As described in Cambourne and Turbill (1990), we believed that this approach provided a suitable model for evaluation of individual student's learning in a whole language classroom. Responsive evaluation was first outlined by Stake (1975) and later expanded by Guba and Lincoln (1981). According to Stake, evaluation is responsive when it does the following:

- is oriented more directly to program activities than to program intents;
- responds to audience requirements for information;

- recognizes different values and perspectives when reporting the success and failure of the program; and
- rejects the concept that objectivity must be— or even can be—maintained.

In a classroom, "program activities" are those things that students actually do in response to teaching and learning; "program intents" are the prescribed learning outcomes found in a syllabus or curriculum. Responsive evaluators would not insist that the learning outcomes of the syllabus be the only frame of reference for assessment and evaluation. Rather, they would argue that when teachers evaluate in classroom contexts with only program intents in mind, they risk being blinded to accomplishments that are not stated as objectives (Stake, 1975). Responsive evaluation recognizes the mind as the most powerful and useful evaluation instrument available. By valuing the mind as instrument, it acknowledges that subjectivity is an essential part of the evaluation process. This does not mean that responsive evaluation is not rigorous or trustworthy. Indeed, the model proposes several procedures that can be used to maintain the credibility of the data and the interpretation. For example, Lincoln and Guba (1986) list procedures such as sustained engagement at the site, persistent observation, triangulation or cross-referencing of evidence, peer debriefing, negative case analysis, and leaving a clear audit trail to maintain credibility. When these procedures are carefully implemented, the rigor of the conclusions drawn is at least as strong as (and often stronger than) the rigor that has allegedly characterized traditional measurement-based methods.

Teachers as Coresearchers

TACOR is a research methodology that involves a mix of people—classroom teachers, university professors, administrators, students, parents, and others who have a stake in education—working together to achieve a common purpose (Barton, 1992). The relationship is one of collegiality; the approach requires equal status among members in the team and recognizes and values the expertise that each has to offer. Previous work about TACOR indicates that it fosters high levels of professional growth in teachers, especially with respect to clear articulation of their beliefs and practices. There is also evidence that it fosters high levels of such development in university personnel because the credibility they gain with teachers and other academics as a consequence of "getting their hands dirty" in real classrooms increases their confidence and their stature as teacher educators. For some, it was also quite humbling to find that grade one and two children didn't think that having a doctorate gave them any status at all!

We used the TACOR methodology to examine our research questions: Is it possible to apply the axioms and practices of responsive evaluation to the classroom context? If so, how? Our project was structured so that team members who were not classroom teachers each worked with four teachers at one of seven research sites. All the coresearchers engaged in personal and collaborative reflection, discussion, debriefing, planning, and sharing and refining of both data gathering techniques and data analysis. Each group of participants collected data on a weekly basis from their classroom sites. They also provided one another with support in regular meetings. The sense of team spirit and joint ownership of the project was clearly evident at whole-group meetings. These meetings also provided opportunities for reflection on the achievements and direction of the project.

Emerging Results

In the first two years of this staff-development project, we generated a great deal of information. Here we discuss two findings that we feel will be most informative for other educators facing problems similar to our own. The first highlights the knowledge that the coresearchers found they needed in order to become effective responsive evaluators, and the second focuses on the processes that helped us begin to take control of this knowledge.

The Knowledge

The first finding that has emerged from our work is a clearer understanding of what is involved in becoming a responsive evaluator at the classroom level. We have identified stages in this journey. In keeping with the journey metaphor, we developed a conceptual map, shown in Figure 1 on the next page, that identifies the understanding, skills, and knowledge that research teams need if they are to implement responsive evaluation effectively. The coresearchers argued that any staff-development program in assessment and evaluation that did not include at least these fundamentals would be inadequate.

The stages that appear on the map only emerged as a consequence of our fumbling. When we ran into difficulties we would slow down, back up, and ask, "What's missing? What else do we need to do?" Each time we did this we came to the same conclusion: we needed to ask ourselves some fundamental questions about what we really believed about literacy. One of our big discoveries was the crucial role that tacit knowledge—that is, intuition, unconscious understanding,

Figure 1
The Conceptual Map for Responsive Evaluators

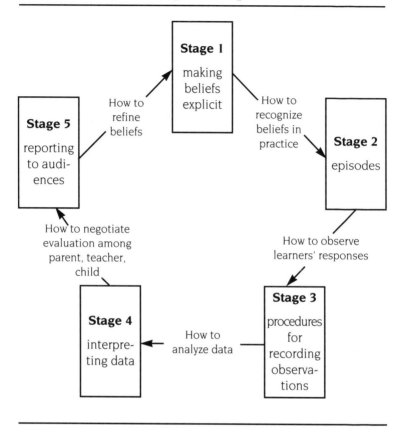

values, beliefs, and the like—played in the processes of assessment, evaluation, and teaching. We began to discover the way that our implicit beliefs influenced how we taught, why we taught what we taught, and how, why, and what we evaluated.

The map begins with an exploration of beliefs, then proceeds to identification of teaching activities, careful observation of learners, interpretation of the observations, and sharing information with others through "negotiated evaluation" (Woodward, 1992). However, we need to emphasize that this map is the result of drawing together the multiplicity of experiences that occurred as we struggled to understand responsive evaluation in a whole language classroom. The processes we went through didn't occur linearly as this map suggests; they were much more complex. It was only after considerable time that our data began to suggest the pattern that eventually emerged on our map.

The Processes

As we proceeded in the project, we experimented with some techniques that seemed to help the few teachers who joined the project late. Essentially these techniques required us to reflect on what we believed. The simplest of these processes was to ask three questions:

1. What is effective literate behavior?
2. How is it best acquired?
3. After it is acquired, what should it be used for?

The process that each of the teachers went through and the end results of this self-questioning were similar in many respects. At first they produced answers such as "Good reading is reading for meaning." We found it necessary to help the teachers refine their answers by suggesting they ask, "Why do I believe that good reading is reading for meaning?" for example, and when they had answered that, to ask again, "Why do I believe that?" Gradually layers peeled away until the teachers reached what one called "an inner core that I couldn't cut into any more. Then I knew what I really believed and why I believed it."

A second process emerged as a consequence of responding to the three general questions listed above. As we worked through the process of digging into our values and beliefs about literacy, we realized that some of our TACOR partners were essentially practical people who needed a way to tie what we were asking them to do more closely to the classroom. In order to do this we established steps to follow:

1. Identify teaching episodes.
2. Ask and answer the question, "Why do I have these episodes in my daily schedule?"
3. Ask and answer the question, "What information-gathering procedures can I employ during each episode that won't break into or stop the flow of teaching and learning?"
4. Focus on one episode.
5. Ask and answer the question, "What indicators will inform me that students are or are not learning in this episode?"
6. Ask and answer the question, "What sense can I make from the information I collect?"

We found this process very effective for helping teachers achieve three things: (1) it helped them make explicit their beliefs, values, and ideologies about literacy; (2) it helped them begin to understand the stages on the conceptual map; and (3) it helped them begin to deal with the logistics of organizing time and resources for controling all the pieces that make up effective responsive evaluation.

An Example

Chris has been teaching for ten years. When this case study was carried out, he was teaching sixth grade.

Chris took a two-hour block of time each morning to teach what he called "language." Within this block Chris identified five episodes:

1. *Teacher reading*. During this episode Chris read to his students, who sat on the floor around him. He typically read for 10 to 15 minutes.

2. *Sustained silent reading*. SSR usually lasted about 20 minutes.

3. *Modeling and demonstration*. This was a kind of minilesson during which Chris modeled or demonstrated what he wanted his students to learn.

4. *Workshop tasks*. This was usually the longest episode each morning, taking up to 50 percent of the available time. Chris had prepared a range of activities that students were expected to choose from according to a negotiated contract.

5. *Discussion and sharing*. This usually took up the last 10 to 15 minutes of each morning. The class gathered and students volunteered to share and discuss what they had been doing during the morning.

Figure 2 is a schematic representation of Chris's attempts to use self-questioning processes to aid in evaluation of students' accomplishments in language. When Chris asked himself the question, "Why do I have these episodes?" he generated a list of reasons that reflected his values and beliefs about learning, teaching, literacy, and children. It is important to realize that these reasons are a crucial first step in identifying basic values. For example, Chris's first reason for reading to his class each morning is that "literature needs to be

Figure 2
Episodes and Evaluation in Chris's Classroom

Episodes	Why These Episodes	Evaluation Data
Teacher reading	• Literature needs to be promoted. • Students need immersion in fiction and nonfiction. • Builds up context for using language purposefully and opportunities to develop ideas, concepts, and understanding that can be drawn on in other topic activities. • Students need demonstrations of how an efficient reader reads fluently, with expression, and makes meaning of the author's text. • Students need demonstrations of a proficient reader using the three cueing systems—they need to see how to use strategies to unravel the mystery of unknown words in a text. • Students need to ask questions about what they are hearing when they can no longer understand what is being heard—they need to be encouraged to interject and say that they "don't understand what that was about" so it can be reread and discussed. • Students need to be alerted to text features. • Reading is enjoyable and a valuable activity for both learning and recreation.	• Teacher observation via anecdotal records • Student learning logs
SSR	• Students need an uninterrupted period to engage with written text in order to make meaning. • Provides students with an opportunity to be immersed in texts of different forms. • Reading is enjoyable and rewarding. • Teacher models reading by reading. • Teacher can show interest in what students like to read. • It provides the teacher with information about students' reading tastes and information about books to read or recommend to others. • Students become responsible for their choices.	• Observation • Reading logs
Modeling and demonstrations	• Focuses on skills identified by the teacher, librarian, or the children themselves in regular demonstrations. • Covers all aspects of language learning and learning in general. • Provides opportunities for children to ask questions and clarify thought. • Assists children in making connections. • Shows necessary structure that children can use when taking on a task themselves.	• Conferences • Interviews • Surveys

Figure 2 (*continued*)
Episodes and Evaluation in Chris's Classroom

Episodes	Why These Episodes	Evaluation Data
Workshop tasks	• Students need an opportunity to work together in groups so they can collaborate on ideas and learn from each other. • They need to use talk for learning. • They need the opportunity to listen to others' ideas. • They need to interact socially and work in a cooperative manner in order to achieve a goal. • They need opportunities to experiece a variety of roles, such as leader, scribe, and group recorder. • They need to use writing and reading to learn. • They can clarify ideas and make connections through role play, drama, music, and dance. • They need opportunities to respond to literature in a supportive atmosphere. • They need tasks that force them to engage in a text or in the modes of language. • They need opportunities to learn the skills of learning and to use language for real purposes and audiences.	• Observations • Retellings
Discussion and sharing	• Focuses on experiences of the day and identifies what learning has occurred. • Shows the problems or difficulties hindering learning. • Shows what needs to be learned next. • Provides students with an opportunity to hear what others think and to ask questions, gain information, analyze, evaluate, and make connections about reading, writing, talking, and listening. • Guides students to respect the opinions of others and accept criticism. • Shows how to solve problems, offer criticism, and give advice sensitively.	• Learning logs

promoted." This reason can be used as a starting point to peel back the values and beliefs that Chris holds about teaching literacy; the next step is simply to ask, "Why?" In answer to "What information gathering procedures can I employ during each episode?" Chris listed a set of options that enabled him to begin organizing himself. He decided he would rely mainly on his own observations, which he would record as anecdotal records, and complement these observations with information collected from student learning logs, conferences, interviews, surveys, and students' written products that resulted from the retelling activities that were a regular feature of his classroom.

Chris found the experience of identifying and justifying his episodes both daunting and rewarding. This is his explanation of how the process of determining episodes began for him:

> What I went through was at first quite daunting. Identifying what all the major episodes were—like a reading episode or a writing episode—was difficult to do. I didn't think in terms of "this is a reading episode, this is a writing episode." I saw them as a whole package. But pulling out all the core components was very important for me to do. I had the plan already there but forcing myself to analyze it—asking myself why I was doing it the way I was doing it—was, in the end, a very valuable exercise. I found that when I asked myself, "Why do I do teacher reading? What do I believe?" I found that my statements were very general. They were big picture statements and I knew that I could refine them again to talk about what I believed about reading and writing and talking and listening and the interconnectedness of all of that.

Chris felt that his initial lack of trust in himself lay in the fact that prior to working in this project he had not been through a process of examining what it was that he believed about literacy teaching and learning and its evaluation. He said, "When you begin to question yourself you find that some of your beliefs are rooted back there in how you went in school and what you believe learning is about. It's a security thing and you don't want to let go. Then you fluctuate for a while, and when you feel really confident you let go and you take on new beliefs." Chris felt that the more he came to understand about language learning and its use, the more he would be able to recognize growth in students' learning through their development of attitudes, knowledge, concepts, skills, and other key learning areas.

Reflections

This project has helped us understand that there is more to assessment and evaluation than putting together portfolios of student work and negotiating with parents and students. While the data collection techniques of portfolio assessment and the inclusive procedures of negotiated evaluation can be important components of evaluation, neither could ever be seriously considered as a complete or total approach to the assessment and evaluation of student learning because both lack theoretical underpinning. Our research together with our interpretation of the literature have convinced us that any theoretically valid or credible approach to assessment and evaluation must deal not only with the logistics of collecting, storing, and reporting information but also must give teachers the knowledge, understanding, and skill to be able to interpret the information they collect, justify the results, and implement procedures aimed at increasing the trustworthiness of their interpretations. Above all, teachers must be able to explain, in theoretical terms, why their methods are rigorous and "scientific."

While we still have some way to go, we believe that the TACOR model we have been using is one way of helping teachers acquire this knowledge and these skills. We believe that we are beginning to identify a staff-development process that will enable teachers to implement, describe, and justify an approach to assessment and evaluation congruent with the principles

underpinning holistic theories and practices of language teaching. Going through the processes described
in this staff-development model leads to the exploration of values and beliefs about learning and teaching. The identification of indicators of effective learning
helps teachers overcome any concern that this approach
to assessment and evaluation is nebulous, subjective,
and nonrigorous. Ginny, a fourth grade teacher, noted
that "the evaluation becomes objective once your markers are in place. You have to know what you are looking
for and why those are important to you. I can now justify what I am doing to anyone who comes in my room."
The knowledge gained in this process of self-reflection,
in turn, provides insight into how classrooms can be
organized and managed and begins the journey toward
improved teacher confidence and more powerful teaching and learning.

References

Barton, B.M. (1992). An evaluation of teacher as coresearcher as methodology for staff development. Unpublished master's thesis, Centre for
Studies in Literacy, University of Wollongong, NSW, Australia.

Cambourne, B., & Turbill, J. (1990). Assessment in whole language
classrooms: Theory into practice. Elementary School Journal, 90(3),
337-349.

Guba, E., & Lincoln, Y. (1981). Effective evaluation: Improving the usefulness of evaluation results through responsive and naturalistic approaches.
San Francisco, CA: Jossey-Bass.

Lincoln, Y., & Guba, E. (1986). But is it rigorous? Trustworthiness
and authenticity in naturalistic evaluation. In D. Williams (Ed.),
Naturalistic evaluation: New directions for program evaluation (no. 30,
pp. 73-84). San Francisco, CA: Jossey-Bass.

Stake, R. (1975). Evaluating the arts in education: A responsive approach.
Columbus, OH: Merrill.

Woodward, H. (1992). Negotiated evaluation. Sydney, NSW, Australia:
Primary English Teaching Association.

John J. Pikulski

COMMENTARY ON *Assessment and Evaluation of Literacy Learning*

Hancock, Turbill, and Cambourne have presented a chapter with many good ideas that bravely approaches the enormous complexity of classroom literacy assessment. Currently much is being written about the assessment of literacy, but my informal observations in classrooms in the United States and my conversations with classroom teachers convince me that teachers are finding suggestions for embedded assessment, performance-based assessment, assessment through exhibitions, the use of portfolios, and so forth to be forebidding and unmanageable. The authors of this chapter very appropriately set out to develop assessment procedures that are, as they say, "doable." The most authentic, valid, responsive, naturalistic assessment procedures are worthless unless classroom teachers find them doable. A significant strength of this project is that procedures are being developed and are evolving as teachers use them in ongoing classroom activities.

The chapter also appropriately stresses the need for developing assessment that reflects the best available theory and research about language learning, achieving congruence between instructional goals and practice, and emphasizing the central role that classroom teachers must play in effective assessment.

Early in the chapter, the authors set out four criteria for effective assessment. It would seem appropriate as a starting point to ask how well the evaluation procedures they describe in the chapter fulfill those criteria.

Evaluating the Evaluation Procedures

Congruence of assessment and theory. One of the criteria indicated that "assessment and evaluation practices must reflect the theories of language learning and literacy that guide our teaching." Bringing about congruence between a "whole language philosophy" and assessment procedures initially seemed like the driving force of this assessment project. Unlike older, traditional, measurement-driven testing in literacy, which relied almost exclusively on psychometric principles and largely ignored curriculum research and theoretical advances, the approach outlined by Hancock, Turbill, and Cambourne attempts to achieve an articulation of literacy theory, practice, and assessment. As the description of the project unfolds, the focus seems to shift, however, from a generalized theoretical position (whole language) to individual teacher's theories and beliefs about language, learning, and assessment (though clearly the teachers in the project are committed to similar philosophical-theoretical positions). Given the ambiguity often associated with the term "whole language" (Bergeron, 1990; McKenna, Robinson, & Miller, 1990), a shift from an emphasis on a vaguely defined term to an emphasis on helping teachers explore and articulate their own belief systems about literacy and the teaching of literacy seems very appropriate.

Yet another shift in emphasis seems to take place later in the chapter. The chapter is consistent in taking the position that the teacher is the single most important instrument in the assessment process, a position that is receiving a great deal of support in literacy publications (Johnston, 1992; Paris et al., 1992;

Winograd, Paris, & Bridge, 1991). Rather than asking teachers to begin the assessment process by exploring and stating their system of beliefs, the chapter suggests that teachers begin by looking at their instructional practices and then asking a central, critical question: "Why am I doing this?" This shift from focusing on belief systems to focusing on instructional practices seems the result of the reactions of classroom teachers, who "were essentially practical people who needed a way to tie what [the authors] were asking them to do [i.e., to state their beliefs] more closely to the classroom." Through repeatedly asking "Why am I doing this?" a system of beliefs emerges and serves as the basis for developing assessment procedures. In this sense, the assessment procedures described in the chapter clearly satisfy one of the criteria for effective assessment: that of basing assessment on a theoretical foundation, though that foundation is an individual teacher's belief system rather than some general theoretical position established within the profession of literacy education.

Informing and supporting teacher decision-making. I do think that the analysis of what a teacher does instructionally serves as an excellent starting point for building an understanding of beliefs and of a philosophy for teaching literacy. However, I am concerned about the potentially self-reinforcing nature of this procedure, which is related to a second criterion that the authors set for effective assessment: to inform, support, and justify teacher decision-making. I wholeheartedly agree that assessment must inform and support teacher decision-making, though I don't think the chapter offers sufficient evidence or examples of how this happens in this project. The only clear example of how the assessment system operates is the case study of Chris, a sixth grade teacher. Chris identified five major "episodes" in his instructional block for language and then thoughtfully analyzed why he scheduled those episodes. However, the emphasis was clearly on understanding and justifying these procedures; it didn't seem that the analysis, or the assessment that supposedly flowed from that analysis, resulted in improved or even modified instruction. The value of understanding why certain instructional activities are engaged in is not to be underestimated, but I'm concerned that a teacher who, for example, scheduled generous amounts of time for students to work on worksheets or for teaching artificial, isolated skills—both of which have been challenged by research findings (Anderson et al., 1985; Taylor, Frye, & Gaetz, 1990)—could build his or her own rationale for maintaining or extending those unproductive instructional activities. Indeed, Chris does seem involved in a self-sustaining system of beliefs; the five episodes that he scheduled for his own classroom are strikingly similar, both in content and time allotment, to those recommended in an earlier publication by Cambourne and Turbill (1990).

The chapter indicates that one important aim of this project was to explore a methodology called "teacher as coresearcher." Teams of teachers, principals, a curricular specialist, a superintendent, and teacher educators were formed. This seems a powerful approach that could be enormously beneficial to all involved; however, almost no information was provided in the chapter about how these teams functioned or what their benefit was. Teams such as these might have helped teachers examine their practices and belief systems critically, which could lead to more informed and improved instruction. Indeed it may be that they did serve this purpose, but the procedures are not discussed in the chapter or reflected in the illustration of how Chris evolved his assessment procedures.

Optimizing learning. A third criterion for effective evaluation that Hancock, Turbill, and Cambourne cite is that it should "result in optimal learning for all involved." This certainly fits with newer concepts of validity, especially the concept of consequential validity (Moss, 1992). As a result of actively involving teachers in ongoing assessment and of bringing about congruence between instruction and assessment, the procedures described seem to hold great promise. But even after two years of work with the project, the focus appears to remain on how to get to the process of evaluation; essentially no examples were given of how assessment data were used to help optimize student learning. A major value of the project is that it truly appears to be trying to address the complexity of literacy development and its assessment. However, given its present content, the chapter doesn't address this third criterion of improving instruction through assessment.

Yielding valid, reliable information. The final criterion for effective assessment is that the findings must be "accurate, valid, reliable, and perceived as rigorous by all who use them." Figure 2, which is the only place in the chapter that gives clues as to the nature of the assessment and the form it will take, suggests an almost exclusive reliance on teacher observations and student learning logs, though reading logs, surveys, and retellings are also mentioned. Certainly observations and learning logs have the potential for being accurate, valid, and reliable; whether they will be perceived as rigorous remains to be seen, especially in environments where psychometric, pseudo-objective measures have been the prevailing assessment devices.

One of the four stated central tenets of responsive evaluation, a cornerstone of this project, indicates that it "responds to audience requirements for evaluation," and Figure 1's conceptual map for responsive evaluation has "reporting to audiences" as one of the five major stages of an evaluation system. Nowhere else does the chapter address how the results of assessment and evaluation in the project were reported or how various audiences (students, parents, administrators, school boards, etc.) responded to them.

The desire to create rigorous assessments in this project may be undermined by the use of the poorly defined word "objective." One tenet of responsive evaluation "rejects the concept that objectivity must be—or even can be—maintained." I would argue that if criteria are clearly stated, made public, and fairly and reliably applied, teacher observations and learning logs can be "objective." Indeed, the authors quote a teacher who has worked on the project as reporting that "the evaluation becomes objective once your markers are in place. You have to know what you are looking for and why those are important to you." It seems unfortunate that the authors of the chapter would reject objectivity as desirable or attainable in their approach to literacy assessment. Perhaps a more expanded concept of objectivity is needed, such as the concept of "dynamic objectivity" discussed by Johnston (1992), who also notes the pejorative connotations of the word "subjective." Rejection of objectivity would seem to raise doubts about fulfilling one of the authors' criteria for effective assessment—that the results be perceived as rigorous by all who use them.

Summary

Overall, it seems that held up against the authors' own stated criteria for excellence in assessment, the system they describe only partially meets the mark. Certainly, however, the project is moving toward fulfilling all the criteria. It also may be that more results are available than could be included in a single chapter with limited space. Nevertheless, more information needs to be reported about how aspects of the framework operate. For example, reference is made several times to the importance of audience reception of assessment results, but it was unclear as to how various audiences might interact with the system. It was particularly disappointing to find no reference to how the students, who I feel are the most important audience, become part of the system. There was no indication of how student self-assessment and reflection would grow.

Hancock, Turbill, and Cambourne have initiated a thoughtful study of an approach to assessment that appears to have great promise. They now need to become clearer about how the system will operate in reality. For example, early in the chapter they state that one of the major issues on which they needed to focus was the outcome-based syllabus being developed in Australia for the first time; yet, except for noting that "the learning outcomes of the syllabus" should not be the "only frame of reference for assessment," there is no discussion of how such syllabi might be addressed in this assessment system. This is a particularly relevant question for educators in the United States, given that national "standards" already have been developed in mathematics (Commission on Standards for School Mathematics of the National Council of Teachers of Mathematics, 1989) and professional groups are actively working to establish standards for language arts and other curricular areas (O'Neil, 1993).

This chapter describes what appears to be a potentially valuable process for approaching the assessment of literacy that appropriately focuses on teachers, students, and classroom activities; the authors now need to describe how teachers and their students can apply that process to gathering information that informs instruction and various audiences.

References

Anderson, R.C., Hiebert, E.H., Scott, J.A., & Wilkinson, I.A.G. (1985). *Becoming a nation of readers*. Washington, DC: National Institute of Education.

Bergeron, B.S. (1990). What does the term "whole language" mean: Constructing a definition from the literature. *Journal of Reading Behavior*, 22(4), 301-329.

Cambourne, B., & Turbill, J. (1990). Assessment in whole language classrooms: Theory into practice. *Elementary School Journal*, 90(3), 337-349.

Commission on Standards for School Mathematics of the National Council of Teachers of Mathematics. (1989). *Curriculum and evaluation standards for school mathematics*. Reston, VA: National Council of Teachers of Mathematics.

Johnston, P. (1992). Nontechnical assessment. *The Reading Teacher*, 46(1), 60-62.

McKenna, M.C., Robinson, R.D., & Miller, J.W. (1990). Whole language: A research agenda for the nineties. *Educational Researcher*, 19(8), 3-6.

Moss, P.A. (1992). Shifting conceptions of validity in educational measurement: Implications for performance assessment. *Review of Educational Research*, 62, 229-258.

O'Neil, J. (1993). Can national standards make a difference? *Educational Leadership*, 50, 4-8.

Paris, S., Calfee, R., Filby, N., Hiebert, E.H., Pearson, P.D., Valencia, S.W., & Wolf, K. (1992). A framework for authentic literacy assessment. *The Reading Teacher*, 46(2), 88-98.

Taylor, B.M., Frye, B.J., & Gaetz, T.M. (1990). Reducing the number of reading skill activities in the elementary classroom. *Journal of Reading Behavior*, 22(2) 167-179.

Winograd, P., Paris, S., & Bridge, C. (1991). Improving the assessment of literacy. *The Reading Teacher*, 45(2), 108-116.

CHAPTER 4

Mary Ann Snider
Susan Skawinski Lima
Pasquale J. DeVito

RHODE ISLAND'S LITERACY PORTFOLIO ASSESSMENT PROJECT

RHODE ISLAND'S PORTFOLIO ASSESSMENT PROJECT is not about sweeping assessment reform, interrater reliability, or the problems with statewide implementation of performance assessment. It is about a small state's fledgling efforts to merge instruction and assessment in a thoughtful yet powerful way. The project began more as an exploration than as the result of a state mandate. It remains that way today, except that now the explorations have moved beyond the walls of the Department of Education and into hundreds of classrooms across the state.

As of this writing, the project's fate is still undetermined. Rhode Island has an assessment program which, at present, does not include portfolios. Higher level subtests of the Metropolitan Achievement Test (MAT) are administered in grades 4, 8, and 10. Students also produce a writing sample that is collected and evaluated by a group of teachers. A new state plan proposes to introduce more performance assessment, but the timeline for implementation is unclear and the necessary budgetary increases are not yet in place.

The portfolio project may be able to fill the need for more performance assessment if its integrity is not diminished in the process. The tension is clear: ours is a state assessment project that is not implemented or aggregated statewide. Teachers who have chosen to participate are addressing issues related to teaching, learning, and assessment through an intensive process. The actual assessment piece is almost incidental to the broader and profound changes occurring in their classrooms. Merely mandating the assessment without supporting the change process would have had a different impact on teachers and their students. Pieces of evidence could have been collected and assessment obligations fulfilled, but the core of the teaching/learning process would, once again, have escaped significant change.

This chapter outlines the project's evolution. It presents a picture of what we think is real portfolio assessment and of Rhode Island's progress toward statewide implementation without the mandates—so far. Despite our state's size, it has taken more than three years for the Department of Education and a number of teachers to form a philosophy and framework for Rhode Island's portfolio assessment project.

The Nature of the Project

In Fall 1989, we began the portfolio assessment project. It started with the concept of portfolio assessment endorsed by the State Education Governing Board, a modest budget from the Rhode Island State Assessment Program, and the general philosophy and belief that using portfolios to assess student progress and to inform instruction made a great deal of sense. We were convinced that for assessment to be meaningful and useful in schools and classrooms, it had to be "hands on"—conceived and developed through collaboration among teachers and Department of Education staff.

As the project has moved through various stages, we have learned and shared our knowledge with other groups who are implementing similar programs (see, for example, Brandt, 1989, 1992; Perrone, 1991; Wiggins, 1989a, 1989b). But when our project started in 1989, the literature offered little enlightenment about classroom models of portfolio assessment and few states could cite experiences with successful designs. Consequently, the project began as an exploratory enterprise characterized by definite purposes and goals but with a less distinct plan for achieving them.

Our primary motivation in undertaking this project was to find ways of better linking assessment with classroom literacy practices. In particular, the imperfect match between an instructional focus on strategic reading or the writing process and an assessment focus on standardized testing was raising concerns about the validity of assessment results. Furthermore, we recognized that teachers maintained a great deal of assessment data, although not always in a formal way, and that this information was as vital as the results collected in more structured formats. Therefore, this project began with a commitment to teacher ownership of assessment and has consistently affirmed that the most meaningful and useful assessment is based in the classroom, where teachers and students collaborate on purposes, forms, and interpretations of assessment.

As we reflect on the first three years of the project, we recognize that a model of process and form has emerged in three stages: exploring possibilities, building collaborative portfolios, and shaping a portfolio classroom environment. Each stage has been characterized by successes and struggles.

Stage One: Exploring Possibilities

With little more than unlimited energy and optimism, we assembled a small group of educators to probe the dimensions of portfolios for elementary teachers and students. A discussion group of eight—four third grade classroom teachers from four Rhode Island districts, three Department of Education specialists, and a researcher from the Educational Testing Service based in Princeton, New Jersey—met once a month during the first year to explore the potential of assessment activities that would reflect authentic classroom practice.

At the start, our thinking was dominated by a need to formalize the "mechanical" aspects of portfolios: What does a portfolio look like? What activities will yield good evidence? Who has access to portfolio information? Consequently, these early discussions revolved around what kinds of information would best describe student growth and which instructional activities presented favorable and meaningful opportunities for assessment.

Our work took a step beyond writing portfolios and moved into integrated portfolios that included evidence of student performance in reading, writing, listening, speaking, and mathematics. In monthly discussions, we framed activities that teachers implemented. As we weighed the merits of activities and results, we found that students were capable of far more than we had originally anticipated and that they revealed remarkable insights about their own learning and progress. For example, in composing a letter describing "All about Me as a Reader and Writer" one third grader wrote, "I am a pretty good reader because I read fast.... I know I am writing well when I write fast and ideas are rushing through my head." When we asked students to keep a log of books they read, we found that the same reader would select books of varying difficulty depending on genre, book topic, and how she or he felt about reading that day. When students were expected to describe the processes they used in solving word problems, teachers were surprised to find that some good problem-solvers were unable to describe their methods very well, while some students who had difficulty in arriving at correct answers had a well-developed understanding of appropriate strategies.

At the end of the first school year, the specialists responsible for the project visited each third grade classroom to conduct conferences with students about their work. Despite the quantity of evidence collected by students and teachers, it was clearly evident that teachers had made most of the decisions about what would go into portfolios; students had been given little input or ownership. This knowledge, and our own expanding notions about portfolios, established the framework for the next stage of development: building collaborative portfolios.

Stage Two: Building Collaborative Portfolios

As we entered the second year, we felt ready to broaden participation in our project to a greater number of teachers. To do so, a "teacher of teachers" approach was adopted. The Department of Education specialists worked directly with teams of "lead" teachers from our four districts, and these teachers shared their knowledge and experiences with "associate" teachers in their schools. In addition, our monthly discussions were more structured and our approach to implementing portfolio assessment was more systematic this year than in the first year. For the most part, student portfolios were pocket-folder expandable files or, occasionally, boxes that could hold a variety of artifacts. To the portfolio activities developed in year one, we added several tasks such as story mapping, written responses to reading, and interviews.

Efforts at this stage revealed two critical insights about the portfolio process. First, while defining the parameters of student portfolios and identifying productive activities were important and necessary efforts, they actually represented a middle point in the process. We recognized that the beginning point was the determining of student outcomes (broad expectations of what students should be able to do), competencies (more specific descriptions of student performance), and criteria (features used to evaluate student performancc). Furthermore, once outcomes, competencies, and criteria were articulated, they needed to be explained and demonstrated to students so learners would have a clear understanding of instructional goals of the classroom and of how they would be judged as learners.

A second insight centered on the significance of collaborative portfolios, or portfolios that represented both student and teacher input. We realized that students unquestionably should retain ownership of their portfolios, but students and teachers must work together to collect evidence, interpret results, and plan future progress. Such collaboration has multiple implications for classroom instruction. For example, in order to assess student performance in particular areas of competence, teachers needed to model strategies that had never before been part of instruction. For example, before asking students to write "All about Me" letters, teachers found they had to describe their own thinking about themselves as learners and demonstrate the language that could express such reflections. In addition, when teachers planned instruction based on what they learned from continually assessing students, instruction became more flexible and fluid, varying from student to student. One teacher summarized this difference by noting that "my plan book is just not useful anymore. I have to organize my teaching around student needs, not around days of the week!"

These changes in perception also influenced our interactions with students about the evaluation process. A team approach was taken to evaluation conferences. Teams were composed of several individuals who shared an interest in students' portfolios: the current classroom teacher, a future classroom teacher, an administrator, and a representative from a local college or university. While we observed many changes in the quality of student work, we acknowledged that the most successful portfolio assessment efforts were nurtured by an environment of flexibility, risk-taking on the part of both teachers and students, and trust.

Stage Three: Shaping a Portfolio Environment

The third stage, reached in year three, represented yet another change in design. Although we still had much to learn, we had developed a richer understanding of portfolio assessment that we felt could be shared with a wider audience. We also knew that the more teachers who shared in our discussion, the greater our knowledge base would be. Consequently, the monthly discussion group was expanded to include 33 lead teachers and 79 associate teachers from 12 districts. We also took a more structured approach to working with teachers by designing a year-long course in which instruction, curriculum, and assessment were discussed.

Discussions with teachers now were directed to a greater extent to exploring the more abstract, philosophical characteristics of portfolios; less time was spent sorting out their concrete, practical aspects. The features of assessment unique to portfolio development and essential to its implementation became the focus.

One characteristic of a "portfolio classroom" was student reflection. Asking students to be reflective about their learning means asking them to examine what they know about themselves as learners, to think about what they are learning, how they are learning, and why they are learning. Such reflection does not often flourish without the understanding and nurturing of the classroom teacher. Portfolio assessment expects students to accept a measure of responsibility for their own learning and to initiate efforts to improve their own performance. Within the context of shared responsibility, the teacher must yield some of the decision-making about instruction and assessment, and students must accept some of the decision-making about their own learning. We discovered that changes such as these are not easily accomplished, and they will not occur at all unless teachers are willing to endure some degree of ambiguity—at least in the beginning.

A second characteristic of the changing classroom environment was evident from the content of the portfolios in year three. Initially, teachers felt most comfortable with portfolio artifacts and activities we suggested. As a result, the contents of most portfolios were limited to only a few activities such as the "All about Me" letter and book logs. However, as teachers began to understand the relationship among outcomes, competencies, instruction, and assessment, and began to relinquish more of the responsibility for selecting artifacts for inclusion to their students, the portfolios became more diverse.

Findings about Portfolios

Throughout these stages, there were several consistent themes. The portfolio process and its physical form were continually revised, and the manner in which teachers and children used the artifacts was expanded. Portfolios were not prepared and shelved until the end-of-the-year portfolio interviews. Teachers were taught how to hold conferences with their students and were encouraged to do so throughout the year. We knew from prior experience that children who had the most successful conferences were those who had many opportunities to practice. Teachers and children modeled for one another how to talk about their work and present their portfolios in a confident manner. They also practiced with several types of conferences—conferences for sharing with their classmates, for assessing specific pieces, or for showcasing their entire portfolio.

Developing a thorough understanding of portfolio assessment has been a slow and sometimes painful procedure. In the beginning, teachers felt most comfortable collecting evidence through activities that we suggested and outlined; their questions and concerns about parent involvement, administrative support, and report card dilemmas were also familiar territory, although we could not always respond with solutions. However, in many ways our efforts have yielded remarkable results. Classrooms became increasingly student centered. Modeling emerged as a crucial part of classroom instruction. Students were much more involved in designing assessment and selecting evidence; they acquired the language of assessment and were able to reflect about themselves as learners. Furthermore, enthusiasm among teachers and students was infectious, as evidenced by one teacher who remarked, "I can't wait until September, so I can really do it right!" Teachers also reported improvements in students' self-esteem and independence. Most important, we learned that portfolio assessment can provide the types of rich, contextual, meaningful information about student growth and achievement that can satisfy the accountability requirements of teachers, parents, and administrators.

Our journey has shown us that portfolio assessment and the manner in which it is implemented constitute a developmental process, not an event. By this we mean that our understanding of portfolio assessment continues to evolve; it is never complete. In the same way, we believe that teachers should adjust continually the content and context of assessment to address the needs of different students at different points in time.

Our work has led us to a "draft" model that is malleable and flexible and will be revised and revised again as Rhode Island teachers learn more about portfolio assessment practices. At the beginning of the model's implementation process is the development of learning outcomes—statements that identify our global expectations of learners. From outcomes, competencies are derived; these describe more specifically the strategies, performances, behaviors, and abilities students will exhibit as they progress toward outcomes. An example of an outcome might be "Students will read age- or grade-appropriate materials with adequate comprehension"; a competency that would contribute to achievement of an outcome could be the ability to retell a story or complete a story map. Competencies clearly delineate the types of evidence that will indicate performance.

Once learning outcomes and competencies have been drafted, attention should focus on generating criteria to evaluate portfolio evidence. Our concept of criteria considers not only the product constructed by the learner, but also the process employed to create the product. Thinking about criteria means thinking about features that depict expected performance in broad strokes. For example, in crafting criteria for a narrative retelling, features such as story organization, level of detailed information, understanding of story grammar, and the awareness of retelling processes could be examined. Criteria must be specific enough to let children know where their strengths and weaknesses lie, help teachers pinpoint "next steps" for instruction, and provide information to plan for revision. Concurrently, they must be broad enough to assess a wide variety of pieces representing many different curricula for potential use at multiple grade levels.

The original plan for the third year of the project scheduled some criteria development during each monthly session. Early attempts at developing criteria were not successful because participants were more concerned with the mechanics of portfolios—how children would access portfolios, record keeping, and who should put evidence in the portfolio. We resisted the temptation to move our agenda along quickly and made adjustments. About midyear when teachers felt their more basic questions had been answered, criteria were developed smoothly and easily.

Once instructional and assessment parameters have been established through outcomes, competence, and criteria development, attention must be centered on classroom implementation. Teachers need to think about the procedures around which portfolios will be organized—what type of folder or box will hold portfolio materials, where they will be stored, what supportive materials students will need, and so on. As portfolio activities are implemented and evidence is collected, forms for summarizing assessment findings and results will emerge. Periodically throughout the year, students and teachers should schedule time for individual portfolio conferences. Students prepare for conferences by organizing materials; then they present their evidence of growth and discuss their profile of achievement with the teacher. The final step in implementing portfolio assessment involves analyzing results to determine growth and to plan subsequent instruction.

Success and Struggle

Many of the project's design features have been the source of both success and struggle. The results of relying on the "form follows function" axiom of our framework provides the best example of this paradox. The portfolio's function has been to allow children to demonstrate progress toward meeting Rhode Island's literacy outcomes in a context that is in harmony with their classroom's natural rhythm; the form within which this might occur has been wide open. Teachers have been invited to experiment with a variety of structures, formats, and techniques to make this happen—a potentially risky and scary situation for educators who traditionally have been given rules and regulations for assessment. Form has emerged from the group of teachers' interactions of the past several years, however. The nature of this form and the issues on which teachers, children, and school systems continue to work have produced their own successes and struggles.

Success and Struggle with Teachers

The first success was internalization of the process by the teachers. Statements such as the following were offered: "In order for me to ask my kids to talk about their writing, I realized I must first model this type of discussion for them" and "I know that we developed this the last time we were together, but it doesn't quite work. Could we change it?" These statements are markedly different from those posed earlier in the project, questions such as "What do you want us to put in the kids' portfolios for our next meeting?"

The portfolio's form also necessitated a shift in responsibility within the classroom. There is much support in current research for the recommendation that classrooms become child centered. Initially, we shared such thinking with the teachers without clearly defining how this might happen for them and their students. As expected, children were becoming responsible for maintaining their own portfolios in very artificial ways because neither they nor their teachers were sure how to make this shift in responsibility happen. In some cases, teachers felt uneasy about letting go of control. After all, who could predict what a third grader might select as his or her best piece of writing? At first, teachers wanted to "child-proof" the potential of disastrous selections.

We acknowledged that some inappropriate selections could not be avoided, especially as children first began to select pieces. The solution is to encourage thoughtful selections by both teacher and students. Evidence may be placed in a portfolio by either child or teacher; however, each entry must be accompanied by a brief narrative describing why the piece was selected. This step marked the development of two important features of the project: first, children were beginning to take responsibility for their portfolios; second, much attention was devoted to metacognition.

Many participants were skeptical about expecting young children to be reflective and analytic about learning. Selecting sensible portfolio entries, discussing work during conferences, or knowing the value of a piece before it is graded by a teacher requires a great deal of insight from an eight year old. Bringing children to this level of ability requires incredible effort from teachers. We modeled for teachers how instruction might look and the language needed to foster metacognition. With some trepidation, teachers carried these tools and new expectations to their classrooms.

No one was let down by this endeavor. A list of teaching suggestions began to take form. One teacher had her students brainstorm a list of reasons why something might be placed in a portfolio. Another practiced holding conferences with one brave child in front of the class. All teachers found themselves posing how and why questions more frequently. Teachers reported that they were reexamining instruction in light of the student learning outcomes they had developed and were instituting changes that better prepared students to meet those expectations.

Success and Struggle with Children

Most children have met expectations and many have surprised their teachers. Second graders have discussed the challenge of reading chapter books, the fun in discovering they like biographies, and the benefits of adding descriptive words to their writing. Children's candor about their learning has informed instruction. A conference with one child revealed an inability to select appropriately challenging books from the library. His book list revealed a series of "too easy" readings chosen, not for this feature, but because his reading competence in previewing was not well developed. The dynamic interaction among curriculum, instruction, and assessment became very real for those involved in this project.

Furthermore, classroom portfolios became vehicles for communicating between students and teachers and between teachers and parents. Children have been very clear about how much they enjoy the portfolio project. One classroom of students who were maintaining portfolios in reading and writing requested an expansion into mathematics!

Success and Struggle with Transition Issues

The transition from traditional approaches to the ones espoused by this project has raised three major issues for educators. The first surfaced as teachers became less content with their reporting systems. One teacher observed that she had never had so few grades but so much information about her students. However, the school system's report card required that the insights provided by all her data be collapsed into a single letter grade. Second, the mismatch between instruction and assessment also was apparent within the state and local testing programs. Many teachers feared that children would be confused by the content and style found in norm-referenced assessments in comparison to classroom practices. Finally, participants talked at length about the daily struggles involved in making the transition to portfolios. At first glance, the portfolio project appeared to require only minor modifications to the classroom—a few folders, a couple of conferences, and all would run smoothly. With experience and insight, teachers realized the project required much more than cosmetic adjustments.

Discussion surrounding these transition issues began when one teacher observed, "This project is about instruction as much as it is about assessment." Participants were now grappling with the appropriateness of their districtwide curricula, the concern of administrators that skills be covered, and the time demands of trying to fulfill old requirements and meet new expectations. Teachers also worried about the mixed messages children would receive if they were promoted to a more traditionally structured classroom at the end of the current school year.

None of these issues has been resolved entirely. Undeniably, the process of change is very difficult. Help must come from collegial and administrative support at the local and school levels. Administrative support must go beyond the nod of approval to participate in the project. Teachers must be provided the time and encouragement to take risks and discuss challenges and accomplishments. Flexibility in relation to daily routines, curriculum, reporting, and local assessment is critical. Understanding and an optimistic attitude from colleagues would be welcomed.

Reflections and Recommendations

Through our project, we have learned a great deal about the issues surrounding portfolio assessment. At times it seemed that tremendous strides were being made; at other times it seemed as if there was no movement at all. The model that has evolved is not so much a formula as a philosophy of instruction and assessment. Making this philosophy come alive in a classroom takes a great deal of time and effort, but it also has the potential to unlock the enthusiasm and zest for learning that have all too often been dampened by years of worksheets, seatwork, and memorization.

Portfolio assessment requires a fragile balance of many factors. This is a new way of operating for many teachers; traditional educational practices often overlook the idea that good assessment looks like good instruction, and vice versa. Fellow teachers often consider teachers who use portfolio assessment to be mavericks who have latched on to the latest fad in education. These teachers, in turn, are often saddled with having to complete all other work required by districtwide curricula and administer multiple-choice achievement tests in their classrooms as well.

In spite of the struggles, however, the teachers and Department of Education staff who have worked and continue to work on the portfolio assessment project are convinced that the benefits are worthwhile and that the principles inherent in such an authentic assessment effort can help guide educational reform in a meaningful way. In this spirit of collaboration and in the hope that the Rhode Island experience will help others, we make the following recommendations:

- There must be a fundamental belief shared by those involved that all students can learn and achieve at high levels.

- Participants must embrace the concept that good assessment looks like good instruction.

- Students must be ready to take more responsibility for their own learning and be willing to accept the teacher as a facilitator or coach rather than solely as a lecturer.

- The support of the school and district administration must be evident for portfolio assessment procedures to succeed.

- Teachers must be given the time to learn about portfolio assessment, to try out numerous activities, and to experience successes as well as failures.

- Teachers must be provided with adequate technical assistance in the portfolio assessment area, for the great majority of classroom teachers are neither trained nor experienced in these procedures.

- Schools and districts should start with those teachers who wish to change the way they assess. At the early stages at least, portfolio assessment should not be required of those who are not ready to accept it.

References

Brandt, R.S. (Ed.). (1989). Redirecting assessment (special issue). *Educational Leadership*, 46(7).

Brandt, R.S. (Ed.). (1992). Using performance assessment (special issue). *Educational Leadership*, 49(8).

Perrone, V. (Ed.). (1991). *Expanding student assessment*. Alexandria, VA: Association for Supervision and Curriculum Development.

Wiggins, G. (1989a). A true test: Toward more authentic and equitable assessment. *Phi Delta Kappan*, 70(9), 703-713.

Wiggins, G. (1989b). Teaching to the (authentic) test. *Educational Leadership*, 46(7), 41-47.

Robert C. Calfee

COMMENTARY ON *Rhode Island's Literacy Portfolio Assessment Project*

STATE ASSESSMENTS OF STUDENT ACHIEVEMENT are going through a paradigm shift. On the one hand is the security of the tried and true. In previous decades, the task of a state assessment department was to develop an item bank for a curriculum domain, establish the reliability of the total test score, collect data, compute summary scores, publish the results, and then pass the baton to policymakers. Now everything is up for grabs. How are those in charge of schools to manage a new game with uncertain rules, where it is not clear who *is* in charge? Snider, Lima, and DeVito identify two significant threads in the tangle: portfolio assessment should be meaningful and valid, and it should be linked to instruction. These concepts presumably distinguish this approach from previous methods used in Rhode Island (and other states and provinces). The challenge is to define the first two terms and to bridge the gap between internally and externally mandated assessment.

The authors of this chapter rely on the narrative, a sensible strategy under the circumstances. In analyzing their story for this review, I looked for themes (the conceptual core) and lessons (the practical outcomes). In these comments I summarize the highlights of the paper and then present themes and lessons.

Highlights

The story comprises seven segments: an opening, three year-long episodes, a list of findings, and final sections on successes and struggles and reflections and recommendations. As the story opens, the authors set the stage for portfolio assessment that is unencumbered by state mandates and accountability. They rightly acknowledge the benefits of the situation and cautiously wonder about the future of the project.

The state hurried to the front of the parade and Snider and her colleagues describe the 1989–1992 program of portfolio assessment from the state perspective. The first year was a pilot study: four volunteer teachers and four consultants. The goal was to promote both teacher and student ownership of the portfolio concept. Monthly team meetings and classroom visits apparently sustained a collegial environment, although the report provides little substantive detail. The authors remark that teachers made decisions and students had virtually no input. More to the point, it appears that teachers looked to the consultants for guidance, and then passed on assignments to students. The consultants encouraged experimentation and risk-taking, but regular classroom teachers, working in isolation from one another, were uneasy with this advice.

During the second year, the state established district teams and injected more structure into portfolio design. The teams were still rather top-heavy, with teachers outweighed by resource specialists, administrators, professors, and the consultants. The structure centered on portfolio mechanics and content. Meetings included some conceptual discussions about curriculum, learning, and instruction, but the authors provide little detail.

The third-year agenda changed because of increased requests from teachers for assistance in implementing portfolios—requests that sprang from instructional needs more than a desire for accountability. The program shifted to a "teacher of teachers" design, the number of participants increased tenfold, and collegial meetings became more like a course. The chapter recounts increasing concern with learner outcomes and student reflection but provides few examples.

The section on findings alludes to "several consistent themes" that are based on experiences and anecdotes rather than more concrete data. My interpretation of this section suggests the following findings from the project: (1) portfolios emerged from an exploratory process; (2) these explorations dramatically transformed the classroom context for both teachers and students; and (3) the ongoing process led the teams to reflect on student learning outcomes, after which evaluative criteria emerged "smoothly and easily."

The final sections attempt to sort out these issues. For instance, the authors make this provocative statement: "The portfolio's function has been to allow students to demonstrate progress toward meeting Rhode Island's literacy outcomes in a context that is in harmony with their classroom's natural rhythm; the form within which this might occur has been wide open." The first primary success of the three-year effort mentioned by the authors was the promotion of "ownership by teachers and students." The authors describe the shift in teachers' discourse from "What do you want us to put in the kid's portfolios?" to "I know that we developed this the last time we were together, but it doesn't quite work. Could we change it?" I wondered whether such exchanges were typical. Professional ownership demands reflective collegiality, which means time for discussion and experimentation. The section on transition touches on matters like time and encouragement, noting that "none of these issues has been resolved entirely."

In the final section, Snider, Lima, and DeVito address several compelling issues, moving from one to another without clear resolutions. For instance, they did not produce a kit and would not recommend it to others if they had; they suggest that each state, district, school, and teacher must recapitulate the process for themselves. They warn about the difficulty of the process and point out that the assessment backgrounds of teachers and administrators are poor preparation for innovative thought and action. The paper concludes with seven generic recommendations; in them, "portfolio assessment" could be exchanged with the name of any other innovation. The exception is the claim that good assessment looks like good instruction, a point to which I will return later.

Themes and Lessons

Although the authors emphasize the uniqueness of the Rhode Island experience, I think their narrative yields lessons for others. I would first like to focus on the open-endedness of the concept of portfolio assessment that is celebrated by its advocates (see, for example, Harp 1991; Tierney, Carter, & Desai, 1991; and Herman, Aschbacher, & Winters, 1992, for rather specific recommendations). This ideology meshes with that of discovery learning (Shulman & Keislar, 1966), in which participants receive a problem with little or no direction and are left to solve it by their own devices. Although discovery learning is slow and discouraging, if you manage to solve the problem, transfer is broad. In directed learning, participants receive detailed instructions about what to do and how to do it; learning is fast but has little transfer. These two strategies combine in "guided discovery," where instruction structures the task while leaving room for participants to experiment with their own ideas.

This principle applies to portfolio assessment. For more than a decade, researchers and practitioners have explored basic concepts that bear on portfolio assessment and that set preliminary parameters for any new program (see the references in Tierney et al., 1991). Some parameters spring from previous paradigms: assessment must meet standards of reliability and validity to be taken seriously, for example. Other parameters are unique to performance-based techniques, but the domains of writing, science, and mathematics provide important examples of practical research on such assessment (see Calfee & Hiebert, 1991, for general comments). For instance, we know that teachers can generate consistent ratings of performance tasks if they have adequate preparation and clearly defined rubrics, whereas different tasks and prompts can yield significantly different images of student achievement. Such principles need not be discovered anew by every district, school, and teacher.

A second theme, purpose and audience, is captured by the phrase "Why are we doing this?" It shows up in teachers' efforts to do what they thought they were supposed to do, frustrating state efforts to promote local ownership. Researchers have contrasted internal versus external mandates in educational assessment (Cole, 1988; Calfee & Drum, 1979; Haertel & Calfee, 1983). If the primary audience for the portfolio assessment program in Rhode Island comprises state policymakers, then eventually teacher ownership will be undermined by demands for standardization and efficiency. If teachers are the primary audience, different requirements move to the top of the agenda, several of which are identified by Snider and her colleagues: replacing isolation with genuine opportunities for collegiality, more equal balance of power between classroom teachers and "experts," substantial professional development opportunities, and resources (including time) for teachers to master what amounts to a new craft.

The authors properly celebrate their success at engaging classroom teachers in ownership of assessment. Missing in their presentation is the bottom line: What will Rhode Island learn about student achievement from this program? Perhaps classroom teachers in Rhode Island will take local control; a century ago, parents and community were the primary audience for assessment, and the idea of state or national accountability had not occurred to anyone. Today's policy environment is different. I have suggested elsewhere how classroom teachers might bridge external and internal accountability by means of a teacher log in which they record student achievements based on portfolio information along with observations and individual assessments (Calfee, 1992).

A third theme builds on the proposal to demonstrate growth in student achievement in a way that allows a seamless merging of teaching and assessment. The chapter provides relatively few qualitative excerpts to make this idea more concrete, but I think the power of portfolio assessment arises from its potential to realize this goal. What would it take to create this merging? For the reading-writing curriculum, portfolio assessment means the accumulation of concrete artifacts such as compositions and book reports, things that can be placed in a folder. Bird (1990) suggests that the portfolio technique is a metaphor not to be taken too literally, that the starting point for a literacy portfolio is not a physical folder but an accumulation of students' achievements demonstrating developmental progress through a curriculum.

What should be accumulated and how? These questions focus attention on curriculum and instruction. Curriculum is the central concern. It makes no sense to amass everything a student churns out during the school year; rather, assessment should build on artifacts that show progress toward curriculum standards. Progress speaks to growth. Unless a school or district lays out a clear progression of developmental learning outcomes at the beginning, it is virtually impossible to design an achievement portfolio. Standards raise the "good enough" question. Passing the end-of-unit test in the basal reader is one touchstone, but its replacement remains to be clearly defined and developed. Finn (1993) has argued persuasively for separate attention to content standards and performance standards. Educators need to be clear about criteria for deciding what to teach; several groups are now laying out content standards to meet this need. Less attention is being given to defining levels of quality achievement. Where such efforts appear, they tend to be relativistic: our students should do better than average, they should be world class. For portfolio assessment to win the day, issues of content, growth, and quality will have to be wrestled to the ground.

The issues falling under this theme are further complicated by the effort to connect assessment with instruction. Instructional practice is moving from rote recitation to more active metalearning, from individualized worksheets to group projects. The teacher's role changes dramatically in this new model, from fount of knowledge to assessor of learning. The consequence is that the student portfolio depends as much on the teacher's observations and reflections as it does on student artifacts. The expert artist's portfolio is a collection of finished products; the developing artist's portfolio consists in large measure of the mentor's reactions.

From this perspective, the student's folder is the tip of an iceberg. Only as these materials are informed by students' reflections and teachers' commentary does a record of achievement begin to emerge. This concept of assessment implies a student who does less and critiques more, who is challenged by authentic tasks rather than uniform assignments, who looks to colleagues and genuine audiences for feedback as much as to the teacher's red pencil. It entails a teacher who observes more and presents less, who relies more on journal entries and less on checklists, and who looks more to colleagues and less to end-of-unit tests in setting standards.

Summary

In summary, Snider and her colleagues have given us a provocative account of Rhode Island's experience in moving into a new world of assessment. Their story has exciting sparkles, ambitious goals, genuine redirections, reassuring honesty. I wished for more concrete excerpts, a clearer picture of the typicality of various experiences, a stronger voice from the trenches. But this is a provocative narrative, with lessons for the many other places now straddling similar paradigm shifts, revolutions, earthquakes. I was appreciative of the great respect in this account for the perspective of the classroom teacher. In this age of "bureaucratic beancounters," it was encouraging to hear the authors' continued and concrete emphasis on "professional ownership." This vision may be workable only in small geographic areas like Rhode Island, but I hope not. The central issues of education—curriculum, instruction, and assessment—are settled not in legislatures and parliaments but in the classroom. Accountability for equal educational opportunity, however, is a responsibility better handled at the governmental levels. A critical challenge for the coming years will be the bridging of this gap.

References

Bird, T. (1990). The schoolteacher's portfolio: An essay on possibilities. In J. Millman & L. Darling-Hammond (Eds.), *The new handbook of teacher evaluation* (pp. 241-256). Newbury Park, CA: Sage.

Calfee, R.C. (1992). Authentic assessment of reading and writing in the elementary classroom. In M.J. Dreher & W.H. Slater (Eds.), *Elementary school literacy: Critical issues* (pp. 211-226). Norwood, MA: Christopher-Gordon.

Calfee, R.C., & Drum, P.A. (1979). How the researcher can help the reading teacher with classroom assessment. In L.B. Resnick & P.A. Weaver (Eds.), *Theory and practice of early reading: Volume 2* (pp. 173-206). Hillsdale, NJ: Erlbaum.

Calfee, R.C., & Hiebert, E.H. (1991). Classroom assessment of reading. In R. Barr, M. Kamil, P. Mosenthal, & P.D. Pearson (Eds.), *Handbook of reading research: Volume II* (pp. 281-309). White Plains, NY: Longman.

Cole, N. (1988). A realist's appraisal of the prospects for unifying instruction and assessment. In C.V. Bunderson (Ed.), *Assessment in the service of learning.* Princeton, NJ: Educational Testing Service.

Finn, C.E., Jr. (1993, January 20). What if those math standards are wrong? *Education Week, 20,* 36, 26.

Haertel, E., & Calfee, R.C. (1983). School achievement: Thinking about what to test. *Journal of Educational Measurement, 20*(2), 119-132.

Harp, B. (1991). *Assessment and evaluation in whole language programs.* Norwood, MA: Christopher-Gordon.

Herman, J., Aschbacher, P., & Winters, L. (1992). *A practical guide to alternative assessment.* Alexandria, VA: Association for Supervision and Curriculum Development.

Shulman, L.S., & Keislar, E.R. (1966). *Learning by discovery: A critical appraisal.* Chicago, IL: Rand McNally.

Tierney R.J., Carter, M.A., & Desai, L.E. (1991). *Portfolio assessment in the reading-writing classroom.* Norwood, MA: Christopher-Gordon.

PART THREE

Elfrieda H. Hiebert
Editor

AUTHENTIC ASSESSMENT IN THE CLASSROOM AND BEYOND

OVERVIEW   Teachers continually gather information on their students. They study students' compositions to decide on foci of upcoming lessons, for example, and they use running records of students' reading to select books for particular groups or units. The results of the standardized tests that many teachers give each year are used quite differently. Typically, scores come back several months after the tests have been given. A principal may congratulate a teacher for high test scores or suggest that test scores could be higher. These comments may lead a teacher to decide to devote more student time the next year to practicing and completing worksheets on isolated skills. Classroom instruction, therefore, is influenced by the standardized tests that are mandated by external agencies such as departments of education or school boards. To date, however, the judgments and decisions of these external agencies have not been informed by classroom-based data—running records, compositions, or literature logs, for example—that teachers and students gather over a semester or year.

Educators and policymakers have become increasingly aware of the consequences of emphasizing standardized test scores and disregarding measures of daily classroom literacy use: the narrowing of the curriculum, fragmentation of teaching, emphasis on lower levels of literacy, and "snapshot" views of learning. Many classroom measures represent students' performances on tasks over time and thereby show their development and progress; many of them illustrate literacy use with more complex texts and responses than the texts and responses of standardized tests.

The underlying aim of the three case studies in this section is to advocate the increased use of assessment that better represents the important literacy tasks of classrooms. The first order of business in all of the projects was for teachers to use the information they gathered for instructional purposes. Critical goals of literacy were identified in districts and educational agencies and common ways of establishing progress toward those goals in classrooms were established. Many teachers were probably already gathering and studying miscue analyses, student compositions, and book logs of home reading. The projects in this section were designed to make the use of these tools more consistent. When teachers in a school are consistent in gathering samples of students' writing or miscue analyses, these measures can inform instruction across grades. The use of a common set of measures can also help parents understand the goals of the school and their children's progress toward those goals.

Although to date only the Kamehameha Elementary Education Project has summarized the results of these measures across schools, all the efforts described in this section could be useful to policymakers and administrators. And, although the underlying aim of these projects was to assist teachers in their instructional tasks, they each have the potential to contribute to the use of "multiple indicators" by external agencies.

A common feature of the projects in this section is the focus on a shared set of measures across classrooms within schools or across schools within a system. The descriptions of the case studies also demonstrate that such efforts require the coordination of various groups of educators. Sometimes assistance came from the district office; sometimes it came from the local university. These partnerships among classroom teachers and educators from central agencies and universities are not without challenges, as the respondents to these three cases point out. With the support provided by a group, however, teachers could work on identifying and implementing a common set of measures in contexts where there was some facilitation of the process. The selection and consistent use of a common set of measures requires teachers' understanding of the functions and instructional interpretations of these measures. A context for negotiation, demonstration, and sharing is most likely much more effective in honing this understanding than are mandates for such assessments without staff development. The three case studies in this section illustrate ways in which these contexts have been created in different school systems.

As other groups of educators work to meet similar challenges, they should keep in mind a theme that the authors of these chapters repeat: each project is still evolving; none claims to be finished. Relationships among educators, between instruction and curriculum, and between classroom teachers and children are always in flux. These case studies should be regarded as chapters in the story of change. A return visit in several years would reveal new relationships and new questions. But a significant feature of these case studies would remain: in these three projects teams of educators take on challenges so that higher literacies can be fostered.

CHAPTER 5

Kathryn H. *Au*

PORTFOLIO ASSESSMENT: EXPERIENCES AT THE KAMEHAMEHA ELEMENTARY EDUCATION PROGRAM

THE WHOLE LANGUAGE MOVE-MENT along with growing evidence of the negative consequences for students and teachers associated with conventional standardized testing (see, for example, Ascher, 1990; Paris et al., 1991) have made the development of alternative systems of assessment and evaluation more urgent. This chapter discusses the implementation of a portfolio assessment system designed to support teachers' use of a whole language–oriented curriculum, the achievement of students shown through the system, and practical implications for others who might be attempting to implement similar systems.

The portfolio assessment system was implemented as part of changes to the curriculum of the Kamehameha Elementary Education Program (KEEP).

Established in 1971, KEEP is aimed at improving the literacy achievement of Native Hawaiian students in public elementary schools in areas of high educational need throughout the state of Hawaii. KEEP seeks to make an impact through inservice efforts that increase teachers' expertise in language arts instruction. Inservice activities, including teacher support groups, workshops, and classroom observation and feedback, are carried out by KEEP consultants based in the public schools. Under a cooperative agreement with the Hawaii State Department of Education, KEEP has worked in public schools since 1978. In 1990–1991 KEEP provided services to 121 teachers and 2,730 students in kindergarten through grade six in eight public schools. (For further background information on KEEP, see Au et al., 1984.)

The Program

In the spring of 1989, KEEP staff members decided to move the curriculum in the direction of whole language (Au, 1990). The main reason for this decision was dissatisfaction with the levels of literacy achievement shown by many KEEP students. Experiences in a small number of KEEP classrooms indicated that a whole language curriculum might advance Hawaiian students' language arts achievement. For example, students' writing seemed to show dramatic improvement in classrooms where teachers used a process approach as advocated by Graves (1983) and others. Research and nationwide trends in the direction of whole language also influenced the decision (Bird, 1989; Tunnell & Jacobs, 1989).

Developers describe the new KEEP curriculum as a "whole literacy" rather than a whole language approach because it incorporates certain features not generally associated with the whole language philosophy. First, although the curriculum includes many activities for speaking and listening, it focuses on reading and writing. Second, the curriculum incorporates standards or benchmarks that spell out expectations for achievement at each grade level (these are discussed later in this chapter). Third, the curriculum emphasizes teacher-guided reading lessons taught to small groups, sometimes formed on the basis of students' reading ability. Fostering students' ownership of literacy, their willingness to use reading and writing in their own lives, is the overarching goal of KEEP's whole literacy curriculum. The five other aspects of literacy emphasized in the curriculum are the writing process, reading comprehension, language and vocabulary knowledge, word-reading strategies, and voluntary reading (Au et al., 1990).

Shifting to Portfolio Assessment

In conjunction with the shift to the whole literacy curriculum, KEEP staff members decided to implement a portfolio assessment system with features such as those described by Valencia (1990). Use of portfolio assessment appears to offer several avenues for improving KEEP's services to students and teachers. First, portfolio assessment creates multiple measures for evaluating the literacy achievement of KEEP students, and hence the effectiveness of the program. Previously, scores on standardized reading tests served as the only measure of students' achievement. Having information on a wider range of literacy outcomes, affective as well as cognitive, gives KEEP staff and teachers a comprehensive overview of students' development. Such information can guide staff and teachers in future curriculum development, inservice programs, and instructional efforts and approaches.

Second, portfolio assessment directs the attention of teachers to major dimensions of students' literacy development that might otherwise be neglected. For example, critics argue that teachers may slight such important outcomes as higher level thinking and motivation to read because such outcomes typically are not assessed on standardized tests (Ascher, 1990). Portfolio assessment makes positive use of the widely reported phenomenon that teachers feel they must teach to the test (Smith, 1991).

Third, portfolio assessment moves the program away from an overreliance on standardized tests. Critics suggest that standardized tests lead teachers to provide students with poor quality instruction because many teachers narrow instruction to focus on the specific objectives in the tests (Smith, 1991). Concerns that testing lowers the quality of instruction are particularly acute in schools with a high proportion of students from diverse backgrounds (Ascher, 1990), as is the case in KEEP classrooms.

Design

Portfolios and other new approaches to assessment draw on current theories suggesting that human abilities are tied to the specific contexts in which they are learned and used (Collins & Brown, 1990). These theories imply that the contents of a portfolio should be drawn from everyday classroom instructional activities, since it is within the context of these activities that students actually learn to read and write. Portfolio assessment differs significantly from traditional assessment that relies on a single testing event in a context markedly different from everyday instruction.

KEEP's portfolio assessment system addresses all aspects of literacy in the curriculum. The specific measures for each aspect are consistent with the instructional practices used by exemplary KEEP teachers, as well as with the whole literacy philosophy. For example, exemplary KEEP teachers have students read and discuss high-quality works of children's literature and write in response to that literature. In the portfolio system, assessment of reading comprehension is based on students' written responses to the stories they have read and discussed with the teacher. Figure 1 presents an overview of the measures used to assess all six aspects of the literacy curriculum in kindergarten through grade three (measures for grades four through six are currently being developed). Measures for the writing process, reading comprehension, and word-reading strategies were adapted from those described in journals and other publications; measures for ownership, language and vocabulary knowledge, and voluntary reading were developed through observations and tryouts in KEEP classrooms.

Figure 1
Portfolio Assessment Measures

Aspect of Literacy	Sources of Data
ownership	teacher observations and student surveys
writing process	teacher observations and samples of writing produced during writers' workshop
reading comprehension	samples of written responses to literature
language and vocabulary knowledge	samples of written responses- to literature
word-reading strategies	running records
voluntary reading	teacher observations and voluntary reading logs

Grade-level benchmarks are a key feature of KEEP's portfolio assessment system. They are used for the purposes of program evaluation to determine whether students are performing at, above, or below grade level in each aspect of literacy. The sources for the benchmarks are the language arts framework developed by the Hawaii State Department of Education, the reading objectives of the National Assessment of Educational Progress (1989), a widely used standardized test series, and recently published basal reading, language arts, and literature programs.

The established benchmarks set the standards for students' achievement in each aspect of literacy at the end of a particular grade level. For example, to meet the benchmarks for reading comprehension at the end of second grade, students must be able to do the following:

- read and discuss a story at the 2.2 level;
- provide a personal response to the story;
- write about story elements including the characters, problem, and solution;
- write about the theme or author's message; and
- write about an application of the theme to their own lives.

To meet the benchmarks for ownership, these students must consistently show that they enjoy reading, recommend books to others, learn from reading, and write outside of school, among other things.

Ideally, data on each aspect of literacy accumulate in students' portfolios on an ongoing basis. Twice a year, in fall and spring, all students in grades one through three are formally evaluated on each of the aspects of literacy. Kindergarten students are assessed on entering school, using five emergent literacy tasks from the test battery developed by Mason and Stewart (in press); portfolio data are formally evaluated only in the spring. This procedure gives kindergarten students a chance to become acquainted with school literacy routines and seeks to avoid the inaccurate labeling that sometimes results when children are tested in mainstream contexts with which they are unfamiliar (see, for example, Labov, 1973).

In the formal evaluations, information in students' portfolios (including teachers' observations) is first summarized on data-collection forms. Each form contains the information needed to arrive at a rating of at, above, or below grade level in that particular aspect of literacy. For example, the second grade form for reading comprehension shows whether the child has written about story elements, themes of stories, and applications to his or her own life. In the spring, if a second grade child shows the ability to write a personal response and to write about story elements, themes, and applications for stories at the 2.2 reading level, that child is rated as at grade level. Figure 2 (overleaf) shows a completed data collection form for the reading comprehension of some second graders.

Each school submits completed data collection forms for each class. Data are aggregated by totaling the number of children rated above grade level, at grade level, or below grade level in each aspect of literacy by class, by grade within school, and by grade across all KEEP schools. Seven bar graphs showing the fall and spring results are prepared for each classroom, one for each aspect of literacy and one showing students' instructional reading levels (operationally defined as the difficulty level of the texts used as the basis for assessing students' reading comprehension).

Figure 2
Completed Data Collection Form

READING/LISTENING DATA COLLECTION CHECKLIST

TEACHER: B. Maeda GRADE: 2 SCHOOL: Kuliouou DATE: 4/91

GRADE LEVEL BENCHMARKS
S=Satisfactory D=Developing
EVALUATION COLUMNS
+=Exceeds grade level benchmarks
/=Meets all grade level benchmarks
−=Doesn't meet all grade
level benchmarks

STUDENT NAMES

COMPREHENSION	Belle	Sean	Charles	Tina	Kawika	Earl					
Participates in small group reading discussions (K–6)	S	S	S	S	S	S					
Shares written responses to literature in small group (K–6)	S	S	S	S	S	S					
Aesthetic											
Writes personal responses to literature (K– –listening)											
Writes personal responses to literature (1–6– –reading)	S	S	S	S	S	S					
Comprehends and writes about theme/author's message (2–6)	S	S	S	S	D	D					
Applies/relates theme to own life/experiences (2–6)	S	S	S	S	D	D					
Makes connections among different works of works of literature (4–6)											
Applies/connects content text information to own life (4–6)											
EVALUATION: Aesthetic response (K–6) [+, /, −]	✓	✓	✓	✓	−	−					
Efferent											
Comprehends and writes about characters & events (K– –listening)											
Comprehends and writes about characters & events (1–2– –reading)	S	S	S	S	S	S					
Comprehends & writes about problem/goal & solution/outcome (1–2)	S	S	S	S	S	S					
Writes summary that includes story elements (3–6)											
Reads different genres of fiction and shows understanding of genres (4–6)											
Understands literary elements [e.g., characterization, symbolism] (4–6)											
Reads nonfiction and shows understanding of content (4–6)											
EVALUATION: Efferent response (K–6) [+, /, −]	✓	✓	✓	✓	✓	✓					
INSTRUCTIONAL READING LEVEL	2.2	2.2	2.2	2.2	1.2	1.1					

Figure 2
Completed Data Collection Form (*continued*)

READING/LISTENING DATA COLLECTION CHECKLIST

TEACHER: B. Maeda GRADE: 2 SCHOOL: Kuliouou DATE: 4/91

GRADE LEVEL BENCHMARKS
S=Satisfactory D=Developing
  EVALUATION COLUMNS
+=Exceeds grade level benchmarks
√=Meets all grade level benchmarks
−=Doesn't meet all grade
  level benchmarks

STUDENT NAMES

LANGUAGE AND VOCABULARY KNOWLEDGE	Belle	Sean	Charles	Tina	Kawika	Earl					
Quality responses during small group discussions (K−6)	S	S	S	S	S	S					
Quality written responses to literature (K−6)	S	S	S	S	D	D					
Notes new and interesting words in small group discussions (2−6)	S	S	S	S	D	D					
Notes new and interesting words during voluntary reading (3−6)											
Uses structure and background knowledge [look−in strategy] (3−6)											
Uses context [look−around strategy] (3−6)											
Uses other resources [dictionary, thesaurus, content text, etc.] (3−6)											
Integrates strategies/resources [context, structure, etc.] (3−6)											
EVALUATION (K−6) [+, √, −]	√	√	√	√	−	−					

WORD READING AND SPELLING STRATEGIES											
Knows letter names and sounds (K only)											
Uses consonant sounds in inventive spelling (K only)											
Attends to print during independent book reading (K only)											
Uses meaning cues (1−3)	S	S	S	S	D	D					
Uses structural cues (1−3)	S	S	S	S	S	D					
Uses visual cues (1−3)	S	S	S	S	S	S					
Integrates cues [meaning, structure, visual] (1−3)	S	S	S	S	D	D					
EVALUATION (K−3) [√, −]	√	√	√	√	−	−					

Reading Level (Running Record)	2.2	2.2	2.2	2.2	1.2	1.1					
% Accuracy (Running Record)	98%	98%	99%	99%	93%	90%					
Self−Correction Ratio (Running Record)	1:3		1:5	1:13	1:3.5	1:6					

Collecting Portfolio Information, Fall 1990

Before the portfolio assessment system was introduced, KEEP teachers and consultants relied on skills-oriented, criterion-referenced tests for the ongoing assessment of students. Teachers were accustomed to using test results to guide instruction. Many were disgruntled when use of these traditional multiple-choice tests was discontinued, and they were slow to accept the new portfolio assessment system (Yumori, 1991). In our system, student performance is supposed to be assessed in a collaborative effort involving the classroom teacher, KEEP consultants, and paraprofessional aides. In fact, with few exceptions, KEEP consultants and aides assumed all the responsibility for the Fall 1990 data collection and evaluation. KEEP staff members rather than classroom teachers administered running records, analyzed the data, transferred the data to summary sheets, and rated students as at, above, or below grade level with reference to the benchmarks. The data collection process took longer than anticipated and was not completed in some schools until November. In some cases information could not be collected because the whole literacy curriculum had not been fully implemented in classrooms. For example, information on the writing process could not be obtained if teachers were not conducting a writers' workshop.

The most serious problem, however, appeared to be one of understanding, not logistics. The vast majority of teachers, consultants, and aides did not appreciate that the whole literacy curriculum and portfolio assessment system were supposed to work hand in hand. Most of these individuals had a positive attitude about whole language and KEEP's new whole literacy philosophy but a negative attitude about the portfolio assessment system (Yumori, 1991; Yumori & Tibbetts,

1992). The difficulty seemed to lie in the holistic nature of the portfolio measures. Teachers believed that the criterion-referenced tests and related scope and sequence of skills told them exactly what to teach next. In contrast, inferring instructional implications from the portfolio assessment measures required the use of considerable professional judgment, which most teachers felt unprepared to exercise.

The specific procedures associated with the portfolio system also caused difficulty, and many consultants, teachers, and aides evidently did not understand the methods for gathering data on students' performance. For example, many teachers had their classes organized in three or four groups, each reading a different work of literature and writing in response to literature almost daily. However, in general they did not think to use students' existing work as the basis for evaluating reading comprehension in the new portfolio system. Instead, for some assessment purposes these teachers had all the students read the same text and write about it in the same format. Various consultants showed similar misunderstanding of the ongoing nature of the data-collection process, as indicated in their statements that certain data were missing because students were absent on the day the assessment was conducted. Most of these misunderstandings seemed to come about because teachers, consultants, and aides treated the portfolio assessment system as if it were traditional evaluation based on one-time testing events.

Another problem was that teachers, consultants, and aides had some difficulty visualizing what a grade-appropriate student response should look like. Although the measures and benchmarks were set for the KEEP program as a whole, the complex nature of most of the measures left considerable room for interpretation. In some schools consultants addressed this problem by involving all teachers at a given grade level in a process of discussion and consensus-building. For example, third grade teachers at one school participated in meetings in which they looked at samples of their students' work and developed guidelines for rating these samples. In other schools, consultants did not establish a discussion process but asked teachers to rely on their individual judgment.

The procedures for rating students as above, at, or below grade level led to considerable confusion. For example, consultants and teachers were likely to report students as being above grade level because of achievement superior to that of other students in the same grade, not because their achievement had met the benchmarks for that rating. This confusion was understandable because the portfolio procedures for arriving at judgments about students' performance were much more complex than those associated with multiple-choice and other familiar forms of assessment.

To help KEEP staff members in the schools develop a better understanding of the portfolio assessment system, meetings were conducted at each school in January. At the meetings, staff members received an explanation of the seven graphs prepared for each classroom and were encouraged to ask questions about the results and the portfolio assessment system. Further explanations were provided about the scoring criteria and the process used to analyze the student data. Problem areas were addressed in detail, including the rationale for the assessment designed for each aspect of literacy and the procedures for conducting the assessment, completing the data collection forms, and evaluating students. In addition, staff members' concerns about the system continued to be monitored throughout the academic year.

Collecting Portfolio Information, Spring 1991

For the next formal evaluation, information was again collected largely through the efforts of KEEP staff members with rather limited teacher involvement. The procedures for collecting and scoring data were the same as those used the previous fall, and some problems continued. Certain information was missing primarily due to oversights in recording. A few staff members again reported data based on a one-time event rather than a collection of student work. In these cases, ratings were made on the basis of a single sample of students' performance, rather than a collection of student work. In one second grade class, for example, the teacher asked students to complete a story frame and rated them in reading comprehension on the basis of this single piece of work. In another second grade class, however, the teacher looked over the writing in students' literature response logs. Overall, the process proceeded much more smoothly than it had six months earlier.

A set of bar graphs was again prepared for each classroom, this time showing both the fall and spring results. Figure 3 shows sample; in this case there were no missing data. Graphs were distributed to consultants in August 1991.

Results

Data were collected for 1,912 students in 6 public schools with 92 classrooms in kindergarten through third grade. As described earlier, results for the fall data collection were seriously flawed due to misunderstandings of some of the procedures for assessing students and for evaluating results against the grade-level benchmarks. Despite these limitations, it is possible to gain some general impressions. As might be expected, the vast majority of students in grades one through

Figure 3
Sample Graph

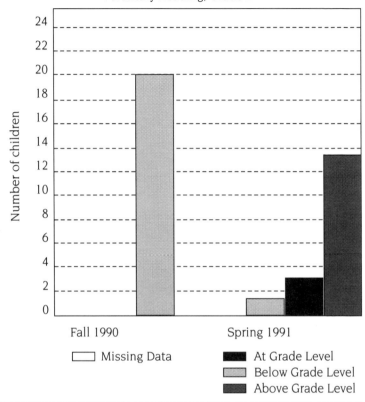

Voluntary Reading, Grade 2

three appeared to begin the year well below the grade-level benchmarks for the writing process, reading comprehension, language and vocabulary knowledge, and word-reading strategies. Most classes at all sites showed many students rated at grade level in voluntary reading, and some classes showed some students rated at grade level in ownership.

Much more confidence can be placed in the portfolio information collected in the following spring.

Only results for second grade classes are discussed here, but they are representative of the results obtained for kindergarten to grade three. (For the complete set of results, refer to Au & Blake, 1992.) Figure 4 reports the results for 499 students in 26 second grade classes. Experienced KEEP staff members estimated that, if the curriculum were having its optimal effect, 25 percent of the students might be above grade level, 50 percent at grade level, and 25 percent below grade level. The actual results obtained differ significantly from this distribution. The strongest results were seen in voluntary reading, with 95 percent of the students rated at or above grade level. Results in ownership were promising, with 30 percent of students rated above grade level, 19 percent at grade level, and 46 percent below. Results in word-reading strategies were also strong, with 39 percent of students rated above grade level, 20 percent at grade level, and 38 percent below. However, the writing process, reading comprehension, and language and vocabulary knowledge were areas of weakness, with few students rated above grade level and 54 percent to 59 percent rated below grade level.

Interpretation and Responses

In 1990–1991, the first year portfolio assessment data were collected, KEEP was in its second year of working with a whole literacy philosophy. The philosophy was not yet well understood by all KEEP staff members and teachers. This was not surprising, given reports indicating that the shift to a whole language or whole literacy philosophy may take from five to ten years (Bird, 1989; Routman, 1991). Results of the first year's implementation of the portfolio assessment system naturally reflected the transitional state of the KEEP program. Favorable results in voluntary reading suggested that there was adequate attention to this aspect of stu-

Figure 4
Second Grade Results, Spring 1991

Percentage of Students

Literacy Aspect	Above	At	Below	Missing Data
Ownership	30	19	46	5
Voluntary reading	71	24	5	0
Word-reading strategies	39	20	38	2
Writing process	0	33	55	11
Reading comprehension	5	31	59	5
Language and vocabulary	3	37	54	6

dents' literacy development. KEEP staff members assisted teachers in all kindergarten through third grade classrooms in implementing lending libraries. In addition, many students benefited from a summer book-mailing program implemented by KEEP staff members. Students' ownership of literacy also appeared quite strong, especially in kindergarten and first grade.

The results on these affective measures appear to be a reasonable estimate of the overall performance of students at the various grade levels, in part because of countervailing trends. On one hand, results in some classes were probably inflated somewhat because, although teachers and consultants were urged to base their judgments about students' voluntary reading and ownership on multiple observations, single observations were used. On the other hand, results were probably underestimated in other classes, particularly those of exemplary teachers who held high standards for themselves and their students. KEEP consultants reported that these teachers had a tendency to rate their students in an overly conservative manner.

The results indicated that many students were developing satisfactory word reading strategies, especially by third grade. This positive effect can be attributed, at least in part, to students' doing a considerable amount of voluntary reading.

Results for the writing process, reading comprehension, and language and vocabulary knowledge were poor across all grade levels. According to KEEP consultants, some results might have been stronger if teachers had a better understanding of the grade-level benchmarks. For example, to meet the benchmarks for writing at third grade, students had to have the experience of editing their own work. Teachers in some classrooms did not prepare students to edit. However, once many of these teachers became aware of the benchmarks, they decided in the future to teach students to do their own editing.

All in all, however, the disappointing results obtained in these three aspects of literacy could not be attributed to lack of knowledge about the portfolio assessment system. Rather, the results pointed to the need for substantial improvement in the instruction KEEP students received in the writing process and in reading comprehension; portfolio results were now perceived as valuable for the purposes of program evaluation. As a result, in Fall 1991, a major inservice effort was launched to better acquaint KEEP staff members and teachers with reading and writing instructional strategies consistent with a whole literacy philosophy.

KEEP consultants had learned that portfolio results could indeed be summarized for program evaluation purposes and could serve as an alternative to standardized test scores. They began to realize that these results could and would be taken seriously by administrators and policymakers.

Meetings were held to acquaint administrators, including principals of the KEEP schools, with the portfolio assessment system. Perhaps surprisingly, administrators did not focus on the relatively low levels of student achievement obtained in the first year of implementation. Rather, they expressed their support for the portfolio system, an understanding of the possibilities it offered for improving the quality of instruction, and optimism that results would improve in the years to come.

KEEP consultants made arrangements to share portfolio results with their teachers and to plan with teachers how the results might be improved during the coming school year. At one school, arrangements were made to release the teachers in grades one to three for a whole-day session on the portfolio results and plans for the coming year. The process of heightening KEEP consultants' and teachers' awareness of portfolio measures as outcomes of student achievement was further reinforced by asking teachers to make predictions about the results students would achieve in Spring 1992 for each of the six aspects of literacy covered by the assessment system.

Curriculum developers prepared a scoring guide, issued in October 1991. Staff members had requested such a guide in order to increase the accuracy and comparability of results across classrooms and schools. KEEP staff members at all schools were asked to submit samples of students' work showing achievement above, at, and below grade level in the writing process and in reading comprehension. Selected samples served as the anchor pieces in the scoring guide. Along with these samples, the guide provided a description of how each sample would be analyzed in terms of the data-collection form and rated in terms of the benchmarks. Figure 5 shows a student's written response to literature at the end of the second grade and an explanation of why this student was rated as performing at grade level.

While the results for students' literacy achievement in 1990–1991 were disappointing, the portfolio assessment system itself proved workable. Principals and other administrators showed a readiness to accept the results produced through the system as valid indicators of students' literacy along with—and even in place of—standardized test scores. Administrators at KEEP's home institution, the Kamehameha Schools, supported use of portfolio measures for evaluating the effectiveness of the KEEP program over a ten-year period.

Reflections

As the KEEP experience indicates, the shift to a portfolio assessment system, while certainly worthwhile, can pose considerable difficulty. The main source of difficulty seems to lie in educators' making the conceptual shift from traditional to new perspectives on assessment. Implementation of the new system got off to a rocky start, and many problems arose during the first data-collection period. However, the second collection went much more smoothly because teachers and KEEP staff members in the schools had become more knowledgeable about the system. A gradual smoothing out of difficulties is anticipated in future years as steps are taken (the development of the scoring guide, for example) to address practical problems encountered at the school level.

The shift to portfolio assessment does not mean that innovative, whole language-oriented programs will immediately be shown to produce positive results in students' achievement. In this case, the KEEP system

Figure 5
Scoring Guide Sample

Response to Literature (2²)

Name Kyle

Date

Story Title The Ledgend of the bluebonet

The problem in this story is When the rain harent come and the land and people are dying.

In the middle of the story the grate spirits told them they have stolen from the earth

The problem is solved when the girl berned the doll and sended the ashes to the north south

At the end of the story is when all the blue bonets growed and the rain came

I think the author wanted me to learn more about the earth and taking care of the earth.

My actions can show that I have learned this. What I can do is to recycle cans and papers

One of the new words my group talked about was ledgend

How did your group figure out its meaning? tai ledgend is a old story or a long journy

Did you like this story? Tell why or why not.
I like this story because it's nice to have a nice earth and a clean earth.

(margin, vertical text): when giving them back east and west and give them back to the land and came back to life.

Explanation of At–Grade-Level Rating

Personal response: Kyle explained why he liked this story.

Critical response: Kyle identified the characters, setting, problem, events, solution, author's message, and application in his response.

Figure 5
Scoring Guide Sample (*continued*)

Language and vocabulary knowledge: Kyle uses language well in his contributions to small-group discussions and in his written responses. He noted a new word from his reading and explained its meaning.

Word-reading and spelling strategies: The teacher's observations of Kyle's reading and the running record show that Kyle can use meaning, structural, and visual cues, and that he integrates the use of these cue systems to help him read. His running record confirms that his instructional reading level is approaching third grade.

relies on a combination of authentic, holistic measures and strict standards in the form of grade-level benchmarks. These measures and standards are not soft or lenient. Our initial results indicated that a significant number of KEEP students were performing well below the grade-level benchmarks in three aspects of literacy. On the basis of these results, corrective measures in the form of intensive inservice efforts were undertaken.

The KEEP portfolio assessment system was originally designed to address the program's need for a variety of measures of students' literacy development. Considerable attention was given to program evaluation issues, such as the aggregation of data across classrooms and schools; less attention was given to issues of teacher and student involvement, such as establishing a process by which students would set goals for their own literacy development. This was due to circumstances surrounding development of the portfolio assessment system, not to a valuing of one set of issues over the other. Pilot studies on student goal-setting within the context of the portfolio system are currently underway. For example, a fifth grade teacher is having her students write about the goals they have for themselves as readers and writers. She is meeting regularly with her students to discuss the progress they are making in moving toward these goals (Carroll & Christenson, in preparation). It remains to be seen, however, if the KEEP system or any other system can function to meet the needs of program evaluation and of teachers and students equally well.

In summary, portfolio assessment systems such as that implemented by KEEP can be used for the purposes of program evaluation in settings where there is a clear commitment to change. On the one hand, such systems are likely to prove difficult to implement, especially in the first few years, and considerable support must be provided to familiarize teachers and others with the theory and practice of the new forms of assessment. On the other hand, with the use of standards such as grade-level benchmarks, these systems can provide valuable information about students' achievement in affective as well as in cognitive dimensions of literacy, making the strengths and weaknesses of a program evident.

References

Ascher, C. (1990). *Testing students in urban schools: Current problems and new directions* (Urban Diversity Series No. 100). New York: Institute for Urban and Minority Education, Teachers College, Columbia University.

Au, K.H. (1990). From reading to literacy: Changes in the KEEP curriculum. *Kamehameha Journal of Education,* 1(1) 1-8.

Au, K.H., & Blake, K.M. (1992). *Development and implementation of a whole literacy based curriculum framework and portfolio assessment system.* Paper presented at the Annual Meeting of the American Educational Research Association, San Francisco, CA.

Au, K.H., Scheu, J.A., Kawakami, A.J., & Herman, P.A. (1990). Assessment and accountability in a whole literacy curriculum. *The Reading Teacher*, 43(8), 574-578.

Au, K.H., Tharp, R.G., Crowell, D.C., Jordan, C., Speidel, G.E., & Calkins, R. (1984). KEEP: The role of research in the development of a successful reading program. In J. Osborn, P. Wilson, & R.C. Anderson (Eds.), *Reading education: Foundations for a literate America*. Boston, MA: Heath.

Bird, L.B. (Ed.). (1989). *Becoming a whole language school: The Fair Oaks story*. Katonah, NY: Richard C. Owen.

Caroll, J., & Christenson, C. (in preparation). *Student goal setting in a fifth-grade classroom*. Unpublished manuscript, Kamehameha Schools, Honolulu, HI.

Collins, A., & Brown, J.S. (1990). The new apprenticeship: Teaching students the craft of reading writing mathematics. In L.B. Resnick (Ed.), *Cognition and instruction: Issues and agendas*.) Hillsdale, NJ: Erlbaum.

Graves, D. (1983). *Writing: Teachers and children at work*. Portsmouth, NH: Heinemann.

Labov, W. (1973). The logic of nonstandard English. In J.S. DeStefano (Ed.), *Language, society, and education: A profile of black English* (pp. 10-44). Worthington, OH: Charles A. Jones.

Mason, J.M., & Stewart, J.P. (in press). CAP *early childhood screening diagnostic tests*. Iowa City, IA: American Testronics.

National Assessment of Educational Progress (1989). *Reading objectives 1990 assessment* (No. 21-R-10). Princeton, NJ: Educational Testing Service.

Paris, S.G., Lawton, T.A., Turner, J.C., & Roth, J.L. (1991). A developmental perspective on standardized achievement testing. *Educational Researcher*, 20(5), 12-20.

Routman, R. (1991). *Invitations: Changing as teachers and learners*, K-12. Portsmouth, NH: Heinemann.

Smith, M.L. (1991). Put to the test: The effects of external testing on teachers. *Educational Researcher*, 20(5), 8-11.

Tunnell, M.O., & Jacobs, J.S. (1989). Using "real" books: Research findings on literature-based reading instruction. *The Reading Teacher*, 42(7), 470-477.

Valencia, S.W. (1990). A portfolio approach to classroom reading assessment: The whys, whats, and hows. *The Reading Teacher*, 43(4), 338-340.

Yumori, W. (1991). Implementation of a whole literacy curriculum. *Kamehameha Journal of Education*, 2(1), 71-82.

Yumori, W., & Tibbetts, K. (1992, April). *Practitioners' perceptions of the transition to portfolio assessment.* Paper presented at the Annual Meeting of the American Educational Research Association, San Francisco, CA.

Ileana Seda

COMMENTARY ON   *Portfolio Assessment:*
Experiences at the
Kamehameha Elementary
Education Program

THE EXPERIENCES OF THE KAMEHAMEHA ELEMENTARY
EDUCATION PROGRAM represent an approach contrary to
those described in most of the literature on portfolio
assessment. Accountability is understandably a major
concern of schools and school systems. Nevertheless,
in the literature on portfolio assessment, accountability
issues are subsumed to assessment of individuals'
achievements. KEEP's portfolio system was launched to
address program evaluation needs, making it the core
of assessment rather than supplemental to the well-
accepted (Mehrens, 1992) but often poorly understood
"formal measures" of learning and program effectiveness. I would argue that portfolio assessment and the
performances represented by portfolios need to be
carefully implemented and seriously studied in various
contexts if they are to gain credibility. The KEEP case
represents an effort in that direction.

Statewide portfolio assessment efforts such as
those that exist in Vermont and California address
instruction and teacher concerns more as an outcome
of the new system than as a process of change. My own
experience working with educators both in schools and
universities indicates that most are sympathetic to
novel ways of assessing (Seda, Miller, & Knaub, 1991).
However, they also seek the credibility of presumably
proven methods and are not supportive of substantial

change. In presenting the KEEP case, Au demonstrates quite effectively the successes as well as the failures of the first year of implementation of portfolio assessment. The forces that worked against full success of the program may be the most informative. As she clearly states, the failures were not the result of the portfolio system but of limitations in instruction.

KEEP's portfolio assessment system is a case of systematic implementation of change. It directly addresses some of the most sensitive and controversial concerns surrounding alternative assessment, namely accountability and well-defined standards. Some of the key features in the model are the institutional process of change, teacher change, and the implementation process. My use of change here is that described by Richardson (1990) as "teachers doing something that others are suggesting they do. Thus, the change is deemed as good or appropriate, and resistance is viewed as bad or inappropriate" (p. 11). Change, in this sense, is often external and imposed on teachers and schools. With this in mind, I will focus the rest of this commentary on the culture of educational change.

In order for change to occur—and assuming change is for the better—educational institutions and programs need to (1) understand change, (2) allow time for change, and (3) provide support structures for change. These concepts are intertwined, often occurring simultaneously. I will address each one in light of the information presented by Au.

Understanding Change

Most educational innovations, reforms, or new methodologies represent changes of the surface structures. Deep structural changes are often avoided because they require different ways of thinking about teaching and learning, take too long to implement properly, and remain tied to unchanged and inappropriate accountability systems. Although KEEP's mission has from its inception been geared toward language arts instruction and inservice education, participating KEEP schools confront challenges similar to those of schools without the "luxury" of such resources. The primary challenge is developing and implementing a process of deep structural change.

Au states that the main reason KEEP moved the curriculum toward whole literacy was "dissatisfaction with the levels of literacy achievement shown by many KEEP students." Thus, the incentive for educational change was low achievement (shown, presumably, by low test scores). However, educational change is risky because it can result in either higher or lower levels of measured achievement. KEEP's curriculum, as described, presents a sensible transition into whole literacy and addresses some of the most serious constraints educational systems face when confronted with radical change. At KEEP, the transitions are guided and shaped through an emphasis on reading and writing outcomes, achievement standards or benchmarks, and grouping practices for teacher-guided lessons. These emphases indicate that KEEP believes that standards are consistent with whole language and alternative assessment. At the same time, KEEP has removed the limiting or detrimental aspects of testing, while maintaining an assessment system that responds to student, instructional, and program-evaluation needs. As noted, it is at the point of program-evaluation needs that portfolio assessment may fall short (Arter & Spandel, 1992).

Efforts for educational change carry the implicit assumption that what exists is wrong (or in need of revision). Even within a discourse of making the good better, change can threaten teachers' professional expertise and effectiveness through the challenge. This is further compounded by some teachers' assumptions that change, especially imposed change, implies more work rather than a change in the manner of working. The assumption is not unfounded since many educational innovations are often add-ons to the curriculum, record keeping, and management. KEEP's strategy to overcome this problem was for aides and consultants to assume the extra load. One could argue convincingly that as consultants and aides work through the transition, teachers will be more willing to embrace the new system. However, the great limitation of this approach is that teachers themselves are outside the process of working through and with the new system "that others are suggesting they do." Although with this approach teachers may still recognize the virtues of a nascent portfolio system (and perhaps be thankful that they are not responsible for its flaws), they also will have less investment in and less understanding of the innovation. Furthermore, their limited involvement may undermine the development of a portfolio assessment culture (Wolf, 1989).

Au makes no mention of future plans to incorporate some of the most provocative features of portfolio assessment such as student-teacher dialogue and the process of selecting representative work (Arter & Spandel, 1992; Valencia, 1990; Wolf, 1989). If it is the case that these features will not be included, then the process will be tied to instruction in terms of work samples and artifacts. It will not directly incorporate the portfolio system into the teaching-learning process. Gradually adding some features that incorporate portfolios into the teaching-learning process would make KEEP's system even more comprehensive.

One feature of the KEEP model is the examination of targeted literacy outcomes from within the culture of teaching and teachers. The models emerge from exemplary teachers. Although not without its problems, this process makes the targets reachable to others. Teachers are often resistant to those not "in the trenches"; thus, the emergence of models from within the trenches is appealing to them.

Time Allotment for Change

During the first year of the project, KEEP's consultants and aides persisted in using single or one-time measures to include in student portfolios. This practice misses a major point about the nature of portfolios (Wolf, 1989). However, it is common to transpose well-known practices to not-so-well-known systems. Those same consultants and aides can probably articulate the premises of portfolio assessment very clearly. However, their actions do not follow suit because they may not have internalized the nature of such changes, nor do they yet understand the whole structure of the change. Conceptual learning and relearning require time. As an example, it is not uncommon to listen to teachers arguing that they are implementing whole language when they mainly have adopted features of a holistic approach without having embraced its philosophical underpinnings. At KEEP, consultants and aides took features of a portfolio system, put certain artifacts in the portfolio, and used their own intuitions within the structure of benchmarks to place students at, above, or below grade level. They have not embraced—or are not yet ready to embrace—the whole portfolio culture. The timeframe (ten years) that KEEP has allowed itself to develop the system will likely permit the change to mature and integrate well into the schools' and teachers' cultures.

Support Structure for Change

The natural resistance to change by teachers is embedded in an institutional process of change.

Teachers, along with their institutions, are resistant to "complex, conceptual, longitudinal changes" (Duffy & Roehler, 1986, p. 55) and do not easily alter their existing culture. The traditional concerns for accountability—how we know we are doing the best for students and how we demonstrate clear outcomes—are major institutional concerns. In the case of the KEEP process of change, such concerns were addressed by a transition process that kept some of the key features of institutional accountability and, at the same time, embraced a new model. The fact that benchmarks were developed, and that scope and sequence charts and traditional tests were used to determine such benchmarks, safeguards the system against total chaos. Thus, the KEEP implementation model can be characterized as cautious and firm.

New Structures for Teaching

KEEP's ten-year commitment at the Kamehameha Schools exemplifies the need to carefully implement and study portfolio systems (as well as other educational innovations). Beyond a thorough understanding of change within an educational culture, this uncommonly wise decision demonstrates a serious commitment from the administration and will likely permeate all levels of the system. This commitment will probably be reflected back to the administration from the staff as they understand, learn, relearn, and go through their own scaffolding process of translating the new structures into their teaching practice. It also will allow the necessary time to respond thoughtfully to general educational concerns of accountability and definitions of high standards.

References
Arter, J.A., & Spandel, V. (1992). NCME instructional module: Using portfolios of student work in instruction and assessment. *Educational Measurement: Issues and Practice*, 11(1), 36-44.

Duffy, G., & Roehler, L. (1986). Constraints in teacher change. *Journal of Teacher Education, 36,* 55-58.

Mehrens, W.A. (1992). Using performance assessment for accountability purposes. *Educational Measurement: Issues and Practice, 11*(1), 3-9.

Richardson, V. (1990). Significant and worthwhile change in teaching practice. *Educational Researcher, 19*(7), 10-18.

Seda, I., Miller, P., & Knaub, P. (1991). Collaboration to enhance curriculum, instruction, and assessment in reading. *Pennsylvania Educational Leadership, 11*(1), 23-28.

Valencia, S.W. (1990). A portfolio approach to classroom reading assessment: The whys, whats, and hows. *The Reading Teacher, 43*(4), 338-340.

Wolf, D.P. (1989). Portfolio assessment: Sampling student work. *Educational Leadership, 46* (7), 35-39.

CHAPTER 6

Sheila W. Valencia
Nancy A. Place

LITERACY PORTFOLIOS FOR TEACHING, LEARNING, AND ACCOUNTABILITY: THE BELLEVUE LITERACY ASSESSMENT PROJECT

PORTFOLIOS ARE A POPULAR TOPIC OF CONVERSATION in many school districts across the nation; Bellevue, Washington, is no exception. Just like other educators, we in Bellevue became disillusioned with multiple-choice tests of reading and writing that did not align with our curriculum and were far removed from the practices and decision-making of daily classroom life. We knew we had to find an alternative: In 1990, we began work on the Bellevue Literacy Assessment Project.

To completely understand both the process and product of our project, it is critical to understand the context in which it was conceived and implemented. Three factors played a powerful role in shaping our work: our starting place, our charge, and the district's philosophy. We did not begin with a focus on assessment; we began in 1990 with an effort to develop a new set of instructional outcomes for our students that would reflect current theory and research in the language arts. As a result of these new objectives and an emphasis on school-centered decision-making, teachers were encouraged to use a wide variety of materials and instructional approaches to teach reading and writing. While supportive of the new student learning objectives (SLOs), teachers, parents, and the school board nonetheless were concerned about how student learning would be assessed. Not only had we given up districtwide use of basal readers and other instructional materials with accompanying assessments, but we had implemented a new set of learning outcomes that were not adequately assessed by the traditional standardized reading and writing tests used in the district. We needed assessments that would help us evaluate student progress toward these outcomes, assess the processes as well as the products of learning, and foster the improvement of both teaching and learning. Portfolios seemed like a reasonable option.

The resulting portfolio project was a district-level effort. Thus, from the beginning, it had the dual obligation of trying to develop assessment strategies that would be useful at the classroom level and could also be used for district accountability. Further, we were required to involve a representative group of teachers so that we would have both broad-based input and an avenue for wide dissemination of information. Although the teachers in our project were volunteers, they represented many of the schools, grade levels, and orientations to teaching in the district. They brought with them a variety of valuable perspectives and a commitment to explore portfolio issues. We were forced to deal with the diversity found in all school districts.

Perhaps the most important factor that influenced our work was the district's understanding of the need for a long-term approach to change. After an initial two-year commitment to developing student learning outcomes, the district committed resources to our language arts assessment project for a minimum of five years; at the time of writing this chapter we had just completed year two. Everyone involved in this project understood that district administrators recognized the complexity of change and were willing to commit time and resources to support quality work. The net effect was a willingness of teachers to get involved, to believe that their efforts were valued, and to work hard to accomplish our goals.

Our charge from the district was to investigate, design, and develop assessment strategies that would help us evaluate student progress toward our new learning outcomes at both the classroom and district levels. Our first year was a "learning year" during which we studied standardized, norm-referenced tests and the possibilities offered by alternative measures. For example, we reviewed the match between our student outcomes and existing tests, discussed the connections between assessment and instruction, explored ways to involve students more effectively in their own learning and evaluation, and debated how to communicate students' classroom performance more completely to others. The products of our monthly after-school meetings were a broad-based understanding of assessment issues by staff and parents and a document stating our assumptions about assessment. This document, along with the district language arts SLOS, provided the direction for the following year's work.

The first year's work enabled us to decide what types of assessment we would pursue in year two. We decided to focus on the use of portfolios built around our SLOS. The concepts and implementation of portfolios intrigued us and seemed to be a logical match with our assumptions about assessment; portfolios provide multifaceted descriptions of students over time that support the improvement of teaching and learning. Our responsibilities to both classroom and district led us to establish several goals for our project, including describing the process of implementing portfolios, their impact on teaching and learning, and their reliability for evaluating student achievement.

Design

Twenty-four teachers of kindergarten to grade 12 from 17 schools met with us, the district language arts specialist and a university-based collaborator, on a nearly monthly basis during release time to discuss the use of portfolios in their classrooms. Each teacher was also responsible for working on portfolios with a group of volunteer teachers at her school and for reporting to the entire school staff about the work of the assessment project. It was important that the learning we were doing not be restricted to a small group of people but be constructed and understood broadly within our district community.

We developed an operational definition of our portfolios, beginning with general discussions about the attributes of a portfolio and the assumptions about assessment we had developed the previous year. We agreed that the portfolios should possess several key features that would allow them to do the following:

- align with the curriculum;
- document authentic instances of students' reading and writing;

- represent learning and progress over time;
- include multiple modes of documenting student ability (samples of work, interviews, observations); and
- provide meaningful opportunities for students to develop ownership for their own learning and evaluation (Valencia, 1990).

These underlying concepts ensured that portfolios would provide a vehicle for expanding the quality and quantity of information available for instructional decision-making.

Once we agreed on these features, we still needed to clarify the purpose, student outcomes, and implementation and management of the portfolios.

Purpose

We had three clear purposes for our portfolio project: (1) to improve instruction; (2) to improve student learning and ownership of learning; and (3) to report to others outside the classroom (Haney, 1991). Our readings in year one had prepared us for the challenges of addressing all three purposes with a single approach to assessment (Haney; Hiebert & Calfee, 1992; Valencia, 1991) and had also acquainted us with several different portfolio models. Our challenge was to develop our own model and definition of portfolios that would help us achieve our purposes.

We drew from four types: the showcase portfolio in which the student has primary responsibility for selecting his or her best or favorite work (see, for example, Paulson, Paulson, & Meyer, 1991; Tierney, Carter, & Desai, 1991); the evaluation portfolio in which most of the contents are specified and scored (Au, 1992; San Juan Unified School District, 1990); the documentation portfolio in which evidence of student progress is systematically placed in the portfolio by the teacher (and possibly the student) to build a rich description of the student without specific attention to clearly established scoring criteria (Carini, 1975; Chittenden & Courtney, 1989); and the process portfolios in which ongoing work for a larger project is chronicled and commented on by the student (Wolf, 1989). We found useful aspects in each type. We were committed to the student involvement and ownership that come with showcase portfolios, the consistency and comparability across portfolios that are assured in the evaluation portfolio, the rich descriptions of students afforded by the documentation portfolio, and the valuing of the learning process and of self-evaluation found in the process portfolios.

We concluded that we needed a composite portfolio that would enable us to address our multiple purposes. Our composite consisted of some work selected by the students and periodic self-reflection and self-evaluation of their progress; several "common tools" that all students would include to permit us to look across the portfolios prepared at a particular grade level; other work and notes included by the teacher or student that were important to understanding that student; and drafts, working notes, and other kinds of evidence of the learning process.

Student Outcomes

We knew we could not address all the student learning objectives during our pilot year, so we decided to sample a range of outcomes that introduced different challenges. Teachers agreed to focus on four of the six SLOs: (1) interaction with text to construct meaning; (2) choosing to read a variety of materials; (3) effective communication through writing; and (4) engagement in self-evaluation and reflection. We were not limited to these outcomes, but we took on an obligation to ensure that portfolios included information about these aspects of literacy for all students.

Implementation and Management

We were committed to making the portfolios useful for teachers and students during the instructional process; we were equally committed that they not be turned into a districtwide requirement that might be perceived as an intrusion. Teachers made individual decisions about how they were going to organize portfolios, what they would look like, how to handle grading issues, how to share the portfolios with parents, and how to coordinate them with other classroom procedures. Although individual decision-making on these issues was critical, other issues had to be agreed on by the entire group so we could examine information across students and classrooms. We argued pros and cons, negotiated, and, finally, all agreed to include the following in each portfolio:

1. Work selected by the student and accompanied by entry slips on which he or she reflects on why that particular work was selected for inclusion in the portfolio, collected at least three times during the year.

2. Portfolio visits during which the student reviews the entire contents of the portfolio and discusses or writes about his or her development in reading and writing, conducted at least two times during the year.

3. "Common tools"—or specific, systematic assessment techniques developed by the group for each of the student learning outcomes to be assessed—administered two or three times during the year. The common

tools were as follows: for the outcome "interact with text," written or oral retellings; for "choose to read a variety of materials," book logs kept for two-week "sweeps"; for "communicate effectively in writing," samples of writing; and for "self-reflection and -evaluation," entry slips and portfolio-visit questionnaires.

4. Work contributed by the teacher or student that would help describe the student more fully, with the type and amount left to student and teacher discretion.

In addition, we agreed that portfolios would be accessible to students, that we would try to use them in parent-teacher conferences, and that we would bring sample portfolios to our monthly meetings as a basis for sharing successes and failures.

After agreeing to use these several common assessment strategies, we then had to develop formats and procedures that were acceptable to our entire team and effective or adaptable for all grade levels. We relied on materials team members were currently using in their classrooms and on ideas gleaned from our readings. We recognized that our common tools had potential to, and in fact should, tap multiple aspects of students' literacy. For example, we developed and tried out several formats for our reading logs and found that they each had their own advantages and disadvantages in allowing us to see different aspects of literacy. Some required students simply to list the names of the books they had read, others included numbers of pages read, and still others included places for comments. In some cases students listed everything they read at home and at school and in others only school reading was listed; sometimes the log was kept for an entire grading period and sometimes it was used only during a "sweep" of any two weeks during the period.

We eventually settled on a reading log that enabled us to determine students' frequency of reading, the variety of reading material, personal responses to reading, and some information about comprehension. In addition, there was a place for students to indicate whether the reading was done at home or at school. (An example of one such log is shown in Figure 1.) Primary teachers included places for students to indicate that books were read aloud to them. Teachers decided that keeping logs all year was ineffective but that using a two-week sweep two or three times during the year would permit them and the students to look for patterns over time.

We also developed these questions for teachers to discuss with students to help them reflect on their own reading behavior and preferences:

- How often did you read during this two-week sweep?
- How many different types of books did you read? What types were your favorites?
- When you look at your reading log, what do you notice about yourself as a reader?
- What was your favorite thing to read?
- What would you like to read next?
- Overall, how would you rate the books you have been reading? Are they easy, medium, or hard for you? Why?
- How would you describe yourself as a reader?
- What would make you a better reader?

These questions were intended to encourage students to use the portfolio actively to reflect on learn-

Figure 1
An Intermediate-Level Reading Log

STUDENT'S NAME _____

BOOK	Type	COMMENTS	DATE	HOME-SCHOOL
Ben Franklin		He's such a good man	Nov 29	S
Paul Rever		I like the Book	30	S
George Washington		it's a great Book	dec 1	S
Jhon Hancock		it's not like my life	2	S
Jhon adams		He is a little Different than most	2	H
Boston tca party		it's exacke What I would Do	6	S
Mother west winds whu stories		Why Billy Possem plays Dead	8	S
Mother west winds whu stories		Why striped School Has stripes	8	S

ing and to set personal goals. The questions also provided teachers with insight into students' reading strategies, which are difficult to observe.

Other common tools—retelling procedures, sample passages, forms, entry slips, and portfolio-visit questionnaires—were developed using a similar process. Our decisions regarding formats and procedures were always guided by what we wanted to learn about our students, to teach, and to assess, and how the tool fit with sound, authentic instruction. We continually struggled to understand whether our tools were capturing important outcomes and how we could sort out whether disappointing student performance was a function of the tool or an indicator that more and better instruction was needed.

Supporting One Another

Our nearly monthly meetings proved to be the lifeblood of the project. We began each meeting with an open period (which often took up much more of our agenda than we planned) in which people could discuss how things were going. Many teachers commented that the meetings gave them the support to continue even when the process was time-consuming and frustrating. One of the primary teachers said, "What I appreciated was that we could talk about it as it really was—hard and frustrating." Although meetings often began with concerns about logistics such as time and space, the conversation quickly moved to deeper issues such as the effect of portfolios on instruction, student ownership, parent conferences, grading, and the structure of the school day.

Early meetings were the most difficult. We spent several months examining our student learning outcomes and asking questions such as these: How will we recognize these outcomes in our students? What instructional strategies and activities do we have in our classrooms that enable students to learn and apply these skills and strategies? Which of the activities might be good candidates for a portfolio? Discussions surrounding these questions led all of us to realize that we still needed to clarify and refine our understanding of the SLOs. Although this was an assessment project, we all ultimately recognized that these questions of curriculum and instruction had to be explored if teachers were going to implement portfolios and make decisions about students' abilities and progress.

Later meetings, when we had samples of children's portfolios, proved to be the most inspiring and most useful—especially when we shared evidence of students' reflections on their work and their progress over time (three examples of such evidence appear in Figure 2). Looking at student work instead of tackling more abstract concepts focused our conversations. We had actual portfolios for the next two phases of our meetings in which we used portfolios to describe children. Pairs of teachers would review the portfolios others had brought as samples. The teacher who had initiated that portfolio would add to the discussion only after she had listened to others discuss their observations. In this way, the initiating teacher could judge how well the portfolio represented a particular child and determine what else might be included or what documentation was needed to help others look at the work. All the teachers then began to compare and find common anchors for their expectations for children.

We spent several months using this process just to describe what we learned about each child from his or her portfolio before we moved to the issue of scoring. Our aim was to focus on the ways in which various teachers understood students as readers and writers and to see if we could develop common, reliable ways to evaluate students' strengths and needs. Predictably, the conversation often turned to instructional techniques and expectations. One initiating teacher commented to her team, "Of course you couldn't have evaluated this child's ability to respond to text personally. It's my fault. I didn't teach it." Turning to her colleagues, she asked, "How do you get your third graders to do it?"

Another key component of the group process was the expectation it developed for intellectual problem solving. Teachers had real concerns that had immediate relevance to their classrooms: Are portfolios something that will have value to me and my students? How do I make them work? What can I do about the fact

Figure 2
Evidence of Reflection on Learning

Entry Slip for a Portfolio Visit (Middle School, End of Year)

Name _____ Date _5-11 – 92_

Self-Evaluation

Have you changed as a reader? What are your strengths and weaknesses?

As a reader I haven't gone through many changes. My only weakness is getting into a book, but once I'm started my strengths take over me. I love to read!!!!

How have you changed as a writer? What are your strengths and weaknesses? As a writer I have relized that it takes many reworkings to come up with a final copy. Spelling is my main weakness and my strengths include sentence structure + punctuation.

Having looked at your work what goals would you set for yourself as a reader and writer? As a reader I plan to widen my spread of books and as a writer I'm going to look more deeply into my work.

Self-Reflection

When you look at your portfolio, how do you feel about yourself as a writer? Tell why you feel that way.

I feel great about myself as a writer. I started off rather slow, but have improved 95%, since the start of this year + I plan to keep improving untill the end.

When you look at your portfolio, how do you feel about yourself as a reader? Tell why you feel that way.

I feel extra great as a reader. I love reading + I love the feeling that I get when I finish a really good book.

---

that this common tool doesn't work at my grade level? How can we use this scoring rubric for ESL children? Because the project involved teachers from many grade levels, the group process fostered a respect for multiple perspectives and an openness to joint problem-solving. As group leaders, we shared any of our disagreements publicly with the group. We wanted to model that we

Figure 2
Evidence of Reflection on Learning (*continued*)

Entry Slip for Individual Piece (Grade 1)

Name *the princess* Date *4-20-9?*

This piece is my favorite because *I add'd details that where interesting to me and "so"they look like it's going to be a winner*

Entry Slip for Individual Piece (Middle School)

Name *The Stranger in the motel* Date *4/3/9?*

After thinking about your choice and why you chose it, complete the following paragraph and attach this slip to that piece of work.

I have chosen this piece of work because it is my favorite or the most meaningful to me. It is my favorite or most meaningful because *this is a true story and it happened to me and a close friend. It is a factual story and it felt very good for me to get it out on paper. I went through the whole writing process, which improved the story and put alot of thought into it.*

enjoyed working together and respected one another, and that our differences were not a problem; in fact, they led to richer conversations and better solutions.

Finally, the most critical part of the process was that teachers in the group participated in every decision and in the development of every common tool. They had a deep understanding of why we were engaging in each activity, a commitment to trying it out, and the understanding that we could modify the tools, procedures, and rubrics as we went along. Teachers were willing to suspend disbelief and, even though the portfolios were difficult, they stayed committed to one another, to us, and to the process.

Findings

At the time of writing, we have been documenting the process and content of portfolios and the perceptions of participants to them over an entire year. (The research design and full report of the results can be found in Valencia & Place, in preparation.) The highlights from a representative subset of the project point to the role that portfolios can have in supporting teachers and students in acquiring critical learning outcomes and the potential portfolios have as assessment tools.

First, the portfolio project assisted students and teachers in establishing a common understanding of reading and writing processes as quests for understanding and pleasurable events rather than the tedious acquisition of abstract skills. Students at all levels reported that they wanted to read more often, read more difficult books, and expanded their choices to include a wider variety of types. Their writing goals included writing more often and writing longer, more interesting pieces with more description, detail, and meaning. Teachers reported similar reading and writing goals for their students. As we would hope, these goals are consistent with the district learning outcomes and with our instructional emphases. It seems that students and teachers are aware of and focused on common goals, a situation that is likely to foster the attainment of those goals.

Second, both students and teachers understood the purposes for portfolios and were committed to continuing with them. Forty percent of students from all grades understood that portfolios helped them look at their growth and achievements over time. As one third grader wrote, "I love seeing what I did in the past and what I need to work on harder." Another 31 percent of students indicated that portfolios helped both them and their teachers understand and evaluate work; another 22 percent thought of portfolios as a place to organize and keep special work. For almost all the students (88 percent), portfolios had been a positive experience, one which they wanted to repeat the following year. One elementary student worried about keeping a portfolio next year because he wasn't sure his teacher would know how it was done. He thought a bit and then commented, "I know! I'll just have to teach her how to do it." The few students who didn't want to continue with portfolios reported that portfolios were confusing and they disliked filling out entry slips for their work. This seemed to be a problem in classrooms where teachers had students keep many other types of work folders (writing folders, art portfolios, and reading journals, for example) along with portfolios.

Teachers, too, wanted to continue with portfolios. One teacher wrote, "I am just beginning to figure out how to make the process an integral part of reading and writing time. I can't stop now." Another commented, "The ups and downs have leveled off. I've begun enjoying the process." At our last meeting of the year, the teachers turned a discussion of this year's project into a discussion about how they were going to make changes in portfolios next year. Many wanted to begin on the first day of school. Although they felt that we had needed the start-up time of a couple of months the first year, they did not want to waste any time getting started next year. In a related discussion, the group vetoed a district plan to disband the large group in order to focus on pilot schools the following year. Instead, they constructed an alternative in which the existing group would continue to meet, each member would work with other teachers in her building to implement portfolios, and we would have several smaller school-based pilot projects. They were unwilling to give up the process and equally unwilling to give up the support of the group; in exchange, they were willing to help their colleagues learn about and use portfolios.

Third, we discovered great variability in the type and number of pieces included in the portfolios. (Figure 3 gives an example of the sorts of materials included in one first grader's and one fourth grader's portfolios.) Although teachers in our group volunteered to participate, willingly attended all our meetings, and contributed to every decision, we found that none of the portfolios contained all of the common tools we had agreed to include. Writing was commonly included, as were book logs and self-reflections on reading and writing. Few portfolios contained more than one reading retelling, and some contained none. For some teachers, the common tools felt too much like a "drop-in" task, outside their typical teaching strategies, although for others, they seemed more natural.

The number of portfolio pieces ranged from 9 to 29, with most portfolios including several optional pieces of student-selected or teacher-selected work. There was great variation in these optional pieces; they included items such as entire reading response journals, research reports, published work, tests, and special projects. When five or more optional pieces were included, a unique and rich portrait of the individual child emerged. No portfolios contained observation checklists or anecdotal notes.

Fourth, we were able to score reliably a random sample of portfolios from all levels. We used a three-

Figure 3
Examples of Portfolio Contents

Grade One

- Story retelling using a story frame

- Writing
  Stories: "There Were 20 Birds," "Play Space" (selected as favorite piece with an entry slip attached), "The Hamster," "The Princess" (with reflection entry slip), "Mrs. Brooks" (selected as favorite piece with an entry slip)
  Poem: "I Have a Friend Named Vanessa"
  Published books: *The School, Dream Again Aliens*

- Free writing and picture about *Charlotte's Web*

- Illustrated book report on *The Dollhouse Murders*

- Reading logs (two two-week sweeps)

- Written response (worksheet) to story *Oliver Pig at School* (characters, important part of story, personal response)

Grade Four

- Reading log (one two-week sweep)

- Written retellings, including personal responses, to "How the Spider" and "Dogs at Work"

- Reflections on reading journal (ongoing personal journal of books read)

- Sample pages from reading journal with comments on *House on a Cliff, Treasure Island, Star Wars, Tales of a Fourth Grade Nothing*

- Writing
  Stories: "Indy Racing" (rough drafts and published version, including writing conference slip), "Goog Breaks Out of Jail" (rough drafts and published version, including writing conference slip), "Ghosts" (with self-evaluation slip attached)

stage process. First, a small team of teachers trained on a practice portfolio for each level (primary, intermediate, middle, high) by reviewing the contents and then moderating, through discussion, a consensus score. After this group calibration process, each team member scored portfolios individually. This process required raters first to describe, in narrative form, their conclusions and supporting evidence found for each of eight categories representing aspects of our SLOS (constructing meaning, writing, self-reflection in reading and writing, etc.). After describing, each rater assigned a score from 1 to 5, with 3 indicating average performance for a specific grade level in a particular category. This process required a focus on the actual content of the portfolio, which then led to a score.

Although the review of work appealed to teachers, the scoring did not. They found scoring difficult and tedious and worried that important insights and information were lost in assigning a number.

With limited training (less than one hour) and limited time spent reviewing each portfolio (15 to 20 minutes), we found that three raters reached agreement within one point 66 to 72 percent of the time. When only the best two of the three raters were considered, adjacent interrater agreement reached 90 to 100 percent. Although the actual training time was brief, the teachers who scored had been team members for two years. It is reasonable to assume that our discussions and work over that time resulted in a common understanding of literacy and of student performance; we do not know if "novice" scorers would have reached the same level of agreement.

The process of scoring led teachers to several conclusions and recommendations for the following year. They strongly recommended that we require and monitor the inclusion of common tools. Although they didn't believe that common tools were sufficient or rich enough to be used as the sole source of information, they believed them to be necessary anchors for understanding and scoring the portfolios. They believed that common tools would add to the interrater reliability and interpretation of student performance. They also recommended more teacher annotation of portfolio entries to help reviewers and parents understand the context in which work was produced. Further, several people in our scoring group recommended that we review and score portfolios several times during the school year. One teacher said, "Scoring forces you to focus on the criteria. You wouldn't necessarily want to publish scores or do anything with them, but when we had to score the portfolios, the conversation was different. Scoring helps you focus on how you want to teach. The scores don't show that, but our debates and conversations do."

Reflections

Our reflections on this project focus on both the product and process of our work. In terms of the product, we learned that if portfolios are to be used for programmatic or district evaluation, there should be a common core of items, strategies, or information that can be found in all portfolios. However, although this common core is necessary, it does not appear to be sufficient to assess adequately the complexity of literacy abilities of individual children. Portfolios are variable and reflect the unique characteristics of both the child and the classroom. Even when teachers and students willingly engage in keeping portfolios, variability is inevitable and the inclusion of agreed-upon contents cannot be assured. Portfolios provide a rich and complex picture of the learner that is likely to help teachers and students with instructional decision-making and goal-setting.

As a process, we have learned that engaging in portfolio assessment is much more than an assessment activity—it requires us to explore and, perhaps, alter our understanding of teaching and learning. The process forced us to confront our own confusions and the gaps in our knowledge of the subject matter of our portfolios—reading and writing. It forced us to articulate our goals and standards for student performance as well as the instructional opportunities we provide in our classrooms. We were forced to become reflective educators—to think deeply and clearly about subject matter, children, teaching, and learning.

It seems that one of the reasons both teachers and students became—and continued to be—committed to portfolios was because the process minimized the distance between instruction and assessment, teacher and child, and teacher and colleagues that has characterized assessment in the past. Implementing and examining portfolios placed assessment in the classroom, close to the child and the instruction. Teachers and students were continually interacting with the assessment-instruction link. Further, the portfolios honored teachers' work in the classroom and helped them better know their students as readers, writers, and thinkers; it honored students' work by encouraging them to take ownership for learning and evaluation. Finally, the process brought teachers together as colleagues, collaborators, and coinvestigators. They came to rely on one another for support, knowledge, and encouragement. The fact that both teachers and students saw this process as useful and important most certainly contributed to its success.

It is impossible to predict the process or product that would have resulted if this project had been implemented under a different set of conditions or in a different context. Had we not had the time, the district's commitment, a group of expert volunteers, the background knowledge, the shared decision-making, problem-solving, and discussion, we are certain the findings would have been different. We learned how important it is for these conditions to be present; the process of implementing portfolios is often difficult and frustrating, and the potential for losing interest and commitment is great. To view portfolio assessment only as a product, another program or activity, would be a mistake. Portfolio assessment is a process, one that has great potential to influence teaching, learning, and assessment and one that requires time, knowledge, commitment, and support if it is to have a positive impact on education.

Authors' notes: The work reported herein is in part a National Reading Research Center project of the University of Georgia and the University of Maryland. It was partially supported under the Educational Research and Development Centers Program (PR/AWARD no. 117A20007) as administered by the Office of Educational Research and Improvement, U.S. Department of Education. The findings and opinions expressed in this report do not reflect the position or policies of the National Reading Research Center, the Office of Educational Research and Improvement, or the U.S. Department of Education.

Special thanks go to the 1991–1992 Bellevue Literacy Assessment Project team teachers who were generous contributors, collaborators, and colleagues throughout the project: Lynne Beebe, Jill Boyd, Sue Bradley, Robin Carnahan, Mary Lou Constans, Julie Copp, Joy Dunham, Marla English, Rosemarie Everett, Betty Hall, Janet La Plante, Marilyn Moudry, Sharon Neal, Marilyn Niemi, Elizabeth Norvell, Sue Osborne, Isabell Phipps, Dodie Righi, Sue Schneider, Eunice Smith, Myrle Summerford, Linda Tipps, Marsh Williams, and Shirley Zapata. Without these committed educators, none of this work could have been done.

References

Au, K.H. (1992, April). *Development and implementation of a whole literacy-based curriculum framework and portfolio assessment system.* Paper presented at the annual meeting of the American Educational Research Association, San Francisco, CA.

Carini, P. (1975). *Observation and description: An alternative methodology for the investigation of human phenomena.* Grand Forks, ND: University of North Dakota.

Chittenden, E., & Courtney, R. (1989). Assessment of young children's reading: Documentation as an alternative to testing. In D.S. Strickland & L.M. Morrow (Eds.), *Emerging literacy: Young children learn to read and write.* Newark, DE: International Reading Association.

Haney, W. (1991). We must take care: Fitting assessments to functions. In V. Perrone (Ed.), *Expanding student assessment* (pp. 142-163). Alexandria, VA: Association for Supervision and Curriculum Development.

Hiebert, E.H., & Calfee, R.C. (1992). Assessing literacy: From standardized tests to portfolios and performances. In S.J. Samuels & A.E. Farstrup (Eds.), *What research has to say about reading instruction* (2nd ed., pp. 70-100). Newark, DE: International Reading Association.

Paulson, F.L., Paulson, P.R., & Meyer, C.A. (1991). What makes a portfolio a portfolio? *Educational Leadership, 49*(5), 60-63.

San Juan Unified School District. (1990). *Reading department curriculum materials.* San Juan, CA: Author.

Tierney, R.J., Carter, M.A., & Desai, L. (1991). *Portfolio assessment in the reading-writing classroom.* Norwood, MA: Christopher-Gordon.

Valencia, S.W. (1990). A portfolio approach to classroom reading assessment? The whys, whats, and hows. *The Reading Teacher, 43*(4), 338-340.

Valencia, S.W. (1991). Portfolios: Panacea or Pandora's box? In F. Finch (Ed.), *Educational performance testing* (pp. 33-46). Chicago, IL: Riverside.

Valencia, S.W., & Place, N. (in preparation). *A study of literacy portfolios for teaching, learning, and accountability.*

Wolf, D.P. (1989). Portfolio assessment? Sampling student work. *Educational Leadership, 46*(7), 35-39.

Kenneth P. Wolf

COMMENTARY ON   *Literacy Portfolios for Teaching, Learning, and Accountability: The Bellevue Literacy Assessment Project*

FROM THE SCHOOL HOUSE TO THE STATE HOUSE, the call for new forms of assessment has become increasingly loud, and much of the attention has focused on portfolios (Valencia, 1990; Wolf, 1989). Efforts are underway to design and implement portfolios in individual classrooms and schools as well as at the state/provincial and national levels. While enthusiasm for portfolios is high, knowledge about the portfolio development process and the effects of portfolios on teaching and learning is still relatively limited. The report by Valencia and Place on the Bellevue literacy assessment project is a big step in addressing that shortcoming. Not only do the authors offer important field-based insights about the challenges of implementing portfolios at the district level for both assessment and accountability, they have also documented a process that could productively serve as a guide for other districts embarking on portfolio adventures of their own. In this response, I will highlight key features of the Bellevue project, discuss a number of issues that emerged in the district's efforts to address systemwide accountability through classroom assessment, and outline major challenges facing the district in future years.

Key Features

Several features appear to be critical to the emerging success of Bellevue's literacy assessment project. The district began with a focus on curriculum and instruction and then selected an assessment approach that fit both its instructional outcomes and assessment purposes. The district deeply involved classroom teachers in all phases of the process and built a broad base of support throughout the school community. In addition, the district made a long-term commitment and maintained an ongoing evaluation of the project.

Begin with curriculum and instruction. As those who are designing and implementing alternative forms of assessment are learning, no matter where you begin in the assessment development process, you always end up addressing curriculum and instruction. The Bellevue project officially began as an investigation into alternative forms of assessment, but its real roots lay in the district's efforts several years earlier to develop desired outcomes more in line with current theory and research in literacy. Only after the new student learning objectives were in place did the district then embark on a search for an assessment approach that would both measure and promote student learning in these areas.

Identify appropriate assessment approaches. Many schools and districts have turned to alternative forms of assessment such as portfolios because of a fundamental mismatch between their instructional goals and the methods used to measure student progress toward those goals. In their quest for a better assessment solution, however, the Bellevue group did not just snatch the portfolio concept out of thin air. They critically reviewed a variety of assessment strategies and chose a portfolio approach because it best fit their needs. Once portfolios were selected, the assessment team carefully defined the concept and clarified the purposes for keeping portfolios, and then structured the contents of the portfolio and outlined a process for implementation.

Involve classroom teachers. Deeply involving teachers in all phases of the design and implementation of the assessment system is vital for a number of reasons. Most important, teachers are the best source of information about student strengths, needs, and progress. Additionally, involving teachers helps ensure that the assessment will be feasible and meaningful, and that teachers will understand and support the assessment system when it is put into practice. Moreover, participating in the assessment process contributes to teachers' professional growth in significant ways. From the beginning, Bellevue involved teachers, and involvement is being deepened by moving to a training and dissemination model in which the original project teachers train their school-site colleagues (who will become trainers themselves).

Build broad-based support. While teachers must be at the center of the assessment development process, other stakeholders should be involved in its evolution and informed of its progress. Bellevue sought to engage the entire school community—a collaboration of students, parents, teachers, principals, and district personnel. Assessment development efforts in which significant groups in the school community are not invited into the process are likely to have limited success at best.

Provide long-term support. Long-term support makes planning and reflection possible. The Bellevue project is in the enviable position of having received a five-year commitment from the district to support its development of a districtwide assessment system. As a consequence, the team was able to spend its first year exploring various assessment systems and its second year wrestling with decisions about the portfolio contents and process. Over the course of the five years, the Bellevue team will have the opportunity to phase in the assessments gradually and make adjustments as more is learned about the effects of portfolios in this particular context.

Conduct ongoing evaluation of the process. Continuous evaluation of the assessment development process is essential, for without regular feedback about problems and successes, it is difficult to determine when to change direction or chart a new course. Bellevue team members met monthly to review their progress, adjust their plans, and set future directions. They took a collaborative, problem-solving approach in their meetings in which they addressed both deep concerns ("Are portfolios something that will have value to me and my students?") and logistical issues ("This common tool doesn't work at my grade level").

District Accountability through Classroom Assessment

The Bellevue School District has taken on the daunting task of addressing the dual, and sometimes conflicting, demands of classroom assessment and district accountability. Balancing both at the same time requires an adept juggler; doing so through a single assessment system calls for a magician.

To promote student learning and improve instruction—the primary goals of classroom assessment—students and teachers need a diverse collection of information gathered in multiple contexts over time from students who are engaged in meaningful learning activities (Wolf, 1993). To provide summary measures of student performance and program quality that can be reported to outside audiences—the primary focus for district accountability—administrators need efficient and reliable evaluation methods. In the past, assessment has been forced to kneel at the altar of accountability, and standardized tests have been granted much greater respect than the assessments that knowledgeable teachers carry out every day in their classrooms. However, in recent years there has been growing recognition that standardized tests are not effective at measuring many important student outcomes and that alternative forms of assessment, such as portfolios, can not only accurately portray but also actively promote student learning by fostering self-evaluation and ownership for both students and teachers.

Bellevue has attempted to address the assessment-accountability dilemma by designing a classroom-based portfolio assessment system that provides students, teachers, and parents with ongoing and detailed information about student learning, and, at the same time, offers the district a broad view of student performance and program quality. The Bellevue portfolios are both individualized and standardized—students are given the freedom to select key pieces of work and write reflective commentaries about their literacy growth ("portfolio reviews"), but students and teachers are also required to include common measures for each of the four learning outcomes under investigation. This approach was intended to preserve student and teacher control over the process, but also allow for districtwide comparisons across students.

While Bellevue's initial efforts at meeting both assessment and accountability needs through the literacy portfolio are promising, several issues related to the design and implementation of the Bellevue project deserve comment, including the lack of common assessment "tools," the absence of anecdotal records and observation checklists, the option for teachers and students to include an unlimited amount of material, and the recommendation for increased annotation.

Despite an agreement by all the teachers to include the common measures in every portfolio, when the portfolios were examined at the end of the school year, the assessment team discovered that none of the teachers included all of the common measures. Why did this happen? A number of reasons are possible. The common measures may have been unmanageable or uninformative, and the teachers chose not to use them; possibly, some of the teachers did not know how to implement them. It is most likely, however, that the teachers did not fully recognize the importance of the common measures for accountability purposes. It was only during scoring at the end of the school year that it became evident that without some shared anchor for understanding and evaluating the portfolios, assigning comparable scores across students is a very difficult task. While the assessment development team needs to explore this issue further, the teachers' recommendation to hold portfolio scoring sessions early in the school year is a sound one. These sessions will highlight the importance of the common tools and have the added benefit of refining the teachers' understanding of the instructional outcomes and assessment process.

Another provocative finding was that no teachers kept anecdotal records or observation checklists—two commonly recommended classroom assessment procedures. What does this tell us? That expectations for teachers to keep these kinds of records are unrealistic? That the pedagogical return on anecdotal records and checklists may not be worth the time investment? I believe that anecdotal records and checklists—when selectively and purposefully used—can provide effective guides and memories for teachers. However, it is very easy to collect too much information for unclear purposes. It is no surprise, then, that many teachers find the process time-consuming and uninformative. The Bellevue team might examine this finding to determine why the teachers did not keep these kinds of records, and then use this information to design methods and materials that will make anecdotal note-taking and checklists feasible and informative.

In addition to student- and teacher-selected works, portfolio reviews by the students, and "common tools," the teachers and students were offered the option to include "any additional pieces or works" in the portfolio. I fear that allowing this option opens the possibility that the portfolio will become a thick and unwieldy scrapbook rather than a selective and reflective collection of work. An alternative approach might be to distinguish between a folio for classroom assessment and a portfolio for district evaluation, in which the folio houses all of a student's work while the portfolio contains a more focused collection. Students, teachers, and parents need a broad and deep view of student performance, but district administrators require only a summary (rather than the entire story). With these different needs in mind, Bellevue might consider a comprehensive folio for classroom assessment that can include all work that teachers and students find appropriate, and a more focused portfolio (derived from the folio) for district accountability that might be limited to, for example, three student-selected pieces of work, two portfolio reviews, and the common tools.

Another finding that deserves comment is the teachers' request for increased annotation of the portfolio contents. The teachers remarked that they found the portfolios difficult to score without more information about the context surrounding the creation of the work in the portfolio. I caution against requiring extensive annotation by classroom teachers, for it is extremely time consuming. However, some annotation of the portfolio is necessary; otherwise its contents are likely to be indecipherable to anyone other than its creators. Annotation helps distinguish, for example, whether a piece of writing was copied from the board or created by a student, or whether it was an individual project or collaborative effort. When a portfolio serves the dual purpose of assessment and accountability, there is a constant tension between making the portfolio useful and manageable for those inside the classroom but also meaningful and interpretable to those outside the classroom. A reasonable approach for Bellevue may be to have teachers and students annotate the student-selected pieces but not the common tools (which are standard across students)—and only for the district portfolio rather than for the entire classroom folio.

Future Challenges

Bellevue has a strong start on the assessment development task, but maintaining its momentum as well as expanding the assessment to all six student learning objectives and to all classrooms (not to mention across the curriculum) will present a new challenge. At present, a core group of knowledgeable and enthusiastic volunteers is exploring portfolio assessment; in the future, teachers of all stripes will be required to implement portfolios. Will these teachers be as willing and able? I believe they will if teachers continue to have a strong voice in the process and if they receive support from the district. However, if the portfolio project is carried out on the backs of already overburdened teachers, then it is likely to stall. Teachers need time—alone, with their students, and with one another—to learn about portfolios, to guide their construction, to evaluate them, and to reflect on the process. The district must provide time for the teachers through a variety of strategies such as school restructuring and redistribution of staff-development funds; otherwise even the most dedicated teachers will be overwhelmed.

The focus in this report was on the development of the literacy portfolio and not on its impact on student learning. The authors did not give us a detailed student's-eye view of the portfolio, but they did report that students had positive reactions to the portfolio, and that there was an increase in the amount and quality of students' reading and writing. These findings suggest that the portfolio is having its desired effect. It is critical, however, that the district constantly monitor the portfolio process to ensure that it continues to advance student learning.

In sum, the Bellevue School District has created a portfolio assessment system for addressing both assessment and accountability that deserves close attention. It is not only the portfolio design, but the process by which the district developed and implemented the portfolio that might serve as a model for others. Beginning with instructional outcomes and then fitting the assessment system to those goals, involving teachers and inviting other stakeholders into the portfolio development process, and providing long-term support and ongoing evaluation of the portfolio process are all critical and effective features of the Bellevue approach. While many issues remain to be resolved, one can only expect that they will continue to be addressed in a thoughtful manner and that the findings of the Bellevue project will insightfully inform us for years to come.

References

Valencia, S.W. (1990). A portfolio approach to classroom reading assessment: The whys, whats, and hows. *The Reading Teacher*, 43(4), 420-421.

Wolf, D.P. (1989). Portfolio assessment: Sampling student work. *Educational Leadership*, 46(7), 35-39.

Wolf, K.P. (1993). From informal to informed assessment: Recognizing the role of the classroom teacher. *Journal of Reading*, 36(7), 518-523.

CHAPTER 7

Teri Bembridge

A MULTILAYERED ASSESSMENT PACKAGE

A FUNDAMENTAL GOAL OF THE ST. VITAL SCHOOL DIVISION IN WINNIPEG, MANITOBA, is to promote learning as a lifelong pursuit. We in St. Vital recognize that assessment is integral to learning: all learners need a way of determining the quality and quantity of their learning. Assessment is most meaningful when it closely parallels instruction and the practice activities that precede it. However, as classroom instruction has changed to reflect the growing understanding of the complexity of learning processes, educators have had to re-examine and question many of our traditional assessment practices (Goodman, Goodman, & Hood, 1989; Monahan & Hinson, 1988; Zessoules & Gardner, 1991). Teachers in St. Vital developed and implemented a reading assessment system when we recognized this need to match assessment to our changing classroom practices.

As is the case with most school district implementations, our assessment tool has a history and an

---

This chapter is based on "A MAP for Reading Assessment" by Teri Bembridge, published in *Educational Leadership* in May 1992. It has been adapted and expanded for this publication.

evolution that illustrate the growth of our professional learning. It also has a future: we view it as a beginning of our process of change toward more authentic assessment of student learning. The tool itself is called the Multilayered Assessment Package, most commonly known by its acronym, MAP. It functions somewhat like a MAP—giving teachers an idea of the literary terrain their students travel and an indication of the direction in which to guide students through reading instruction. This chapter describes the MAP's chronology, specific components, and classroom use, and includes a brief discussion of future directions.

Development

In the early 1980s, resource teachers in St. Vital recognized the need for an assessment tool that could be used in classrooms where whole language practices were being implemented. The consultant at our divisional learning center helped us by sharing research and compiling dossiers about alternative assessment and instructional strategies. In addition, a local informal reading assessment was created and resource teachers were trained in miscue analysis (Goodman & Burke, 1972). These techniques were effective for detailed diagnostic assessments, but they required a highly trained teacher and considerable time.

By the mid-1980s, resource teachers were frustrated by isolated assessment practices that kept us out of the classroom at a time when we were advocating a collaborative model to deliver resource services. We were becoming aware of the literature on alternative assessment (see, for example, Valencia & Pearson, 1987) and recognized that our tools for reading assessment were not in harmony with the exciting literature-based, child-centered learning that was occurring in many of the kindergarten to grade six classrooms in our school division. As a result, a committee was formed to locate an assessment device that would meet the following conditions:

- was literature based so students would have to read actual books or stories rather than contrived texts created with controlled vocabulary for testing purposes only;
- would be administered in the classroom by either a resource or classroom teacher;
- allowed for observation of reading behaviors and discussion of these behaviors with the student;
- produced scores meaningful to the child, parents, and teachers; and
- suggested when a more in-depth assessment was needed.

We soon realized that no commercially available assessment met all of these requirements; however, we did locate and purchase one assessment package, The Diagnostic Reading Program (Alberta Education, 1986), that met *some* of our needs.

Filled with the optimism of the naive and with information gathered from other whole language practitioners (particularly Ken and Yetta Goodman, Carolyn Burke, and Dorothy Watson), we decided to pull together our own assessment package that might fulfill more of our division's needs. Over the course of four years we met, researched, questioned, argued, shared, wrote, rewrote, and edited our package. These years had many frustrations, including turnover of personnel. Nevertheless, because of the committee's determination and belief in the project, we were able to secure a budget and release time from the superintendent's department. The enthusiasm of other resource teachers aided the committee's resolve to complete the project. In Spring 1989, the committee presented the results to the entire group of St. Vital resource teachers.

Description

The MAP is a method for individual assessment of oral and silent reading and listening in kindergarten through grade six. We call it "multilayered" because when it was originally conceived we envisioned a tool that would cover the four strands of language development as outlined in our provincial language arts curricula guides: reading, writing, speaking, and listening. The MAP in its present form assesses reading and listening; writing is part of our current exploration of portfolio collections. The MAP is also considered multilayered because it recognizes the components, or layers, involved in reading—the cognitive and affective processes. The four cueing systems—graphophonics, semantics, syntax, and pragmatics (Goodman, Burke, & Watson, 1987)—can be thought of as one set of layers. They are not necessarily hierarchical layers that build on the mastery of a previous layer, but interactive layers that grow in relation to each of the others.

Another set of layers important to a child's reading involves emotional and motivational factors. The MAP attempts to address these issues by assessing a student's reading in the safe, comfortable environment of the classroom and by using books similar to those found in the classroom's own collection. In many cases, the student can even make a choice of which book to read. Such conditions tend to add a measure of informality to the potentially stressful situation of reading assessment. Stress can be further reduced if the resource teacher is well known to the student through regular work in the room, or if the teacher can administer the assessment to an individual while the resource teacher works with the rest of the class.

The MAP is best described as a four-part package of books and manuals:

- Collection of books—56 books/stories used for assessment, each labeled with the grade in which it is typically read and an indication of whether it is meant for oral reading, silent reading, or listening assessment;

- Guidebook one—St. Vital's philosophy of instruction and assessment, references, administrative and scoring procedures for the MAP, plus suggestions of additional assessment tools;

- Guidebook two—record-keeping forms, transcripts, and retelling outlines for each item in the collection; and

- Strats Pac—a collection of instructional strategies for teachers to use with elementary students.

Once these materials were identified, purchased, and collated by the committee, a complete set was supplied to every elementary school in the division. Every resource teacher has been trained in the materials' use. Each school staff has had a short workshop about the MAP. Professional development is continuous as the MAP procedures are modeled in classrooms and individual teachers are trained by the school's resource teacher. The package is designed to supplement techniques used by classroom teachers to evaluate students' reading and listening.

A vital feature of the MAP is the use of literature that the students actually hold and read during the assessment. A subcommittee began the formidable task of selecting these stories and books by creating pilot collections and gathering feedback from colleagues. Each of the books finally included had these features: narrative story form; problem-oriented plot; reasonable length; natural vocabulary and grammar; ample context for understanding; picture clues that match text; clear typeface and font; and cultural diversity. All books were purchased, and the publishers' permission to retype each into transcript form was secured. Teachers are asked to keep the MAP books out of general circulation to ensure that students read new material for the assessment. Most are storybooks but some of the selections are stories from anthologies or basal readers. Although we tried to meet all the criteria for every grade, finding books of reasonable length at the intermediate grades was difficult. Consequently, stories and passages rather than complete books tend to dominate the collections at grades four to six.

Books and stories were assigned grade levels based on our collective professional judgment and on actual classroom use rather than by relying on publishers' suggestions for grade levels or on readability scores. Numerical formulas to determine readability levels were discounted because our study of the professional literature showed their inability to reflect the complexity and elusiveness of language structure (Zakaluk & Samuels, 1988). For this reason the books are sorted into groups of material typically found at specific grades, from preprimer level to grade six. At the first, second, and third grades there are separate selections for the beginning and ending months of these grades—a label of "1-1," for example, means the book is typically read by children during the beginning months of first grade. These divisions are subjective and are meant only as guidelines. Each level offers four to six selections.

Guidebook one contains the essence of the MAP; it outlines the theoretical constructs and practical procedures fundamental to the MAP's delivery. Professional reference books needed by all St. Vital resource teachers are listed, and the final section contains additional assessment suggestions.

The procedures written for the MAP assume it will be conducted in the child's classroom. We acknowledge that some situations require the assessment to be administered in a separate space, but the classroom is the ideal location because it is in this everyday setting that the most realistic picture of students' reading behaviors and activity will emerge. A typical scenario has a teacher sitting in the classroom's library corner with a tape recorder and asking the student to read a book. The book is introduced without using the title, but the child is provided with the proper names found in the text. The first book is determined by observing the kind of books the child typically chooses to read or having the child bring a book that she or he particularly likes or can read well. It is expected that the teacher administering the assessment knows the child well enough to make a professional judgment about starting points.

During the session, the teacher introduces a discussion about typical reading strategies the student uses, such as how he or she figures out the meaning of unknown words. In most of our classrooms, students have been taught to use one of several techniques, but many develop their own personal strategies as well. We believe it is important and informative to allow students to talk about their reading strategies.

The audiotape allows for observation, while postponing coding and scoring for later. Taping seems less stressful for children than knowing the teacher is taking notes while they read. Most students like to hear themselves later, and this provides an opportunity for the teacher to point out the useful strategies individual students employed in the reading. For example, the teacher might note how a student dealt with unfamiliar text by using picture clues, slowing down, or rereading to clarify meaning.

After reading, the child is simply asked to tell the story. This is more natural than the teacher asking or the child answering specific questions. We liken the procedure to discussing a movie with friends: we talk about it; we don't answer a quiz. The retelling can be guided by the teacher if the student needs some prompts to continue talking. The student's retelling is recorded on a form, adapted from Morrow (1988).

Guidebook two contains transcripts of the MAP stories and "Retelling Analysis" forms for each story or book. Complete transcripts of each story make the MAP quick to administer. Each story is retyped, double-spaced for coding miscues, with room for notations at the end of each sentence. Each transcript page also notes the number of words and sentences, bibliographic information about the story or book, and typical grade level. (A brief example taken from one such transcript appears in Figure 1.)

The retelling forms (an example of which appears in Figure 2) were developed by analyzing each story for components relating to setting, plot, resolution, theme, and sequence. A total possible score is assigned to which students' retellings can be compared. Blank retelling forms are also included in the package so teachers can adapt the technique to other materials.

As can be seen from the preceding description, the MAP provides scores in addition to observational and anecdotal data. A record sheet for individual students contains space for oral reading, silent reading,

Figure 1
MAP **Oral Reading**

Student's name: _____

Date: _____

Tester: _____

Grade: _____

Word accuracy score: _____

Sentence comprehending score: _____

Retelling score: _____

Title: "Breakaway"

Series: _Diagnostic Reading Program_

Publisher: Alberta Education

Number of words: 250

Typically used at the grade 5 level

Number of sentences: 24

Sally longed to be a goalie like her older brother, John, but whenever the regular goalie was unable to play, someone else from her hockey team was chosen.___ Rather than become discouraged, she spent hours practising in her backyard.___ She could hardly wait for a chance to show her skill as a goalie.___

Then one night just before the playoff game the coach announced, "Unfortunately our team's regular goalie is ill.___ Sally, I hear you've been practising, so I want you to be our goalie."___

What an opportunity!...

Figure 2
Retelling Analysis

Student's name: _____ Date: _____

Recorded by: _____

Grade: _____ School: _____

Story: "_Breakaway_"   Level: 5R

Points in Story Setting:	Story Structure	Student's Points
_1_ wants to be a goalie	(a) begins story with introduction	
_1_ Sally	(b) names main character	____
_2_ coach/brother/team	(c) score for other characters	____
_1_ hockey rink/night	(d) includes statement about time and place	____

Plot:

_1_ to play well as a goalie	(a) refers to primary goal(s) or problem(s) to be solved	____
_2_ chance to be goalie; the game	(b) number of episodes	____
_1_ makes the save	(c) names problem/solution/ goal attainment	____
_1_ brother says "great save"	(d) ends story	____

Theme:

_1_ practice pays	(a) main idea/title	____

Sequence:

_2_	retells story in structural order: setting, theme, plot, episodes, resolution (score 2 for proper, 1 for partial, 0 for no sequence evident)	____

Highest score possible __13__   Student's score ____

$\dfrac{\text{Student score} \times 100}{\text{Highest score}} = $ _____%

Note: Actual retelling can be recorded on the back of this form. Prior to hearing the student's retelling, the Points in Story should be determined and recorded on the form.

Adapted from Morrow, 1988

and listening scores. For oral reading, for example, three scores can be derived:

- Word accuracy score reflects the child's ability to identify specific words read in context. It is calculated by dividing the number of correctly read words by the number of words in the story, and multiplying by 100 to yield a percentage. Mastery is 95 percent.

- Sentence comprehending score examines the child's use of the four cueing systems and of self-correction. It has been adapted from information in Goodman, Burke, and Watson (1987). The teacher uses the last version read by the student (including self-corrections) and counts the number of sentences that make sense within the context of the story read to that point. It is calculated by dividing the number of accepted sentences by the number of sentences in the story, and multiplying by 100. Mastery is 85 percent.

- Retelling score (illustrated in Figures 1 and 2) reflects comprehension, sense of story structure, and understanding of language complexity through the reader's reconstruction of the textual information. It allows the reader to formulate a response according to personal experience, a factor which can give an observant examiner considerable information to help construct the picture of the student as a reader. Mastery is 85 percent.

The mastery percentages attached to each score were, and continue to be, a source of debate. Many teachers feel that some numerical cutoff point was needed to indicate acceptable performance, while others feel that satisfactory performance should be based on teacher judgment. It was decided to use the mastery indicators found in many informal reading inventories. During training sessions we stress that these percentages are only guidelines and must be interpreted within the context of the classroom.

The fourth part of the MAP is a collection of 16 instructional strategies for classroom use. The strategies include the Directed Reading-Thinking Activity (Stauffer, 1969), reading conferences (Atwell, 1987), and sustained silent reading (Buchanan, 1980). None of these is new or unique to St. Vital; some even spring simply from the common sense of whole language teachers. But each strategy included is basic to sound instruction from the holistic perspective. The descriptions in the Strats Pac were written to act as support material for teachers using the whole language approach and as invitations to those teachers and parents who are beginning to learn about it.

The Strats Pac is not a cookbook of sure formulas, but rather a representation of basic instructional strategies useful in all classrooms. The package is meant only as a guide, and teachers are encouraged to adapt, expand, experiment, and share with colleagues to create strategic learning situations that fit the context of their classrooms. At no time is it implied that the strategies be used in isolation or learned for their own sake. The goal is always to help students become independent readers. A strategy is a means of achieving that goal, not an end in itself. We believe that a strategic learner knows many strategies, is aware of personal style, and understands when a particular strategy needs to be employed. The Strats Pac provides a composite set of instructions to help a teacher model and use strategies. It also emphasizes that learning a strategy does not spring from a one-time lesson or event but is an ongoing process.

Classroom Use of the MAP

As is obvious from the preceding description, the MAP is based on and has many similarities to informal reading inventories and miscue analysis techniques. The procedures, coding of miscues, and even the scores are adaptations from these assessment tools. We are indebted to the educators and researchers who laid the groundwork for our adaptations.

The procedures we developed from this earlier work, however, are consistent with instructional practices found in most of our classrooms. One difference between the MAP and other techniques is the generic nature of the procedures and their flexible content. The procedures and scores can be used with any narrative material a teacher selects. The student's reading ability guides the choice of book to be used; the selected text may or may not be one of those found in the collection.

Consider this hypothetical example. A teacher decides to use different books for assessment because she is working with adolescent English as a Second Language readers who aren't interested in the selections included in the MAP. She decides to use magazine and newspaper articles but keeps the MAP criteria in mind when selecting them. She analyzes each on a retelling form and has them retyped into a transcript. She follows the MAP procedures and scoring formats for oral reading. She can then sit down with each student and talk about his or her reading in terms of word accuracy, sentence comprehension, and retelling. From this point, some specific strategies can be suggested and an instructional plan can be devised. Follow-up assessment can demonstrate growth.

Another major difference is that the assessment is conducted in the environment where the student usually reads: the classroom. This provides a realistic picture of reading behaviors the student displays when surrounded by classmates and typical activities. For example, the teacher may notice that the student seems distracted by the talking of classmates. This observation can be discussed with the student and may lead to some suggestions for focusing strategies, which may be as simple as moving to a quiet place in the room. The discussion may even lead to discovering the types of books the student would prefer to read, since being easily distracted may indicate a simple lack of interest in the book.

The MAP presents information in the form of scores that are meaningful to everyone concerned. For example, the use of three scores for oral reading, as opposed to a single score provided by some traditional assessments, illustrates the complex nature of the reading process. The MAP recognizes that reading cannot be reduced to a single number. Discussing scores with parents provides an occasion to talk about the nature of learning and our philosophy of instruction. Through the explanation of the scores and our observations we can heighten awareness about ways in which reading can be enhanced at home. To reinforce this, the strategies in the Strats Pac are designed to be shared with parents and students so everyone understands the rationale behind instruction in the classroom.

Students must understand the purpose and results of the assessment as well. Talking to youngsters in kindergarten or first grade about the different cueing systems is as important as doing so with sixth graders. The details of the conversations will be different, but the message about reading is the same: we all use several systems to make sense of the printed text. Readers of all ages need to be aware of their personal styles, strengths, and weaknesses in order to make decisions about reading. Reading is an active, thinking activity, and all readers need to perceive it as such.

Finally, using the MAP in the classroom provides time for the resource teacher and the classroom teacher to interact and work together with the students. Depending on the situation, the resource teacher may administer the assessment at the request of the teacher, providing an opportunity to model the procedures. In other cases, the teacher may wish to administer the MAP, in which case the resource teacher could assist by teaching the class, interpreting the scores, or suggesting appropriate strategies. The main point is that the MAP is intended to be used in the classroom with students and teachers.

Reflections

Working on the creation and implementation of the MAP and the Strats Pac has been one of the professional-development activities of my teaching career. The learning that occurred as I read, discussed, questioned, challenged, reacted, and responded to information about reading, learning, and assessment would not likely have happened in a university lecture hall. My hope is that students in my classes have similar learning experiences, including the opportunity to reflect on their achievements. Reflection is a necessary part of assessment. We all must be able to think about our learning if we are to learn from our "mistakes." The process we engaged in to create the MAP has resulted in learning that will continue to be applied in the future.

As resource teachers, all members of the MAP committee learned and practiced skills to foster collaboration through communication and interaction within our school teams. We used our problem-solving abilities to create the MAP. In fact, we exercised what in retrospect looks almost like a textbook example of a collaborative working relationship (see, for example, Friend & Cook, 1991), but we did it without conscious regard to our process. As we take on new projects, we will attempt to reflect on all the elements of collaboration: personal qualities, communication skills, interactive processes, programs, and context.

Because the MAP was developed locally, we tend to be proud of it, but that does not blind us to its shortcomings or to criticism. For example, some have suggested that a section on interpretation of combinations of scores should be included. Such a section could provide teachers with suggestions on what strategies to pursue when a child obtains a certain combination of scores, and this might simplify the interpretation of scores and make the MAP more useful to classroom teachers. Such a section has been purposely omitted, however, because neither the MAP nor the Strats Pac was developed to be used dogmatically. It is expected that teachers using the MAP have a strong background in learning theory, reading assessment, and language acquisition. We feel this should allow interpretation of the scores and meaningful observations based on experience and professional judgment. We will continue to discuss the advantages and disadvantages of offering such interpretive information as part of the package, however.

We would like to be able to expand the MAP to include writing and speaking; we may also begin to use materials other than narratives. Expository texts would be very useful, particularly at the upper elementary grades where textbooks become commonplace. Of course, adding materials and increasing the range to grades seven and eight is another goal for the future.

The MAP is not a tool or a package that can be transplanted from St. Vital to another school district; it is a set of procedures and materials that fit our local population. Educators in other districts must examine their own instructional and assessment practices and develop assessment tools appropriate for their circumstances. The descriptions in this chapter were written with the purpose of supplying information that may assist other groups of teachers in the development of their local assessment packages.

We believe that the MAP is a useful tool for helping to assess the reading process of children. It meets our local needs and has become an integral part of reading assessment in our elementary classrooms. But, as stated at the beginning of this chapter, we are continuing to change as we learn more. Recently, after reading *The Unschooled Mind: How Children Think and How Schools Should Teach* (Gardner, 1991) I realized how much more dramatically instructional and assessment practices must change in order to meet future challenges. We feel that the MAP is a step in the right direction.

Author's note: Many people contributed to the development of the MAP. Betty Anderson, Susan Blauer, Heather Burkett, Louise Clark, Joan Dary, Janice Foster, Eric Frank, Connie Graham, Sheryl Harris, Orysia Hull, Ann Ingalls, Claire Jewers, Myma Jubinville, Nancy Keys, Lois Koop, Diane Krahn, Don MacIntosh, Madeline Noyes, Terry Parsons, John Pura, Sally Robin, Elaine Sharpe, Audrey Siemens, Bonnie Southern, Shelly Struthers, Lana Warren, Rosanne Wasylyniuk, and Bev Wilson are all acknowledged for their work on and contributions to the project.

References

Alberta Education. (1986). *The diagnostic reading program*. Edmonton, Alta.: Author.

Atwell, N. (1987). *In the middle: Writing, reading and learning with adolescents*. Portsmouth, NH: Heinemann.

Bembridge, T. (1992). A MAP for reading assessment. *Educational Leadership*, 49(8), 46-48.

Buchanan, E. (1980). *For the love of reading*. Winnipeg, Man.: CEL Group.

Friend, M., & Cook, L. (1991). *Interactions: Collaboration skills for school professionals*. Toronto, Ont.: Copp Clark Pitman.

Gardner, H. (1991). *The unschooled mind: How children think and how schools should teach*. New York: Basic.

Goodman, K.S., Goodman, Y.M., & Hood, W.J. (Eds.). (1989). *The whole language evaluation book*. Toronto, Ont.: Irwin.

Goodman, Y.M., & Burke, C.L. (1972). *Reading miscue inventory manual: Procedures for diagnosis and evaluation*. Chicago: Richard C. Owen Publisher.

Goodman, Y.M., Burke, C.L., & Watson, D. (1987). *Reading miscue inventory: Alternative procedures*. Chicago, IL: Richard C. Owen.

Monahan, J., & Hinson, B. (1988). *New directions in reading instruction*. Newark, DE: International Reading Association.

Morrow, L.M. (1988). Retelling stories as a diagnostic tool. In S.M. Glazer, L.W. Searfoss, & L.M. Gentile (Eds.), *Re-examining reading diagnosis: New trends and procedures*. Newark, DE: International Reading Association.

Stauffer, R. (1969). *Directing reading maturity as a cognitive process*. New York: HarperCollins.

Valencia, S.W., & Pearson, P.D. (1987). Reading assessment: Time for a change. *The Reading Teacher*, 40(8), 726-732.

Zakaluk, B.L., & Samuels, S.J. (1988). *Readability: Its past, present, and future*. Newark, DE: International Reading Association.

Zessoules, R., & Gardner, H. (1991). Authentic assessment: Beyond the buzzword and into the classroom. In V. Perrone (Ed.), *Expanding student assessment* (pp. 47-77). Alexandria, VA: Association for Supervision and Curriculum Development.

Marjorie Y. Lipson

COMMENTARY ON *A Multilayered Assessment Package*

THE CRITICISMS OF TRADITIONAL ASSESSMENT are now well understood by most educators. In particular, critics have charged that when conventional tests are used, there is (1) a lack of correspondence between instruction and assessment; (2) a limited match between authentic literacy activity and test selections and tasks; (3) a narrow view of students' abilities resulting from a single assessment; and (4) limited information upon which to base instructional decisions about students (see Valencia & Pearson, 1987; Wixson & Lipson, 1986). Consequently, teachers, schools, and districts across the country are engaged in efforts to improve their assessment practices. The vitality and local control of these efforts are critical for encouraging teacher development. This is especially important because so many teachers have come to distrust their own judgment, relying instead on test scores and the views of "experts" (Valencia & Pearson). The success of some innovative assessment projects may be threatened by an early insistence on uniformity. In this context it is especially delightful to read Teri Bembridge's account of assessment development efforts in St. Vital School Division.

The Local Context: Strengths of the MAP

Increasingly, both researchers and other educators are coming to see that knowledge, skills, and strategies are not easily transferable; they tend instead to be learned and used in specific situations. As pointed out by Brown, Collins, and Duguid (1989), "Knowledge is situated, being in part a product of the activity, context, and culture in which it is developed and used." Dyson (1991) argues persuasively that children's language can be sensibly assessed only when purpose and situation have been clearly described. In the same way, discussions of school and classroom assessment only make sense if we consider the particular purposes and situations within which they exist.

It seemed to me that these issues were especially evident in the assessment project described by Bembridge. The Multilayered Assessment Package (MAP) is a home-grown project that draws on contemporary ideas and practices but is designed for use by a particular group of resource teachers in a specific setting. In a nutshell, this project might be viewed as "situated assessment" similar in some ways to what we have come to recognize as "situated knowledge."

As Bembridge notes, the project has both a history and a future. Although it is not yet complete, there are several identifiable outcomes of this project. The most obvious is the reading and listening assessment package itself. However, other notable outcomes include professional development for the MAP planners and opportunities for ongoing reflection for all parties. None of these outcomes can be discussed in any useful way unless the purpose and situation are carefully considered. In the following section, I react to several notable accomplishments of this project.

Utility and functional value. Perhaps the overriding reason to view this effort as successful is that "it works for them." No matter what others might imagine the value or limitations of this assessment plan to be, it has obviously proved functional and valuable to the members of this education community. The idea that local conditions are important to making instructional decisions has been forcefully argued by Goldenberg and Gallimore (1991). They note that research and policy can only tell us what to do, "all things being equal. But all else is rarely equal...to understand how things work, it is necessary to have direct experience of them" (p. 2). This project works because the participants were clear about what they wanted from the assessment in the first place and then sought to devise a plan that met their needs.

Content and procedures. The content of the MAP represents a significant improvement over traditional practices. Students read books that conform to a rigorous and reasonable set of selection criteria. The materials are selected by teachers who can make decisions about what to include and whose judgments about difficulty can be informed by their knowledge of school programs and practices. This represents a significant step in the right direction since the reading performance of students in this district is no longer tested using short, poorly written, or truncated selections. As a result, the processes evaluated using the MAP will more closely resemble the reading processes students actually need when they read outside of assessment events. Similarly, the procedures for using the MAP approximate the types of reading contexts students encounter during the course of normal school activities. Students read in their own classrooms from materials that are familiar in form and type; then they engage in story retellings and have conversations about the books. The process appears to be relatively unobtrusive and results, according to Bembridge, in diminished anxiety and improved motivation. Finally, the assessment practices are familiar and well-tested ones that result in scores for oral reading accuracy, sentence comprehension, and retelling.

Relationship between assessment and instruction. One of the most striking features of the MAP is the

extent to which it is similar to the instructional programs in these schools. There seems to be a clear relationship between the assessment formats and the
instructional situation. This not only increases the like-
lihood that students' reading abilities will be fairly
reflected in the results, but it improves the usefulness
of the information for both classroom and resource
teachers. Teachers won't be left to wonder whether students would have performed better or less well if the
test had been more like what students were learning to
do in their own classrooms. Everyone will have information that can be used to make some general instructional decisions.

Flexibility. The MAP procedures are, as the author
notes, "generic." Although there are texts that have
been identified for assessment use, a teacher is free to
employ the same techniques with other texts. Thus,
teachers can adapt the assessment procedures to gather information about students' reading and listening
abilities using the most appropriate texts—not necessarily the most common ones. This also opens the way
for teachers to use the MAP with books or stories that
the *child* selects. Because learning as a lifelong pursuit
is a stated goal of this school district, students' ability
to make wise choices is a critical aspect of literacy
development. (Indeed, one school in Vermont values
this ability so highly that students are *always* evaluated
using a book they select from among the available
assessment books [O'Keefe, 1990]. "Rightness" of the
selection is one aspect of reading evaluated during the
assessment.)

Revisiting the Purpose to Extend the Procedure

Clearly the MAP represents an important improvement in assessment practices for this school division.

The development of professional expertise and reflection of local context are especially noteworthy. As the MAP moves into its future, there are several issues that should probably be considered, both because doing so may improve the quality of the assessment information produced and because there may be new settings in which the assessment could be used.

Using the MAP. In Bembridge's words, the MAP is designed to give teachers an idea "of the literary terrain their students travel and an indication of the direction in which to guide students through reading instruction." The "terrain" and the manner in which it is mapped are a bit ambiguous, however. Some of this ambiguity is perhaps the result of limited space for reporting specific assessment procedures (for example, it is not clear how many stories students read during any one assessment or whether students read both orally and silently). Some of this may also result from the fact that this project is not really complete; in general, the promise of a multilayered assessment is not yet realized.

Although teachers do seem to receive more overall information from the MAP, it is not entirely clear that teachers receive more detailed information on which to build specific instructional responses. For example, the MAP does not appear to provide assessment of strategy use (either comprehension or word-level), and it doesn't seem that patterns of miscues are described. Similarly, although the assessment procedures are sensitive to motivational factors, the MAP does not provide any direct measures of attitude, motivation, or prior knowledge. Bembridge implies that teachers make story selections based on their knowledge of students, but it isn't clear whether students always read equally familiar materials.

This leads to an important concern about the use to which the results of the assessment are put. Because the assessment materials are divided along grade level lines, teachers presumably use the results to place children in reading materials and to guide their book selections; it also appears that results are shared with parents and others. As the MAP is used to communicate with more groups about more aspects of literacy, teachers and resource personnel will need to be sure that the purposes don't outstrip the nature of the information. And, as development of the MAP continues, it will be important for the school division to consider how large a picture is desirable.

Mapping more terrain. Bembridge points out what is probably the most serious limitation of the MAP: students read only one type of text and respond in the same way to that text. The exclusive use of narrative is a particular concern at the upper grade levels, as Bembridge notes. However, there is considerable evidence that comprehension abilities vary *within* students as they read different types of narrative, about different topics, or familiar versus unfamiliar materials, or complete different types of tasks. People have a range of reading abilities, not just a single ability; assessment practices need to capture this dynamic nature of reading (Lipson & Wixson, 1991). Although the MAP has been responsive to many other concerns about assessment, it does not reflect the variable and interactive nature of reading and listening in its present form.

As development continues, it seems likely that the MAP might promote a view of assessment as continuous and involving multiple sources of information (Valencia, 1990; Wixson & Lipson, 1986). At the moment, the MAP does not provide for continuous assessment during instruction or on other occasions. Moving the MAP in this direction is likely to promote additional professional development among classroom teachers (as opposed to resource teachers). In addition, this direction would probably improve the quality of information available on students. As Dyson (1991) points out, "Assessment of a child's language use cannot be made by observing children's performance in any one action or on any one day; rather it is through daily encounters that new questions emerge, revealing a tentative, sharpened, and then blurred vision of each child" (p. 21). Finally, developing procedures for ongoing assessment would permit the MAP to look at another layer in the process—students' self-directed and volitional reading and writing. At the moment, there is no way to capture how much reading and writing students do or to assess the nature of that reading and writing.

A Final Note

The MAP's success rests largely on the involvement of committed teachers. It is an impressive project, but it cannot make sense if transported elsewhere. Other teachers and support personnel in other schools can learn from the *process*, but specific forms and procedures must be cultivated and decided on in the local context. If recent efforts to reform assessment and instruction are to thrive and survive, they must not only create products but also professionals. We have abundant evidence that no assessment tool is better than the people who use and interpret it. As Pinnell (1991) says, "Teachers need assessment tools that help them become 'noticing' teachers who recognize children's competence and progress through specific evidence" (p. 81). Assessment projects such as that described by Bembridge are investments in people as much as projects—people who notice.

References

Brown, J.S., Collins, A., & Duguid, P. (1989). Situated cognition and the culture of learning. *Educational Researcher*, 18(1), 32-42.

Dyson, A.H. (1991). Faces in the crowd: Developing profiles of language users. In J.A. Roderick (Ed.), *Context-responsive approaches to assessing children's language* (pp. 20-31). Urbana, IL: National Conference on Research in English.

Goldenberg, C., & Gallimore, R. (1991). Local knowledge, research knowledge, and educational change: A case study of early Spanish reading improvement. *Educational Researcher*, 20(8), 2-14.

Lipson, M.Y., & Wixson, K.K. (1991). *Assessment and instruction of reading disability: An interactive approach.* New York: HarperCollins.

O'Keefe, J. (1990). *Classroom assessment in a literature-based program.* Unpublished manuscript, University of Vermont, Burlington, VT.

Pinnell, G.S. (1991). Interactive assessment: Teachers and children as learners. In J.A. Roderick (Ed.), *Context-responsive approaches to assessing children's language* (pp. 79-96). Urbana, IL: National Conference on Research in English.

Valencia, S.W. (1990). A portfolio approach to classroom reading assessment: The whys, whats, and hows. *The Reading Teacher*, 43(4), 338-340.

Valencia, S.W., & Pearson, P.D. (1987). Reading assessment: Time for a change. *The Reading Teacher*, 40(8), 726-732.

Wixson, K.K., & Lipson, M.Y. (1986). Reading (dis)ability: An interactionist perspective. In T.E. Raphael (Ed.), *The contexts of school-based literacy*. White Plains, NY: Longman.

PART FOUR

Peter P. Afflerbach
Editor

LARGE-SCALE AUTHENTIC ASSESSMENT

OVERVIEW   Authentic reading assessment at the state- or province-wide level poses a unique set of challenges. Large numbers of students must be assessed effectively and efficiently, and issues of validity and reliability are crucial when results are to be used to determine educational accountability and program effectiveness and to inform funding and resource decisions. Districts and classroom teachers find these issues important to their alternative assessment efforts; they too must struggle with developing trustworthy assessments.

Each chapter in this section reports ongoing efforts to meet these challenges of large-scale assessment. The development process, content, and format of these particular assessments are representative of what we are likely to find in the next generation of commercially published and state- or province-developed tests. Each of the three chapters and chapter commentaries that follow provides detailed information that helps us appreciate the progress that has been made and the hard work that will continue.

The chapters included in this section present the current and evolving reading assessments used in Arizona, California, and Maryland. Throughout the chapters, there is a tentativeness to the conclusions the authors are willing to draw about the successes of the specific assessments, and of the assessment programs themselves. This is appropriate; reading assessment templates should retain a flexibility that allows integration of new learning about reading and literacy, and about new forms of assessment.

Each of these projects has approached the development of its assessment in a slightly different way and each has produced a unique format and structure for the authentic assessment of reading. Despite these differences, there are common themes that run through the chapters. A first theme is that "authentic tasks" complicate the reading assessment picture. There is nothing more likely to create a yearning for the classic standardized, multiple-choice test than finding oneself squarely in the middle of an assessment that encourages students' multiple responses to multiple texts and involves group discussion and writing as natural accompaniments to authentic acts of reading. The messiness of such assessments can be daunting, but it may also help us reflect on what has been previously accepted as "reading assessment." These authentic tasks yield information about many complex—and often untapped—aspects of students' reading development. Each of the assessments described in this section is clearly tied to stated student outcomes that define what students should know and be able to do. The outcomes frame the assessments and provide a touchstone when the complexities of authentic assessment may obscure the questions "What exactly is being assessed?" and "What are we looking for?"

A second theme is that the development of valid and authentic reading assessments requires sensitivity to the variety of peoples, cultures, and languages that students represent. When easily administered and easily scored tests are abandoned, there must be a consistent and careful monitoring of the assumptions of the developers of new assessments, and these assumptions must be compared with the worlds of the students required to take the assessment. In this area, the assessments of Arizona, California, and Maryland have made notable accomplishments.

Communication plays an important and often underappreciated role in initiating, developing, introducing, using, and refining a large-scale authentic reading assessment program. For authentic reading assessment to be useful, clear, and consistent, communication about its nature and purpose is critical. And to the extent that an authentic reading assessment program represents a radical departure from the traditional program, communication is crucial for helping gain acceptance for the new approach. Because province- or statewide assessments are most often imposed by policymakers, communication is imperative for the potential usefulness of the assessment to be realized. The assessment programs described in this section make varied attempts to include teachers. This approach—in contrast with traditional approaches in which assessments are developed and scored by test companies—is intended to provide teachers with valuable professional development, a sense of ownership of the process, and a greater understanding of the instruction-assessment connection.

In summary, the three programs described in this section are designed with the intention of making large-scale reading assessment more authentic in terms of the texts, tasks, and contexts of reading. The ongoing efforts in Arizona, California, and Maryland are deserving of encouragement and reflection. The assessments described in this section are also notable for their sensitivity to students and teachers. These may be examples of a new form of reading assessment with a conscience, in that the consequences of assessment for students and teachers and issues of inclusion and exclusion from the development process are being considered. Other states and provinces will surely pay close attention to the accomplishments and challenges of these programs. As these large-scale reading assessments move toward authenticity with responsibility, they are well worth watching.

CHAPTER 8

Barbara Weiss

CALIFORNIA'S NEW ENGLISH– LANGUAGE ARTS ASSESSMENT

Effective English–language arts programs include a wide range of assessment techniques to evaluate student's growth in understanding challenging literature, confronting important social issues and values in literature and their own lives, writing clear and lively prose, speaking thoughtfully and effectively, and listening critically, all of which enable students to participate fully in society (from *English–Language Arts Framework for California Public Schools, Kindergarten through Grade 12*, California State Department of Education, 1987, p. 36).

ENGLISH AND LANGUAGE ARTS TEACHERS at all grade levels have long recognized that students use language actively, interactively, strategically, and fluently as they construct and communicate meaning. Authors of *California's English–Language Arts Framework* (adopted by the California Board of Education in 1986) and subsequent model curriculum guides and

---

Portions of this chapter have appeared in other California publications.

standards envisioned a literature-based English–language arts program that actively engaged students in reading, writing, and reflecting on a wide range of significant literary works and human experiences. At the heart of the new framework was a paradigm shift that replaced "gaining knowledge" with "constructing meaning" as the primary goal of English–language arts.

The shifting focus of English–language arts curricula called for changes in instructional strategies. The *English–Language Arts Framework*, along with the state model curriculum standards and guides, repeatedly describe English and language arts programs that "encourage students to read widely and in depth, write often in many formats, study important writings from many disciplines, and relate these studies to their own lives in meaningful ways." A change in vision and in instruction requires a change in assessment as well. Where once one correct answer to a generic question about the text was used to determine comprehension, now a single answer is considered too constricting, not very informative, and probably not a sufficient indication of the student's thought processes. The *Framework* speaks specifically to the need for assessment to mirror the integrated parts of the language arts that contribute to the wholeness of understanding:

> With the revised curriculum in place, assessment of its effectiveness must depend on tests that reflect the purposes of the curriculum. Teachers and others responsible for assessment will create tests based on significant works whose meanings have import for all students; tests will integrate all of the language arts by including significant reading and writing and reflecting the students' oral skills as well; and tests will focus on students' meaning, not on formalistic features such as plot and character (p. 33).

Since the construction of meaning is the essence of both reading and writing, the critical question becomes how to construct an assessment that allows students to become participants in the outcome rather than simply to identify correct meanings that testmakers have posited.

Background

The first step toward a comprehensive and integrated English–language arts assessment for California began in 1985 with the passage of major educational reform legislation that allowed for the expansion of the California Assessment Program (CAP) to include the development of a direct writing assessment for grades 6, 8, and 12. This effort was spearheaded by the California State Department of Education in conjunction with assessment advisory committees that consisted of elementary and secondary teachers, curriculum specialists, testing experts and administrators from district and county offices, university professors, and representatives from the California Literature Project, the California Writing Project, and the National Assessment of Educational Progress. In addition to the advisory committees, a writing-development team composed almost entirely of grade 8 and 12 teachers and California Literature Project and California Writing Project representatives was constituted to lead the test- and staff-development activities.

The state's first writing assessment was introduced at grade 8 in the spring of 1987 through a phase-in process that was completed in 1989. A similar phase-in process was used for the grade 12 writing assessment launched in December 1988; however, state budget constraints in 1990 prevented the implementation of the final two writing types for this grade level. All the components of CAP, including the writing assessment, were halted for one year until legislation calling for the development of a new state assessment program was passed in October 1991. This legislation called for major changes in the state-mandated assessment program, the most significant being the provision to return individual student test scores in addition to school and district program evaluations.

An Integrated Approach

In response to this legislative mandate, a more comprehensive, integrated testing program for California public schools is currently being developed. It will employ performance-based assessments in addition to enhanced multiple-choice items to produce valid and reliable scores. The new program will assess reading, writing, and mathematics at grades 4, 8, and 10, and history–social studies and science at grades 5, 8, and 10. For the first time, the state assessment is to report levels of individual student achievement relative to statewide performance standards for each content area; school, district, county, and state scores are to be reported in percentages of students who have reached these performance levels.

As of this writing, the English–language arts assessment does not solve the problem of using a large-scale reading and writing assessment to ascribe scores to individual students. This assessment, to put it in perspective, represents the first step toward a much larger vision—a comprehensive system that places the classroom teacher at the center of the assessment. Serving as one aspect of such a program, the on-demand assessment can provide teachers and students with a checkpoint, a snapshot into the performance of a particular student on a particular day reading specific texts for given purposes and writing to a specific prompt. Because the design of the prompt and the scoring-guide criteria are based on teacher expertise supported by research, this assessment will make a valuable contribution to an overall picture of a student's performance over time and across a broad range of reading and writing experiences.

Within this perspective, the new English–language arts assessment has three major purposes: (1) to establish standards of excellence for students in reading diverse kinds of materials for defined purposes and in writing of a variety of types; (2) to measure how well students are able to construct meaning through integrated and dynamic interactions among reader, writer, text, and context; and (3) to improve the instructional program by providing an assessment that reflects the *Framework* and is based on the expertise of some of California's best teachers.

Development of the Assessment

The English–Language Arts Assessment Advisory Committee—a Department of Education committee representing the spectrum of California's educators—working with internationally recognized leaders in the field, developed the guidelines for a new integrated English–language arts assessment that would align with the *Framework*, mirror exemplary English–language arts programs, and build on CAP's writing assessment. To carry out this vision, the development team of classroom teachers was expanded in 1989 to represent English and language arts teachers from grades 1 through 12 as well as teachers of science, history, and math. These development-team teachers have been responsible for shaping the test format, developing prompts for the assessment, and constructing scoring guides. Team members representing the elementary grades were charged with a more complex assignment because the statewide writing assessment for younger students had not yet been developed. While middle and high school teachers were able to build on the existing writing assessment and the writing types established for grade 8 and high school, the grade 4 test developers were required to create all components of the new integrated English–language arts assessment.

The Assessment Emerges

In preparation for designing the reading component of the English–language arts assessment, development-team teachers steeped themselves in work sessions with leaders in the field, read and discussed current articles and books by theorists and researchers, and engaged in thoughtful analyses of their own classroom practices. From these activities, a working definition of reading as "the process of constructing meaning through bringing personal experience into transactions with text" emerged. In this view of reading, the individual reader assumes the responsibility for interpreting the text by building on an understanding of the contexts (historical, cultural, linguistic, psychological) of both the text and his or her personal experience. Rather than believing that meaning lies in the words on the page, this view of reading depends on the role of the individual to construct a meaningful interpretation from the transactions among text, context, and experience.

Readers and writers have related but different purposes within four major groupings of events that encompass a spectrum of mindsets or reader "stances." These are the purposes for the new assessment identified by teachers from their work with students as well as from their own experience as readers and writers. These basic reader and writer purposes are described in Figure 1. The figure shows, for example, that from an aesthetic stance, one can express one's own experi-

Figure 1
Basic Reader and Writer Purposes

Nature of Event	Reader Purpose	Writer Purpose
Aesthetic: Narrative	to live through an aesthetic experience; to connect to the universalities of experience	to give shape to an idea or an experience, real or fictional
Expressive/ Personal	to connect with another's personal experiences or ideas	to create, reveal, or clarify ideas or experiences for self or another
Efferent: Informative	to understand information; to gain new knowledge	to convey information; to explain ideas, facts, or processes
Persuasive	to consider and evaluate another's point of view	to influence or convince another of one's ideas or judgments

ences or connect with another's. From an efferent stance, one can understand and convey information to influence or persuade and to evaluate another's point of view.

Key to the development of appropriate tasks for the assessment is the selection of texts for the reading component. The development team has been committed to finding texts that are challenging to all students while being accessible to most. The team looks for texts that represent the points of view of different ethnic or cultural groups, both sexes, and of urban and rural perspectives, as well as texts that accommodate a wide range of reader purposes. Once a text is selected, a group of three or four team members discusses the selection in depth, exploring its multiple dimensions prior to beginning the work of developing a prompt. This exploration of a text enables the teachers to determine its suitability for a prompt; it must engage and challenge readers as they respond to questions and activities that will invite them to show evidence of their reading ability. The final evaluation of a text's suitability is determined after field testing when the team reviews the responses of hundreds of students representing a cross-section of California's diverse population.

Texts selected for the assessment are stories, articles, and poems typically taught in each of the tested grade levels. Texts may, on occasion, be excerpts of long pieces; they are always, however, complete in themselves. Occasionally two related texts—a story and poem or an article and story—are paired. While it is not possible to match specific texts to individual pupils, the assessment does draw on a range of materials deemed suitable for classroom instruction in English–language arts classes. Due to the time constraints of an on-demand assessment, length of text remains an important consideration. The texts used in the new assessment are many pages long and often take students up to 20 minutes to finish reading. Other key factors in determining the use of a particular text include the complexity of positions or arguments presented in the text, the accessibility of form or structure, the abstractness of ideas, and the presentation of shifting points of view or timeframes. Texts that rely on heavy use of dialect or outmoded English are not considered for the assessment. Since students will construct meaning for a text based on transactions among text, context, and experience, selections for the assessment center around concepts familiar to students. For example, a passage about a snowstorm may seem appropriate and interesting for fourth grade students; many California students, however, could have difficulty with it due to their lack of prior experience with snow. In all cases, teachers weigh the appropriateness of subject matter and the complexity of the text for most students in each of the tested grade levels.

Collaborative Group Work

Teachers on the development team wanted to ensure that this assessment was sensitive to both instructional strategies used in the best classrooms in California and those described in the *Framework*. Early in the assessment-development process the issue of collaborative group work and student "talk" emerged as a critical element deserving attention. Should students be allowed to discuss a topic or the text before, during, or after the reading assessment?

While teachers can discuss a reading passage with their students at several points in typical classroom events, discussion after the reading seemed the only logical place for assessment purposes. The first field test of the assessment in 1990 included prompts with collaborative group work after reading and prompts without such subsequent group work. Development-team members were attempting to determine how group work would affect student writing and found that the students who had an opportunity to collaborate with peers produced more proficient writing. Using the students' performances and reviewing the surveys of the field-test teachers led team members to believe more strongly in the value of incorporating speaking and listening into the assessment.

The Writing Component

The eight types of writing used in the CAP writing assessment since 1987 for grade eight and high school were maintained in the new assessment; four broader categories of writing were selected for the writing assessment for grade four. Criteria for selecting the types of writing to be assessed at elementary, middle, and high school levels included emphasis on what California's best school writing programs use, relationship to students' reading experiences, consistency with students' cognitive development, appropriate curriculum sequencing, and appropriateness for assessment purposes. Figure 2 shows the types of writing selected. Grade four categories are the more broadly based divisions developmentally appropriate for nine-year-olds, while the middle and high school categories reflect the finer distinctions of writing types appropriate for those age groups.

The development team conducted numerous task tryouts and several field tests as the assessment took shape. Each field test brought new insights into what worked and what did not and contributed to the modification of the test design. Spring 1992 field testing for grades 4, 8, and 10 involved 836 teachers and 23,926 students statewide. Some classrooms worked through integrated task prototypes that required three periods to complete; students in other selected classes tried out test models that extended to five periods. Reactions of students and teachers to the different formats were gathered and these results were used to make decisions about future assessments.

The Prompt Format

The design of the integrated English–language arts assessment calls for students to read and respond independently to a text selection, to work in small col-

Figure 2
Types of Writing at Each Grade Level

	Grade 4	Grade 8	Grade 10
Expressive:	X		
Autobiographical incident		X	X
First-hand biography		X	
Reflective essay			X
Persuasive:	X		
Problem-solution		X	
Evaluation		X	X
Speculation about causes			
or effects		X	X
Interpretation			X
Controversial issue			X
Informative:	X		
Report of information		X	X
Observational writing		X	X
Narrative:	X		
Story		X	

laborative groups, and to respond individually to a writing prompt. Each section is intended to take approximately one class period. The following example of the procedure is based on John R. Gardiner's *Stone Fox*, a fourth grade reading selection, and illustrates the format and content of the assessment. The responses of a single student—one who was evaluated as giving a high-range performance—are included. Some assessments involve more than one text, but the fundamental components of the assessment are present in this example.

Section I: Reading. Students read an excerpt from *Stone Fox* that is a complete and critical part of the story. In it, Little Willy, who has the lead in the race, stands beside his dead dog, Searchlight, as the sled of Stone Fox, who had been in second place, pulls alongside him. Creation of the full context for the passage is supported through a summary of what has happened prior to the excerpt. A statement directs students to read the text and invites them to mark the text in any way that helps them better understand what they are reading. The reading text appears on the left-hand side of the page with the remaining space available for any notes or annotations that the student wishes to write or draw while reading. In the wide right-hand margin, the student whose work will serve as an example here wrote, "I agree with the crowd. I don't want Stone Fox to win the race. That was very sad, that Searchlight died. Why did you have to make her die, John Gardiner?"

After the reading, an initial response question or drawing activity elicits students' immediate responses—feelings, questions, opinions, memories, ideas. Four to seven additional questions or activities help students move beyond their initial response to a deeper exploration of meaning by connecting with, challenging, and reflecting on the text. One such question and the student's response are shown in Figure 3.

Some of the strategies used to elicit individual responses include double-entry journals, listing, clustering, drawing, and completing charts or diagrams. Students are invited to bring their own experiences to their transactions with the text in many ways. Each prompt presents an opportunity ("This is your chance to tell anything else about this story," for example) that allows students to address any insights, issues, or concerns that developed during the reading process and to express any responses that might not have been elicited by other activities. Students may, through their writing or drawing on this page, come to closure or discover

Figure 3
A Question and One Student's Response

Select a line or lines from the story that interest you or make you think. Write the line or lines in the box below.

> Little Willy's sled seemed to lift up off the ground and fly.

Tell why you chose these lines.

> I chose these lines because, I know you can't fly. But I like the way it sounds. I can just see it lift up off the ground and feel like it is flying.

new insights emerging from the text or from their reading experience. A reading score is determined from the evidence of each student's performance on the reading section.

Section II: Group work. Students who have read the same text selection(s) form groups of not more than five. Currently, this section is not scored; instead, these activities serve to extend students' reading experience of text and to initiate prewriting activities that they will use in the writing assessment. Guidelines contain specific directions for collaborative activities such as sharing individual experiences with the text, exploring the text further, making group graphics, role playing, writing informally, sharing drafts, and responding to one another's ideas for writing. For the *Stone Fox* prompt, the group tasks begin with a discussion of what was read and the endings that each group member envisions for the story. The author's ending is read and students discuss it. The content of the passage is extended to group members' experiences through discussion of ways in which people help one another and how they have helped or been helped by others.

Section III: Writing. The writing assessment section may be linked to the reading assessment in one of two ways. Some writing prompts link directly to the reading section by asking students to move beyond their initial interactions with the text to write a longer, more fully developed essay expressing their understanding of the text or evaluating the selection or a character. Other writing prompts are more loosely tied to the reading by using the selection's topic or theme as a springboard to an essay based on personal experience and knowledge.

Each prompt has two parts and is designed to elicit one of the types of writing tested at a grade level. The first part of the prompt establishes a framework for the writing prompt and provides students with a context for writing. It orients students to a type of writing and provides specific background about the topic. The reason for writing is also specified, preparing students to think about their intended audience. The second section gives the specifics regarding the assignment's topic, intent, potential audience, and any other information students need in order to respond to the prompt. For the *Stone Fox* selection, getting ready to write and writing activities revolve around a time when the student helped someone or was helped by someone. Each student receives two writing scores for the essay written in response to the writing prompt: one for rhetorical effectiveness and one for conventions.

Variations on the format. This integrated task format of reading–group work–writing can be adapted or repeated, allowing students multiple opportunities to demonstrate their reading and writing abilities. For example, a reading prompt could be used independently from the other two sections. Likewise, a writing prompt that is not directly linked to a reading text can be administered in addition to a more connected prompt so students have two opportunities to demonstrate their writing abilities; each opportunity could require a different type of writing.

Challenges and Concerns

Developing an assessment of the size and scope required for California is a complex process with numerous issues to be addressed. Although space limitations preclude a discussion of all the challenges, a description of some of the major issues follows.

Meeting the Needs of Population Diversity

One of the great concerns of development-team members is the effect of the new assessment on California's diverse student population. Teachers are determined that the impact of the assessment on curriculum be positive. With the advent of the reporting of individual test scores, teachers are also concerned that the new assessment provide the opportunity for students to demonstrate their best reading and writing abilities and not be a minimum competency test.

Some Californians have expressed the opinion that performance assessment is unfair to minority students and that since multiple-choice tests rely less on a student's proficiency in English they are fairer to these students. The intent of California's new performance assessment is to expand the potential for student response and to allow all students to demonstrate their abilities to construct meaning through a variety of activities that include graphics, writing logs, and other strategies. Teachers on the development team are very aware of the necessity of designing an assessment program that meets multicultural needs in concert with the ideas formulated in the *English–Language Arts Framework*. Every available means has been employed to ensure that the assessment content—texts for reading, activities for group work, and topics for writing—reflect California's diverse population.

The Value of Group Work

As the development team worked through design of the format for the new assessment, concern was expressed over the impact of the group-discussion section on test validity. Much debate ensued over this issue, and a variety of format models were designed to address the potential problem of contaminating the reading or writing scores. The proposed format, field tested for implementation, allows individuals to demonstrate their ability to construct meaning from reading and to interact with text prior to the group-discussion sequence. Group-discussion activities are designed to clarify issues from the reading section and to create a natural bridge to the writing task that is an individual effort.

While there are no plans at this time to grade group discussion, its value has continued to be evident. Occasionally we see instances where students were confused by a reading selection. Their much-improved performance on the writing assessment signals that a clearer understanding of the passage has come from discussion with classmates.

Handling Sensitive or Offensive Papers

The California writing assessment has tested as many as 80 different topics across 8 types of writing.

Occasionally topics—"a remembered childhood experience" or "something that changed my life," for example—elicit student essays that reveal sensitive issues such as child abuse or threat of suicide. These essays are directed to the chief reader for consideration and usually are forwarded to the Department of Education. A member of the department staff will contact the appropriate school administrators to apprise them of the potential problems. In many cases, the school administrators are already aware of the problems, and the situation is already being addressed.

Sometimes scorers will come across student essays containing offensive language or descriptions that can cloud unbiased evaluations of the work. An established policy calls for a table leader or chief reader with years of experience to read extremely offensive papers and assign scores to their components.

Scoring Site Design

Prior to the summer of 1992, most of the student essays were scored centrally, under the direction of the state writing assessment contractor. Some regional sites were established in 1990 that extended the staff-development benefits inherent in the scoring process, but again most of the work was coordinated by the scoring contractor. The scoring site design initiated in 1992 brought to fruition a major goal of the writing assessment program: to have all papers scored by teachers at regional sites through the coordinated efforts of the scoring contractor and the California Professional Development Program Resource Agencies and Consortia. The design called for the contractor, under the direction of department staff, to select and train chief and assistant-chief readers. This team would be responsible for the training of readers at the scoring sites and for facilitating the scoring of papers. Site coordinators and document handlers selected by the regional consortia were provided with a detailed procedure manual outlining security measures, the logistical needs of scoring facilities, processes for moving and returning student essays, directions for using the scoring documents, and more. Regional site coordinators and their staffs set up the sites, selected teacher readers, provided meals and hotel accommodation when needed, and oversaw the scoring operation. Teachers were paid an honorarium to score student work.

The feedback from teacher-scorers indicates that the scoring session provides excellent staff development. Teachers become familiar with one of the eight types of writing being assessed by the state and the scoring rubric for that type of writing; they read and score a wide range of student writing from across the state; they share teaching strategies with peers representing other schools and districts in their region.

In addition to the scoring session, many sites offer an additional day of staff development to the teacher-scorers. Often there is not time to discuss the wide range of student performance that readers see as they score thousands of papers or how they will use what they have learned from the scoring experience to improve their own teaching of writing. The additional day of staff development allows time for these discussions. Also, teachers in the field want to hear about the new assessment, and since the chief readers are often development-team members, this provides an opportunity to spread the word about the new English–language arts assessment.

Individual Student Results

A component in CAP assessment has been the use of matrix sampling in which each student takes only one version or one part of a total test in any given content area. In the writing assessment, matrix sampling allowed the state to assess eight kinds of writing at grades 8 and 12. Now as a full spectrum of grade-level assessments with the additional legislative requirement to report individual student scores is being developed, alternative designs are being considered. One design being explored would retain matrix sampling for some aspects of the assessment while including a uniform component for all students. This amalgam would provide the latitude to retain the existing writing assessment as part of an integrated design with the addition of the new grade-level designations. It also would provide an additional way to strengthen test reliability.

Reflections and Next Steps

California's writing assessment has been recognized nationally as the first large-scale performance assessment to be successfully implemented in public schools. Key to the program's success has been its close relationship to state frameworks and model curriculum guides for English–language arts, the leadership role of teachers in the test development and scoring, the availability of instructional materials and other support materials, and multiple opportunities for staff development.

Many of the components that received positive recognition in the writing assessment have been incorporated in the new integrated assessment, such as the continued emphasis on maintaining a strong alignment between the state curriculum framework and assessment. Special features of the integrated English–language arts assessment include a full range of carefully defined reading and writing types and purposes; the focus on reading and writing assessments as dynamic activities that involve the construction of meaning; assessment activities that call for students' interactions with texts and with other students and provide opportunities for prewriting; the bringing together of teachers to design tasks, scoring guides, and support materials; and a commitment to staff development and scoring support by regional consortia, the California Writing Project, and the California Literature Project.

Initial field responses indicate that the new integrated assessment is being well received by California's educators. The successful implementation of this once-a-year, on-demand examination, however, will represent the accomplishment of only one goal in the full vision of the English–language arts assessment. A broader goal of the California State Department of Education is that within the next five years the on-demand assessment given each spring will become one of three sources of data for measuring individual student achievement. The second source, identified as curriculum-embedded assessment, would allow classroom teachers to select tasks from an approved pool and administer them during the school year at times when they fit naturally into the curriculum. The third source of information would come from a portfolio-type assessment that would draw from student-selected work, class projects, and other teacher-initiated and -scored assignments. Common statewide performance standards currently under construction would be used as the basis of measurement for all assessment components. These different sources of information will be accompanied by different levels of information produced from the results—from individual student and parent reports to school and district reports to a reporting of statewide results to the legislature and the governor's office. In addition to the test reports, each student will have compiled an individual record of accomplishment by the end of grade 12.

Much has been done in California to move toward this vision, but much still is to be accomplished. The far-reaching goals for assessment are made possible through the dedicated efforts of many outstanding educators who see teaching tomorrow's leaders as an admirable and valuable profession.

Author's Note: The material in this chapter draws on the work of Fran Claggett, advisor to the English–Language Arts development team. Her work appears in the article "Reshaping the Culture of Testing: A New Reading and Writing Assessment in California," published in *Reading Instruction Journal*, Fall 1990. I thank Fran for her extensive research, guidance, and continuing work with the development team.

Reference

California State Department of Education. (1987). *English–language arts framework for California public schools, kindergarten through grade 12.* Sacramento, CA: Author.

P. David Pearson

COMMENTARY ON *California's New English–Language Arts Assessment*

THE TEACHERS OF CALIFORNIA have started a revolution in reading and writing assessment. The effort chronicled by Barbara Weiss is revolutionary on several counts, including these:

- the basic conceptualization of the assessment;
- the social context of the assessment—that is, the role of teacher scaffolding and peer interaction in the assessment process;
- the pervasive involvement of teachers in the entire assessment process, from conceptualization to text selection to task development to scoring; and
- the format and content of the assessment.

While these attributes bode well for this revolutionary effort, the most difficult challenges for this approach to assessment have yet to be encountered. Thus far, the California effort has had the luxury of experimental or pilot status; it has carried no consequences for teachers or students in the way that other high-stakes assessments have. If, and when, it changes status and assumes the burdens of a high-stakes assessment, it will be interesting to see whether most—or even many—of its current attractive features survive.

In this review of the California effort, a section that elaborates on each of these positive attributes is followed by a section that details the challenges that face it and all other performance-based assessments as they move from experimental to operational status.

Positive Attributes

The basic concept. Like most recent assessments (see, for example, Valencia et al., 1989), California's English–language arts assessment is based on constructive (Anderson & Pearson, 1984) or transactive (Rosenblatt, 1985) views of language communication. As such, it is committed to a highly contextualized view of language and learning. In such a view language users construct—rather than passively receive—meaning of the texts that they read and write. Their meaning construction is influenced by the entire array of factors present in the learning environment: texts, knowledge, and values they bring to learning; the intentions of authors whose texts are being read or consulted; the views of other learners (teachers and peers) in the learning environment; and the very nature of the learning environment itself (different classrooms nurture different stances toward text).

In this view, interpretation is the norm, not the exception; indeed, without interpretation, there is no comprehension. It also makes reading and writing inherently social acts even if they are performed in solitude; there is always a reader or a writer lurking in our minds as we construct meaning. But more important in the case of classroom learning, reading and writing often involve overt social negotiations of meaning. In fact, there is no apparent purpose for classroom discussion of texts unless we believe that the models of meaning we build as we read and write can be revised during discussion.

The social context of the assessment. Given California's commitment to a transactive view of learning, we should not be surprised to learn that teacher scaffolding and peer interaction play a pivotal role in its assessment process. More conventional assessment environments are notoriously and intentionally lonely. The label we apply to the act of consulting others during a test is "cheating." And teachers are instructed to deny help to those who are confused about the test— "You'll have to figure it out for yourself. I can't help."

Contrast those conventions with the role of peer and teacher consultation described in the California assessment. The California assessment encourages, even demands, classroom discourse in both large- and small-group contexts. It can occur prior to reading, as a follow-up to reading, as prewriting, or as peer response to writing. In short, the roles of discussion and conversation in this assessment are identical to their roles in everyday classroom instruction. As Weiss suggests, collaborative group work is incorporated in "ways that are natural to good instruction." In comparing the social contexts of conventional assessment with the performance assessment tradition exemplified in the California case, it is almost as though performance assessment allows inferences about an individual's performance in everyday social learning or problem-solving situations while the conventional assessment tradition permits inferences about how an individual performs in a completely isolated environment devoid of any human or material resources. Of course, the benefit of authenticity provided by a rich social context carries a heavy cost (that I will discuss in more detail later) when it obscures the contributions of a particular student to his or her own work.

One other aspect deserves mention. Because these tasks last anywhere from three to five days, there is no way they can be shrouded in the veil of secrecy accorded to conventional tests that arrive sealed in plastic with instructions about preserving test security.

These assessments become by their nature and duration quasipublic events. Students see them, discuss them, perhaps even share the activities with parents over the duration of their administration. So the social context of these assessments can extend well beyond the classroom community.

The pervasive involvement of teachers. Perhaps the single most appealing attribute of the California assessment is its commitment to teachers. Teachers control, monitor, and implement all aspects of the process from conceptualizing the framework that undergirds the assessment to text selection to developing the assessment tasks, rubrics, and scoring guides for reading responses and writing efforts to scoring the student responses. As Weiss suggests, the extensive involvement of teachers has several benefits beyond the obvious and important sense of ownership that it gives them. The biggest benefit is the development of professional expertise among the teachers in the state. Those teachers who have worked on the framework and test development encounter new ways of thinking about curriculum and assessment. Furthermore, because they are learning by doing, they develop the competence needed to nurture similar expertise among their peers in local staff-development efforts. Having conducted a few scoring and task-development sessions with groups of teachers, I agree with the assessment of the positive potential of this approach for professional development. By actually creating tasks, developing rubrics, and rating the quality of responses, teachers gain a deep understanding of reading and writing and the reasoning processes students use to respond to complex tasks.

The format and content of the assessment. There is much to applaud in the assessment tasks themselves. My list of favorite features includes opportunities for students to engage in extended written responses to reading, opportunities to respond with marginal notes and reactions while reading, and extensive use of graphic organizers to scaffold students' individual responses and cooperative learning activities. For many students, especially those with long histories of failure in verbal tasks, the visual display provides a more inviting, less threatening format. In addition, I have seen many of the assessments piloted at grades 4, 8, and 10, and am impressed with the teachers' selection of texts. As Weiss puts it, they tried to find texts that would be "challenging to all students while being accessible to most." Such texts also lead quite naturally to engaging writing prompts.

Future Challenges

As I noted earlier, the experimental status of the California assessment has shielded it from the type of angry criticism typically hurled at any high-stakes assessment used to sort or rank districts, schools, teachers, or students. In the final analysis, the California assessment—along with the entire crop of new performance assessments and portfolio approaches—will be judged not by their contribution of "interesting" alternative approaches, but by whether they allow the constituencies concerned about education (parents, students, teachers, administrators, and policymakers) to make better decisions and whether they bear positive consequences for the ultimate clients of our system—the students.

Creating scores for individuals. The real issue here is how much information one can gather in a three- to five-day assessment about the range of literacy competence of a particular student. While students may write extensively in response to a single text in that time, one is left with information about a given student's performance on a single text. Given what we know about the influence of knowledge on comprehension and composition, any generalization about that student's overall competence is dangerous—if not irresponsible.

The situation is different for a class. Using a technique known as matrix sampling, in which different students respond to different parts of the entire curricular space for which one might want to make an inference about performance, it is possible to gather sufficient information on the population of, say, eighth grade students in a typical school to feel comfortable with some sort of judgment about typical performance. Traditional standardized tests confront this problem by exposing students to many brief multiple-choice questions about an array of short texts on a range of topics.

The truth is that the sorts of on-demand tasks in the California assessment (as well as in most other performance assessment efforts) cannot be used by themselves to fashion a portrait of an individual student. Not only can't performance on specific tasks be generalized to other literacy tasks, but these on-demand performance measures must be surrounded by other, more comprehensive data sources. Most performance assessment efforts echo the logic of the California designers in suggesting that any assessment system that purports to make valid judgments about individuals must use portfolio entries and curriculum-embedded assessments along with the on-demand assessment.

Equity issues. Issues of equity, especially as they apply to groups that traditionally have been marginalized by tests designed for mainstream or politically dominant groups, have risen to the top of public discourse about assessment. In fact, one of the key arguments used by those who criticize conventional approaches to assessment is that those approaches are biased against particular ethnic groups or—in the case of mathematics assessment—women. Recently, advocates of conventional assessments have counterattacked, pointing out that the extreme writing demands of performance-based reading assessments are likely to place students from minority cultures at a particular disadvantage in relation to their dominant-culture peers.

The problem is that we now have a great deal of rhetoric and precious little direct evidence to support either claim. If ever there was a need for careful research on an important policy question, this is the question. We need good studies, both large-scale evaluations of the comparative performance of different groups on different tasks and close analyses of the cognitive and linguistic strategies that individuals from these groups use to cope with task demands. Otherwise, we will continue to engage in empty rhetorical exercises about problems that may or may not exist. California needs to confront these questions of equity directly and immediately, most certainly before high stakes are tied to the assessment.

Task difficulty. The California assessment developers tried to choose texts and design tasks that were challenging to all and accessible to most. But "accessible to most" does not mean accessible to all. One of my greatest fears is that many students will be challenged right out of the assessment process. Also, because the texts are chosen to typify certain grade levels (in fact, they are often chosen from existing curricula), students with marginally developed literacy skills will have great difficulty reading the texts, let alone responding to challenging tasks that require intertextual reasoning and authorial critique.

Without emulating what we take as negative and narrowing features of standardized tests, new assessments need to incorporate the logic of those tests in dealing with text and item difficulty. Texts used on standardized tests begin with passages that are several grades lower than the target grade and then become successively more difficult until they are well beyond the target grade. We need to find a way to incorporate the notion of text difficulty into performance assessment so that all students who are asked to undertake these tasks find activities that they can respond to with confidence and perhaps even a sense of personal mastery. To the degree that we want to use these tests to draw inferences about the performance of individuals rather than groups, this issue is all the more critical.

An internal contradiction. Weiss reminds us that the California assessment respects the idiosyncratic nature of individual responses to literature. Indeed, its designers value scoring rubrics that reward students for engaging in imaginative interpretation and in risk-taking behaviors. Yet rubrics and scoring guides, no matter how open or flexible or imaginative, are still external impositions on the interpretive process. They inherently give privileges to particular interpretations over others and to certain response strategies over others. They ultimately make this assessment process, like most other assessment processes, a matter of one individual or group judging another individual or group.

Some Questions

As I read and reread the Weiss chapter, several questions kept popping into the back of my mind. I raise them as challenges to our thinking as we move ahead to the next generation of performance assessments.

> 1. If discussion is a valued activity and if it is used to solidify comprehension and response to literature prior to writing, why is it not used

to help students revise their individual reading responses? In other words, why not invite students to edit, add to, or completely recast their initial reading responses after a discussion? They could leave their first responses intact but demonstrate the type of response they are capable of with "a little help from their friends."

2. If we build new state and national systems with milestone assessments at key grade levels (4, 8, and 10 emerge most commonly), what are we going to use for on-demand assessment at the other grade levels? Will standardized tests continue? Will teaching staffs or testing companies develop interstitial clones of the state assessments? Will states publish practice assessments?

3. What are the other hidden consequences of using a group assessment for individual purposes? I have already discussed one problem—the fact that time-intensive, on-demand tasks provide too narrow a portrait of an individual. Are there others? Some approaches work well for group decisions (e.g., matrix sampling) but cause problems for decisions about individuals.

4. How will we ever develop a language that will enable us to convey to students what is truly valued in these approaches to assessment? One of the potential virtues of this approach is that it enables us to move assessment out of the plastic-wrapped bundles of secrecy hidden in school closets and on warehouse pallets and into a public forum in which student work is displayed for everyone—including students—to see. But it is not enough to make

these assessments and our underlying values public. We must also render transparent the criteria on which students will be judged. If we do not or cannot achieve complete transparency so that all students have equal access to the criteria and to examples that make the criteria concrete, then we will have achieved nothing more than another means of extending privileges to some students at the expense of others.

These concerns notwithstanding, I find much to applaud in the California experiment. The assessments described by Weiss are enlightening, challenging, and engaging. The processes through which they have been developed are equally enlightening, challenging, and engaging; more important, they are respectful of the wisdom and concern for children that teachers bring to the table. I am confident that through the collaboration of teachers, students, parents, policymakers, and scholars, we can meet the challenges of the future and answer the questions that currently puzzle us. We can, I believe, have assessments that match our aspirations for high-quality curricula and thoughtful students. The California language arts assessment certainly moves a long way toward meeting that goal.

References

Anderson, R.C., & Pearson, P.D. (1984). A schema-theoretic view of basic processes in reading comprehension. In P.D. Pearson, R. Barr, M. Kamil, & P. Mosenthal (Eds.), *Handbook of reading research: Volume I* (pp. 255-291). White Plains, NY: Longman.

Rosenblatt, L. (1985). Transaction versus interaction: A terminological rescue operation. *Research in the Teaching of English*, 19(1), 96-107.

Valencia, S.W., Pearson, P.D., Peters, C.W., & Wixson, K.K. (1989). Theory and practice in statewide reading assessment: Closing the gap. *Educational Leadership*, 46(7), 57-63.

CHAPTER 9

Mary W. Garcia
Kathy Verville

REDESIGNING TEACHING AND LEARNING: THE ARIZONA STUDENT ASSESSMENT PROGRAM

As SHIFTS HAVE BEEN MADE IN CURRICULUM TO REFLECT HIGHER LEVEL LITERACIES, assessments need to change as well. Arizona's experience is an important one for teachers in other states and countries to know about. A new state performance test that uses multiple indicators of student accomplishments has been put in place. It is similar to those described in other chapters in this section in that it provides opportunities for students to write and respond with alternative formats such as semantic maps; but in other ways, the Arizona Student Assessment Program (ASAP) has some unique features. For one, it has different forms to reflect difficulty levels—a neglected feature on most state assessments. It also allows teachers to use the instrument on an ongoing basis in their classrooms rather than having to wait until the end of the year for a one-time administration. As important, the ASAP has not forgotten other forms of assessment. Local districts can participate by providing material developed within the district. Further, standardized tests continue to have a place—but alongside other measures. It is truly a system that encourages multiple indicators.

The ASAP was designed to be inclusive. There is an expectation that all students will participate and a provision that enables this to happen. In the past, districts frequently exempted limited English proficient (LEP) students and all special education students from the state achievement testing and, by extension, diminished expectations that these students would learn the reading outcomes. Now, only those students whose individual education plan requires an exemption are excluded from the assessment. This results in the expectation that all will learn and be assessed on all the reading outcomes.

The philosophy of inclusion prompted the development of mediation as a strategy for those students who are classified as LEP and special education. The rule of thumb is that when administering an assessment, teachers can provide the same modifications of instruction usually employed in the day-to-day classroom setting. This might include more time for completing the assessment, an alternate setting, translation into a student's primary language, paraphrasing, taking dictation from a student, and using visuals such as pictures in a dictionary.

Approximately one-third of Arizona's kindergarten to grade 12 students are Hispanic; many speak Spanish as a first language and are in bilingual classrooms. To meet the needs of Arizona students, all 67 assessments included in the ASAP are available in

Spanish. In some instances, translations of the English assessment are used, and in other instances original Spanish-language literature or poetry is included. The Spanish assessments measure the same outcomes as their English counterparts.

Aims and Origins

The goals of high levels of literacy and other proficiencies for all students in the state motivated Arizona to initiate Goals for Excellence legislation in 1987. That legislation resulted in the creation of a committee charged with setting goals that included increased student achievement in kindergarten through grade 12, graduation rates, and success beyond the completion of high school. When goals are established it is necessary to develop some means by which it can be determined if and when they are reached. So it was that the ASAP came into being as part of the initiative to increase achievement and meet goals.

The implementation of a curriculum framework preceded the development or identification of assessment tools. While called the *Language Arts Essential Skills*, the framework emphasizes meaning-making and the integration of reading and writing with other language processes, rather than a listing of discrete skills. Three processes are emphasized across all the grades: building background, comprehending, and presenting. Benchmarks or outcomes have been identified within three grade-level clusters (K-3, 4-8, 9-12) and for each of the three processes. "Competency indicators," which tell what a skill looks like when demonstrated, are given, as are suggestions for evaluation. With the processes, students are able to become proficient in or perform the outcomes; the outcomes are tangible signs of learning that indicate what a student must demonstrate at each of the benchmark grades. The outcomes, competency indicators, and suggestions for evaluation for the process of comprehending for kindergarten to grade 3 are presented in Figure 1 to illustrate the new framework.

The success of a state project like the ASAP depends on participation of as many groups as possible. While the Arizona State Board of Education took responsibility for the framework, concerned citizens, educators, and representatives of business and industry were part of the process of its development. The goals and the resulting framework document were discussed at public forums across the state and revised on the basis of recommendations from various groups.

The next step was to obtain assessment measures that captured those outcomes. Outcomes can be comprehensive and broadly conceived, but if instruments for monitoring them are limited, they will not be translated into practice. Riverside Publishing Company (RPC) was awarded the contract to assist the curriculum specialists in the Arizona Department of Education (ADE) with the task of developing assessment tools that represented the outcomes. Interaction between the testmaker and the Arizona educators was continual. At the outset, examples of assessment items developed by Arizona educators were shared with RPC. These included such tasks as having students listen to and discuss an audiotape of Martin Luther King, Jr.'s "I have a dream" speech to compare the effect of hearing the speech to the effect of reading it. In eighth grade, students read a newspaper article entitled "N.M. Cave Find a Deepening Mystery" and make predictions and formulate opinions about an issue raised in the article by creating an advertisement to attract tourists to the cave or a poster protesting tourism. In another eighth grade assessment, students read a magazine article and a summary of the article and judge the summary's faithfulness to

Figure 1
Framework for Comprehending, ᴋ-3

Process	Products/ Outcomes	Competency Indicators	Suggestions for Evaluation
Comprehending	uses the relation-ship between letters and sounds as a strategy to promote fluent reading		oral reading that shows fluency and understand-ing
	uses knowledge of useful familiar words		oral reading that shows fluency and understand-ing
	uses strategies to understand unfamiliar words	analogy to familiar words, context	oral reading that shows fluency and understand-ing
	uses strategies to self-correct when necessary	checks under-standing against predictions: oral rereads; uses con-text (including pictures); "holds" to read further; asks for help	reading that shows under-standing

the original in terms of main idea, critical details, and underlying meaning; then they rewrite the summary. In twelfth grade, students read Anton Chekhov's short story "The Lament" and a critique of the story; they are then called on to write a brief evaluation of the critique. Specialists at ʀᴘᴄ also examined trade books, maga-zines, and anthologies to find more material on which to base assessment and developed questions that cap-tured the critical processes. ᴀᴅᴇ specialists then dis-cussed these items with one another, teachers, and the testmaker. Through this process, the various forms of the assessment were developed.

The Nature of the Assessments

Each reading assessment is an integrated series of items based on high-quality literature and built around a core problem or product. Literature selections are both fiction and nonfiction and are chosen on the basis of interest level, readability, and appropriateness of content. The topics range from wildlife preservation to art to spelunking; the genres include personal narrative, autobiography, fiction, informative reports, letters, poetry, summaries, essays, persuasive writing, and critiques. The primary tasks of the assessments include the following: sentence completion and short answer; distinguishing fact and opinion; true/false items requiring correction of false statements; ranking and sequencing; completion of charts, diagrams, and tables; drawing; and composition of single- and multiparagraph essays with the aid of editorial checklists. One task may involve reading several different types of text. In a third grade assessment of comprehending, for example, children are given a letter from the school principal describing a bicycle accident and an article on safe bicycling. The texts, which are presented in Figure 2, create a realistic context for third grade students.

The presentation of the assessment follows an interactive model of reading. Each assessment begins with a prereading activity designed to stimulate students' interest and activate background knowledge of both the content and the genre of the reading passage. The prereading activity for the bicycle safety task, for example, is guided by discussion questions such as "How did you get to school today? Did you walk? Did you come by car? By bike?" Children's responses are listed on the board and a follow-up set of questions

Figure 2
Texts Used in a Third Grade Comprehending Assessment

Please read carefully.

Notice To All Students

Dear Students:

Yesterday, there was an accident near our school. One of our students was injured while he was riding his bicycle. Luckily, he was not seriously hurt. But this accident might have been prevented if the student had followed bicycle safety rules.

I have listed these rules on the next page. Please read them carefully. They will be posted in every classroom in our school. Your teacher will also be reviewing them with you in class this morning. Once you have learned the rules, be sure to follow them each time you ride your bicycle.

Remember, bicycling can be fun. But if you're not careful, it can also be dangerous. Know the rules for bike safety and always keep your bicycle in good shape.

Sincerely,

Dr. Sandra Cook

Dr. Sandra Cook, Principal
Lincoln Elementary School

Bicycle Safety Rules

1. Obey all traffic signs and signals. Be sure to stop at all stop signs.
2. Ride single file on streets and highways.
3. Keep to the right side of the street. Ride with the traffic, not against it.
4. Ride in a straight line. Never do stunts or weave in and out of traffic.
5. Slow down and look carefully before crossing intersections. If traffic is heavy, get off your bike and walk.
6. Use proper hand signals in traffic.

Left turn   Right turn   Slow or stop

7. Watch out for cars, especially ones that may be pulling out from the curb. Keep a safe distance from traffic in front of you.
8. Don't carry another rider.
9. Be sure your bike has good brakes. Keep your bike in good repair.
10. Do not ride your bike at night unless you have a headlight in front of your bike and a reflector in back.

leads them to think about safety rules. Students are then asked to make predictions about the passages before reading, to set reading goals, and to recall their prior knowledge of the topic and genre. For the bicycle safety task, support for engaging in these processes is provided through an illustration of a bicycle. On the illustration, parts of the bicycle are labeled. The teacher refers students to the illustration and notes that some parts of the bicycle make it move while other parts make it safe. The teacher then describes the task children are to do independently—in this case, study the parts of the bicycle and circle the names of parts that make it safe.

The reading phase—when students make meaning of the text, confirm predictions, and clarify ideas—occurs next. After reading, students demonstrate their ability to construct meaning by responding to several different kinds of questions. They are asked to look back at the reading selection as they work and to explain the reasons for their answers. Questions tap comprehension at the literal, interpretative, critical, and appreciative levels. At the appreciative level, students go beyond the selection by relating the content of the assessment to their own experiences.

As these two items from the bicycle safety task illustrate, the questions are written to encourage a variety of response modes:

1. What does the principal talk about in her letter? Finish the sentence below in your own words.

You may look back at the letter.

The principal talks about _____

_____

_____

2. What steps did Dr. Cook follow when she wrote her letter? Put a "1" in front of the first thing she wrote about. Put a "2" in front of the second part. Put a "3" in front of the third part of her letter. You may look back at the letter.

_____ She tells her plan for posting and reviewing bicycle rules.

_____ She tells students about an accident.

_____ She reminds students how to have safe fun on their bicycles.

A balance of scaffolded and open-ended response types are available as students write sentences, sequence a group of sentences that summarize key parts of the letter, and complete a paragraph summary of the letter using the cloze procedure. The final two exercises of the bicycle safety task give children the opportunity to make extensions beyond the text. In the first, students write a note to a friend who does not ride his bicycle safely that explains the consequences of not following appropriate rules. Examples of student responses identifying the qualities that would be expected at four points on a scoring rubric (which is discussed in the next section) are illustrated in Figure 3.

The final task encourages creative responses as well as extensions of the meaning students have made from the reading. In this exercise, students draw a poster that illustrates one or more bicycle safety rules to remind other students of the importance of riding safely.

There are four forms of each assessment: Form A is targeted for grades 3, 8, and 12 but may be used by the district at any appropriate grade level; Form B is parallel to Form A but intended for use one to two

Figure 3
Student Responses to an Open-Ended Question

I would say your not riding by the rules
why   becouse she is not
I am being Kind
I may Like her
She may be nice

1

She can get ran over
She can get hurt
She can hurt someone
or an animal

2

Stop at a stop sigh and
Keep your bick strty.
Ride single file on street
and highways.

3

①Stop at a stop sine. If you
dont stop at a stop sine you
may get hit by a car
②Dont ride with a flat tire If
you ride with a flat tire you
may fall off of you bike

4

grades prior to grades 3, 8, and 12; Form C, also parallel to Form A, is intended for use two or more grades prior to grades 3, 8, and 12; Form D is parallel to Form A but includes different content that allows it to be used for the state-administered assessment each spring. For example, if Form A had students formulate opinions about an issue raised in a report on spelunking in New Mexico, Form D might have had them formulate an opinion about an issue raised in a report on ever-increasing numbers of tourists in the national parks.

Forms A, B, and C were distributed to schools over a two-year period for teachers to use in the classroom. The objective was to help teachers see how the assessments mirrored good instructional practices. Assessment becomes an instructional tool when teachers discover the link between what they are teaching and the content of the assessment texts and tasks.

Scoring

Each scoring guide provides a "rubric," the term we use to describe a hierarchy of acceptable responses. It identifies the qualities one would expect to see in a response at several points along a scale. Each score is matched to an "anchor," an example of a student response at that point. Points are awarded by matching the student's response to a point on the scale and to an anchor.

Rubrics are preceded by a "headnote" that provides general ground rules for using this approach. These features of the rubrics are illustrated in Figure 4, which presents the scoring guide for the "What would you say to a friend who does not follow bicycle safety rules?" item on the bicycle safety task.

The extensive training of scorers involves their using the rubrics, anchors, and a common set of papers with the goal of attaining standardized scoring on any performance. As scorers work, they award points on the basis of how closely a performance matches the rubric and anchors for a particular score. Scoring is calibrated by different methods: second readings, prescored papers that are mixed in with unscored papers (seeding), timed review of the rubrics and anchors, and table leaders' review of papers.

Figure 4
A Scoring Rubric

Task question: What would you say to a friend who does *not* follow the bicycle safety rules of your community? Why? Give as many reasons as you can.

Headnote: The primary evaluation should be on the content of the student's response to the situation and on the logical explanation of the need for rules and the reasons for following them. Sentence-level problems (e.g., punctuation, spelling, capitalization, etc.) should not impede understanding. There should be no serious language problems in a "4" or "3" response.

A "4" response indicates that the student understands both bicycle safety and the consequences of not following appropriate safety rules. It is distinguished by its unity of purpose and expression (e.g., it might present the information in paragraph form despite the fact that the question does not stipulate the need for a paragraph response.) A "4" response presents persuasive reasons for following bicycle safety rules and organizes the advice logically.

A "3" response indicates that the student understands bicycle safety, but it may fail to present reasons for following the rules or to equate failure to follow the rules with the consequences.

A "2" response tends merely to express the writer's advice (e.g., "you should follow the rules") without providing reasons—compelling or otherwise. It may exhibit sentence-level problems sufficiently severe to hinder the reader's understanding.

A "1" response may momentarily address the situation posed, but then diverge into loosely related or wholly unrelated issues (e.g., the writer might begin by focusing on the friend's failure to adhere to bicycle safety rules but quickly shift to an unrelated personal narrative). On the other hand, a "1" response may propose wholly insupportable explanations for following the rules (e.g., "If you follow the rules, you'll get a new bike for your birthday"). It may also be hampered by sentence-level flaws so severe that the reader has difficulty comprehending the writer's ideas.

Assign a "0" if the student has failed to address the question in any way.

Assign an "N/S" (Not Scorable) if the response is illegible or unreadable.

Other Components

Prior to the ASAP's inception, norm-referenced tests were administered each spring to Arizona students at every grade level. With the advent of the new curriculum framework, it became apparent that norm-referenced tests alone could not measure the reading outcomes since the correlation between the tests and the outcomes was minimal. While the ASAP requires students to construct their own responses to real-life situations, norm-referenced tests are designed to measure the skill acquisition of large numbers of students in an efficient manner. However, since there was a continued interest in comparing the general academic achievement of Arizona students with that of students from across the country, norm-referenced testing remains a component of the ASAP. But to reduce its impact on curriculum and to lessen or eliminate the classroom time spent on test preparation, administration was moved from the spring to the fall of each academic year and only a partial battery of the tests is now given at each of three grade levels.

District performance assessment is also part of the ASAP. Each Arizona district is required by statute to complete a District Assessment Plan (DAP) and to submit this plan to the ADE. The DAP requires that districts report how and when they will assess students on the reading outcomes for K-3, 4-8, and 9-12. Districts have the option of using Forms A, B, or C of the performance-based assessments, their own criterion-referenced tests, or portfolios. The first step in creating the assessment component of the DAP is curriculum alignment—how will the curriculum framework be matched with grade level expectations? The next step is to determine when and how the outcomes will be assessed. While districts have options for assessment instruments, they must ensure through the forms they submit to the ADE that students demonstrate both process and product. Teachers teach, assess, and keep a record of student mastery of the K-3, 4-8, and 9-12 outcomes; districts will report each spring the percentage of third, eighth and twelfth grade students mastering these outcomes. The DAP is, however, an evolving plan. As districts implement their assessment decisions, they are encouraged to continue to elicit teacher input so appropriate plan modifications can be made over time.

Findings: A Statewide Pilot

The ADE conducted a statewide pilot of 67 reading, writing, and mathematics performance assessments in March 1992; 21 of those were reading assessments. Over 500 Arizona teachers volunteered to score the over 115,000 assessments. Measurement, Inc., under a contract with ADE, trained teachers to use analytic trait scoring to assign points to student responses. Once assessments were scored, they were summarized to produce a statewide report of students' accomplishments for each of the outcomes at grades 3, 8, and 12.

To illustrate the manner in which results were reported, we return to the bicycle safety task. There were six components in the task, each of which could be assigned a maximum of four points. Unlike standardized test scores that provide summary data on how many students were above or below the mean, the aim of this assessment is for all students to attain high levels of proficiency. The summary of third grade students' performances on the bicycle safety task begins with the description of the outcome and the task, as indicated in Figure 5; the figure also shows the nature of reporting when high standards for all students are the aim.

Several studies of reliability and validity were conducted as part of the pilot study. Validity of the ASAP was evaluated through a content review of the assess-

Figure 5
Report Summarizing Performance on the Bicycle Safety Task

Essential Skills Group: Reads and comprehends a communication. Students read a letter and an instructional article on safe bicycling. In the prereading activity, students discuss safety features of bicycles. They then read the letter and the article and answer comprehension questions about them. Finally, students draw a poster, applying what they have read. Students are scored on their ability to comprehend the communication they have read. They are judged on their ability to write a response that is distinguished by its unity of purpose and expression, which indicates the student both understands bicycle safety and the consequences of not following appropriate safety rules, and to draw an accurate visual portrayal of one or more bicycle safety rules. Students are not judged on their artistic abilities.

The information that follows is a summary of student performance on the assessment derived from the essential skills group identified above. Because each ASAP assessment independently evaluates a specific grouping of Arizona's essential skills, the information presented here cannot be directly compared with the outcome of any other assessment.

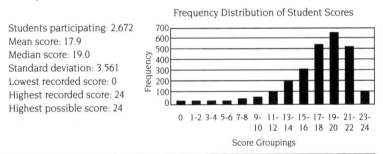

Students participating: 2,672
Mean score: 17.9
Median score: 19.0
Standard deviation: 3.561
Lowest recorded score: 0
Highest recorded score: 24
Highest possible score: 24

Frequency Distribution of Student Scores

ment, a comparison with norm-referenced reading tests, and test-item analyses. The tests went through an iterative review process over their three years of development, and several groups of experts reviewed them for content and fairness. Other statistical studies indicated that correlation with norm-referenced tests is substantial and that item analyses yielded highly acceptable values for this kind of assessment (Riverside Publishing Company, 1992). Scorer bias, examinee error, and generalizability were among the reliability issues studied. The median reliability indices across all types and all three grades ranged from .67 to .90. In general, these values indicate that these performance assessments can be scored reliably by a single rater and that little is lost by having papers read by a single rater rather than two raters (Riverside Publishing Company):

> The data show that, in general, these instruments meet acceptable psychometric standards for providing information that may be useful for making decisions about instructional programs and individual students. However, no testing instrument can provide *all* the information required for making such decisions. Whenever decisions about individual students or educational programs incorporate test-score data, it is important that the limitations of the instrument be known. This pilot study was conducted under relatively low-stakes conditions. To the extent that these conditions can be preserved in future ASAP administrations and that ASAP scores are used in conjunction with other performance indicators, these instruments generally display the technical strength to make positive contributions to the decision-making process (pp. v-vi).

Reflections

The ASAP is entering its fourth year of implementation. Every day more evidence of the impact of this reform project comes to light: a review of one DAP reveals a model plan; administrators and teachers call or stop by to share positive changes occurring in their schools; requests for more technical assistance and staff development roll in; students' letters arrive expressing enjoyment in participating in the spring pilot; teachers share their pleasure at finally having assessments that measure what they teach. It must be noted, though, that developing performance-based assessments, administering the assessments statewide, and scoring 115,000 assessments was a monumental task that should not be undertaken without a strong commitment of time, effort, staff, and money. Development of the assessments, while contracted to a publisher, required months of editing and reviewing.

Along with evidence of success, certain areas for improvement have come to light. In designing and revising the reading assessments, the match between items and outcomes is critical. If this match does not exist, problems occur in the corresponding rubrics used to score student responses and in the checklists students use to edit work. One problem that occurs with this one-to-one matching of outcomes and tasks, however, is that change in one necessitates a corresponding change in the other. During the assessment review process, teachers at all levels questioned the validity of a comprehending outcome measured by having students read a poem. The issue of whether comprehending a poem is relevant to real life will have to be addressed when the curriculum framework is revised.

Choosing reading selections for the assessments is a difficult task. Major issues include relevance, student interest, and attending to cultural, sex-role, racial, and religious bias in selections. A revision process such as the one that exists with the ASAP is critical in addressing these issues. It is imperative that such concerns be discussed and resolved prior to final decision-making.

The original assessments had specific time requirements for the prereading activity and for completing the entire assessment. In keeping with the philosophy of measuring what students know and can do and not how quickly they can perform, subsequent revisions provided for more flexibility in administering the assessments. However, test schedules become complicated and adjustments to schedules can frustrate administrators and teachers who have to deal with students who finish the assessment early.

As teachers provide feedback on the use of the assessments, they become more involved in evaluating and modifying their DAPS to reflect a more appropriate alignment of the assessments with grade level expectations for learning. The DAPS have therefore begun to take on more importance as Arizona educators see how they map curriculum and assessment decisions and set the stage for reporting achievement. In addition, as teachers score the assessments and use them for instruction, they come to know the criteria that define mastery of curriculum outcomes and recognize the importance of aligning instruction to the expected outcomes. The scoring rubrics accompanying each assessment clearly articulate the differences between score points and are used by teachers for evaluating student performance and for helping students become critical reviewers of their own work. The links among curriculum, instruction, and assessment that have emerged from these processes are becoming more evident in Arizona classrooms. New learning environments that reflect the curriculum frameworks, the use of the ASAP for instruction as well as assessing achievement, and the accompanying instructional approaches needed to match outcomes and assessment are transforming teaching and learning in Arizona.

Any state or district entering into a performance-based assessment program must be willing to live with the ambiguity and the discomfort that change brings. The ASAP components discussed in this chapter, especially the development of the performance-based assessments, set the stage for restructuring teaching and learning in Arizona. The high standards for achievement set forth in the curriculum framework and measured by the assessments, the reflection and collaboration needed for making curriculum and assessment decisions, the reporting of achievement data tied to identified outcomes, and the reporting of achievement data to parents and the public have the potential to transform the teaching and learning in our schools. We now know that we can successfully assess students statewide using valid curriculum-referenced, performance-based assessments. We know that Arizona teachers can reliably score these assessments. We also have baseline achievement data for goal-setting at the state, district, and school level. Our aim now is that this reform effort will result in graduates who are prepared for a competitive world.

Reference

Riverside Publishing Company. (1992). *Arizona student assessment program, March 1992 pilot study: Technical report.* Phoenix, AZ: Arizona State Department of Education.

Charles W. Peters

COMMENTARY ON *Redesigning Teaching and Learning: The Arizona Student Assessment Program*

ANYONE WHO HAS ATTEMPTED to reform large-scale assessment deserves credit for trying to do what at times seems like an impossible task. What the Arizona Student Assessment Program (ASAP) has accomplished builds on the foundations laid by other states that have undertaken similar reform projects (see, for example, Peters et al., 1992; Valencia et al., 1989). What these programs have in common is that they are constructed around sound theories of learning, cognition, and assessment. Each effort represents another step forward, one that moves assessment away from overreliance on traditional measures of performance toward more innovative performance-based tasks that are part of an integrated, multidimensional assessment system. As this transition occurs, large-scale assessment moves closer to capturing Brown's (1991) idea of thoughtfulness in schools.

While there is still progress to be made, change continues to occur at an accelerated pace, and the ASAP is at the forefront of that movement. What follows is a discussion of the significant contributions of the ASAP as well as questions and problems associated with the development and implementation of new and innovative assessment programs.

Significant Contributions

The ASAP is an assessment system that relies on multiple measures. One of its strongest components is its performance-based assessments. The performance-based portion of the ASAP measures students' application of skills embedded in a single realistic task that requires students to read high-quality literature and nonfiction to solve complex problems. Students have to produce original thoughts about issues or problems rather than reproduce or recognize information. As a result, the ASAP requires higher order thinking skills. Additionally, the assessment tasks are introduced in a context that models good instructional practice; for example, students engage in a prereading activity that helps set the stage for the tasks that follow. This approach to assessment contrasts sharply with standardized multiple-choice tests.

Another centerpiece of the ASAP is its multidimensional approach. It provides local school districts and teachers with a variety of assessment options. For example, in the District Assessment Plan (DAP) districts are given various assessment options—norm-referenced tests, criterion-referenced tests, performance-based assessment tasks, or portfolios—for evaluating student performance. These options permit performance data to be gathered on larger segments of the curriculum, thus allowing for a more comprehensive method of assessing student growth. All assessment options are guided by the *Language Arts Essential Skills*, a document that includes processes and products for reading, writing, speaking, and listening. By permitting options, the state creates the potential for teachers within buildings and across districts to work together to develop standards for evaluating student performance. Furthermore, local districts can avoid the single-method approach as a panacea to assessment problems. As Valencia (1990) cautions, no one single type of assessment can capture all learning behaviors. The ASAP seems to have taken to this sound advice.

Another important feature of the ASAP is that its development is guided by the state-adopted curriculum framework for language arts. The advantage here is twofold: first, a more direct link between curriculum and assessment is possible; second, because the competency indicators that grow out of the framework focus on the functional use of knowledge, a traditional standardized test would be an inappropriate assessment technique. For this reason, the ASAP relies on assessment tasks that capture real-life situations and on portfolios that contain a broad sampling of student work.

Similarly, the link between the ASAP and instruction is enhanced by providing teachers with alternative forms of the performance-based assessment. Teachers are encouraged to use Forms A, B, and C, and to view them as models for good instruction and assessment. Forms B and C are directed at grade levels below the targeted testing grade so that teachers and students have access to these models years before statewide testing. Only Form D is kept secure; the other forms are widely distributed.

The ASAP also uses mediation of assessment for those students classified as limited English proficient (LEP) or special education. The purpose of mediation is to provide more students with the opportunity to participate fully in the assessment process. In part, this mediation addresses the issue of fairness and equity by going beyond traditional approaches to fairness questions. Teachers are permitted to use the same instructional strategies when administering a mediated assessment that they employ daily in their classrooms. This support might include translation of students' primary language, paraphrasing, taking dictation, or using visual material. By allowing mediation in assessments, the ASAP ensures that one set of standards can be applied to a larger segment of the student population.

This will help reinforce the understanding that all students should be provided with equal opportunities to learn and attain the state standards.

Issues and Concerns

As Linn, Baker, and Dunbar (1991) point out, the increasing emphasis placed on performance-based assessments such as the ASAP has generated a need to rethink the criteria by which direct assessments of complex performances are judged. Three major concerns are the complexity and comparability of the assessment tasks, the alignment with curriculum, and the process of development and resulting decision-making.

Complexity and comparability. The real-life tasks on the performance-based assessment portion of the ASAP are designed to tap complex cognitive processes. However, it is difficult to judge the complexity of many tasks. The analysis needs to take into consideration students' familiarity with the problems and the ways in which they attempt to solve them. It should also evaluate the cognitive processes, strategies, and knowledge students must have to complete these tasks successfully and the nature of the responses called for. It is critical that the cognitive complexity of tasks be judged systematically so that task developers and teachers have a clear understanding of what should be taught and assessed (Linn, Baker, & Dunbar, 1991).

Although the design of the assessment calls for parallel forms of the performance-assessment (Forms A, B, C, and D), comparability may be difficult to achieve. For example, on Form A students may be asked to formulate opinions about an issue raised in a report on spelunking in New Mexico and on Form D they formulate opinions about issues raised in a report on increasing numbers of tourists in national parks. While on the surface these seem like similar tasks, it should not be assumed that both require the same level of higher order thinking. The critical question is whether students might have personal knowledge of one task and not the other. As Newmann (1991) suggests, higher order thinking is not the reproduction of ideas but the production of new and original thoughts on the part of the learner. If the texts for these two tasks are not equally explicit, familiar in style, or relevant to the student's prior experience, then it is possible that one task might result only in knowledge refinement while the other might require a higher level of application and extension (Marzano, 1992).

A related concern focuses on generalizability— that is, does performance on the performance-based assessment provide an accurate picture of student achievement? How well does a particular performance assessment capture the aspects and scope of literacy that we think should be assessed? These considerations are especially important because students will only respond to a limited number—in some cases, as few as one—of complex, extended performance-based tasks. Variations in performance due to difference in tasks given year to year also must be guarded against. Research suggests that there is greater variation on tasks than in raters (Shavelson & Baxter, 1992). It is not clear how the ASAP has addressed this concern or how it might deal with it in future.

Curricular considerations. Important curricular considerations may not have been adequately explored in this project. For example, the framework lists tasks, products, and processes but doesn't appear to include guidelines that pertain to content coverage. Content is defined here as both the "big ideas" in the literature and knowledge of how literature is structured. How are teachers to determine the breadth and depth of coverage? If there are content gaps on the assessments, teachers are not likely to cover what has been omitted. For example, what specifically should students know about literature? There are no outcomes or standards for literature. Literature is treated as a type of material rather than a discipline that contains ideas that must be learned, understood, and applied to the world outside school. The nature and quality of content is an important consideration (Peters, 1991).

This means the framework must be clear about content—that is, about what students are expected to know. Without a clear delineation of outcomes, the assessment activities rather than the outcomes become the focus. Clear parameters and guidelines for making decisions about the type of content associated with each product are needed. One of the criteria used for the selecting of tasks and products should be how they will advance knowledge in a systematic manner. Without depth of understanding, critical reasoning is impossible.

Process and decisions. The ASAP was developed with continual interaction among Arizona Department of Education specialists, the Riverside Publishing Company, and Arizona educators. Over time, decisions were made regarding the format and content of the test, but not all of those decisions are explained. For example, it is not clear how or if metacognition is handled in the ASAP. Similarly, the importance of prior knowledge is acknowledged in the format of the assessment but not reported to teachers. Decisions such as these have implications both for assessment and instruction. Their consequences may suggest that some decisions need to be reconsidered.

An ambitious decision to use multiple measures at the district level may create some problems. For example, it is not clear how portfolios implemented at the district level could be aligned with the language arts standards and outcomes, the curricular framework, the performance-based assessments, or the DAP. If this is an integrated system, then it must be clear how all the components are tied together by a common set of standards and outcomes. This question will need to be addressed quickly or else one component, the portfolios, may be destined to take a back seat to the others or to be lost altogether.

Supporting the Initiative

The success of a new state initiative such as this often rests on the the help and support of local professional organizations (Peters et al., 1992). Dissemination of information about both the assessment and the accompanying instructional issues also will be important to the success of this program. State leaders will want to pay special attention to communication and information about the ASAP.

In the end, we must ensure that assessment supports and does not detract from quality education. Assessment practices themselves must be accountable to criteria that force attention not only to technical issues but also to the consequences of the assessment and to students' opportunity to learn what is assessed. Changes in assessment are only part of the answer to improved instruction and learning. Schools need support to implement new instructional strategies and to institute other changes to ensure that all students can achieve the complex skills that these new assessments strive to represent. In the long run, assessment cannot be a constructive means of reform unless we invest in more educationally useful and valid measures of student learning (Darling-Hammond, 1991).

References

Brown, R.G. (1991). *Schools of thought: How the politics of literacy shape thinking in the classroom.* San Francisco, CA: Jossey-Bass.

Darling-Hammond, L. (1991). The implications of testing policy for quality and equity. *Phi Delta Kappan, 73*(3), 220-225.

Linn, R.L., Baker, E.L., & Dunbar, S.B. (1991). Complex, performance-based assessment: Expectations and validation criteria. *Educational Researcher, 20*(8), 15-21.

Marzano, R.J. (1992). *A different kind of classroom.* Alexandria, VA: Association for Supervision and Curriculum Development.

Newmann, F.M. (1991). Classroom thoughtfulness and students' higher order thinking: Common indicators and diverse social studies courses. *Theory and Research in Social Education, 19*(4), 410-433.

Peters, C.W. (1991). You can't have authentic assessment without authentic content. *The Reading Teacher, 44*(8), 590-591.

Peters, C.W., Wixson, K.K., Valencia, S.W., & Pearson, P.D. (1992). Changing statewide reading assessment: A case study of Michigan and Illinois. In B.R. Gifford (Ed.), *Policy perspectives on educational testing* (pp. 295-385). Norwell, MA: Kluwer.

Shavelson, R.J., & Baxter, G.P. (1992). What we've learned about assessing hands-on science. *Educational Leadership, 49*(8), 20-25.

Valencia, S.W. (1990). A portfolio approach to classroom reading assessment: The whys, whats, and hows. *The Reading Teacher, 43*(4), 338-340.

Valencia, S.W., Pearson, P.D., Peters, C.W., & Wixson, K.K. (1989). Theory and practice in statewide reading assessment: Closing the gap. *Educational Leadership, 46*(7), 57-63.

CHAPTER 10

Barbara A. Kapinus
Gertrude V. Collier
Hannah Kruglanski

THE MARYLAND SCHOOL PERFORMANCE ASSESSMENT PROGRAM: A NEW VIEW OF ASSESSMENT

IN MRS. BROWN'S EIGHTH GRADE CLASSROOM, student-led discussions of short stories and novels are taking place. Students bring response logs to the groups in order to begin the discussions. The logs are one means that Brown uses to encourage a range of interactions with the novels students select for themselves. The students observe and assess one another in the discussion groups. The following is an example of a student observer in conference with another student:

> Student 1: As I was watching today in discussion, I noticed that you were an active listener and when somebody

elaborated on something, I could tell if you agreed or disagreed by a little nod of your head.

Student 2: I need to work some more on agreeing or disagreeing.

Student 1: You might want to try a personal example because that's pretty easy. I think that the elaboration you gave today sort of livened up the discussion. What did you get out of the discussion today?

Student 2: I started to understand the beginning of the story better. It sort of jumps in—like, into the middle—and you can't really understand it.

Brown meets with each student at least once every two months to discuss the contents of logs, performance in discussions, and individual goals for the coming quarter. She uses summaries of peer observations of the discussions as one of several tools for assessing students' progress (the form she uses as a guide for assessment is shown in Figure 1). Along with her students, she continually considers the quality and depth of the responses to what has been read as evidenced in both discussion and log entries.

This classroom is not unusual. However, the notable aspect of all of this is that Mrs. Brown is teaching to a test, the Maryland School Performance Assessment Program (MSPAP).

What Is the MSPAP?

Administered to every third, fifth, and eighth grade student in the state, the MSPAP reports scores and background information in reading, writing, language

Figure 1
Guide for Assessing Discussion

Student's Name

(Date)

Discussion Model

Global understanding:									
Author's purpose									
Important idea or event									
Developing interpretation:									
Elaboration									
Asks for clarification									
Personal response:									
Agrees									
Disagrees									
Personal example									
Critical stance:									
Author's craft									
Technique									
Technique									
Strategies:									
Active listener									
Rereads from text									
Poses questions									
Visualizes									
Makes predictions									
Recalls prior knowledge									

Comments:

Developed by Gretchen Brownley and Monica Smith, Carroll County Schools usage, mathematics, social studies, and science. All of these domains are tapped in one assessment administered for 90 minutes each day over 5 consecutive days. The assessment focuses on broad educational outcomes adopted by that state in 1990 with the goal of attaining them by 2000. In reading, the outcomes addressed by the assessment include (1) demonstrating positive attitudes toward reading; (2) constructing, extending, and examining meaning when reading for literary experience; (3) constructing, extending, and examining meaning when reading for information; (4) constructing, extending, and examining meaning when reading to perform a task; and (5) demonstrating awareness of strategic behaviors and knowledge about reading. The second, third, and fourth outcomes are tapped by open-ended items designed to allow students to demonstrate high proficiency in these behaviors with evidence of a wide range of thinking skills. Information about the other outcomes is gathered through questions that provide background information.

The purpose of the MSPAP is to assess how well public schools educate Maryland students. The state reports performance at the district and school levels. The emphasis is on school performance, not on individual student or teacher performance. The data from the assessment—both cognitive and background information on attitudes and strategies—are used together with other school statistics such as average daily attendance, number of suspensions, teacher-pupil ratios, demographics, and activities promoting parent involvement to consider the effectiveness of schools. Thus, multiple indicators are used to determine school success.

School performance scores are reported in each of the content domains: reading, writing, language usage, mathematics, social studies, and science.

Additional data on each of the reading outcomes are available to districts and schools. Individual student data are made available to districts and schools for analysis at that level. However, individual data is not comparable across students since students receive different parts of the assessment; individuals are not compared or diagnosed for instruction based on the MSPAP scores. Schools and classroom teachers are responsible for gathering comprehensive individual student assessment data. Some districts are exploring portfolios in order to do this. At present, a consortium of representatives from the districts is working with the Maryland State Department of Education to help teachers develop district and classroom assessment activities congruent with the state outcomes and the MSPAP. Products developed by the consortium help teachers gather extended information about the performance of individual students.

The state data includes both quantitative and qualitative information. Reporting categories were developed by sorting scored items into five groups based on each item's relation to students' overall scores. Then a group of teachers, reading supervisors, and outside experts in reading analyzed these groups and the student responses and generated descriptions of student performance for each of five proficiency levels. Figure 2 gives these descriptions for reading in the third grade.

The descriptors were intended to make the results more informative to the public as well as to educators by describing what students at each of the proficiency levels could do. State and school proficiency levels were reported in terms of the percentage of students in each band. The following chart gives an example from the 1991 report:

Reading	Level 1	Level 2	Level 3	Level 4	Level 5
Grade 3	0.2%	2.1%	25.0%	34.9%	37.8%
Grade 5	0.6%	3.1%	24.4%	31.7%	40.1%
Grade 8	1.2%	4.0%	22.4%	33.3%	39.2%

The data are released with accompanying guidelines about appropriate uses of scores, and districts are trusted to exercise responsibility in this area. For example, the results above were published with a caution that the state outcomes adopted in 1990 were a goal for 2000. Therefore, local curriculum and instruction could not yet have been adjusted to reflect the outcomes, nor would we expect 1991 scores to reflect attainment of the goals.

What Does the Assessment Look Like?

The assessment focuses on broad-based cognitive, educational outcomes in each of the content areas assessed. Traditional large-scale assessments have used items organized around subskills and snippets of contrived text to measure reading. The Maryland assessment uses naturally occurring, unedited texts and focuses on tasks that readers are likely to address both in and out of the classroom. The activities or questions in the tasks reflect real-life reading by involving the use of several reading strategies in considering important aspects of texts.

The reading material used for assessment includes stories, poems, articles, directions, and chapters from trade books. We seek passages that are engaging, rich, thought-provoking, and linked to other test passages about similar topics. Materials for the student tasks, including maps, charts, and directions for hands-on science, are integrated around themes such as the importance of rain forests, communicating with friends,

Figure 2
1991 MSPAP Proficiency Levels: Grade Three Reading

Students at a particular MSPAP proficiency level are likely to be able to display most of the knowledge, skills, and processes at that level and at lower proficiency levels.

Level 1
Readers at Level 1 construct, extend, and examine the meaning of third-grade–appropriate texts by:
- building a complex understanding of the text;
- making judgments, connections, and extensions of the text that are substantially supported;
- explicitly connecting personal experience to the text and providing substantial text support for the connections;
- making extensive inferences about the author's craft and purpose with substantial text support.

Level 2
Readers at Level 2 construct, extend, and examine meaning of third-grade–appropriate texts by:
- building an extended understanding of the text;
- making connections and extensions of text with adequate text support;
- making logical judgments of the text with some text support;
- identifying elements of the author's style;
- making inferences about the author's craft and purpose with limited text support.

Level 3
Readers at Level 3 construct, extend, and examine meaning of third-grade–appropriate texts by:
- building an adequate understanding of the text;
- providing connections of ideas or information when given a structure for responding;
- making relevant inferences with some text support;
- relating personal experience to the text with some explicit text support.

Level 4
Readers at Level 4 construct, extend, and examine meaning of third-grade–appropriate texts by:
- building some understanding of the text;
- making limited, relevant inferences with implied text support;
- providing some relevant text information to support inferences that are provided in the assessment task;
- making logical judgments of the text with little or no text support;
- providing examples of elements of the author's craft.

Level 5
Readers at Level 5 are likely to have provided some responses to assessment activities at Level 4 but not on enough activities to place them at proficiency Level 4.

energy-conservation problems, and struggles for survival. In addition, we have begun exploring students' responses to the complex directions for mathematics, science, and social studies tasks as possible sources of scores for the reading outcome "reading to perform a task."

The implementation design of the assessment randomly assigns students at each of the three grade levels to one of three different clusters of assessment activities. When the activities from the clusters are pooled, they reflect all the outcomes to be assessed in all the domains. Each cluster contains activities from each of the six domains but does not sample the whole domain. Thus, while no one student takes the entire assessment, the entire assessment is administered in each school so that a complete profile of how well a school program addresses all the learning outcomes can be reported.

A student responds to thematically related activities in a cluster of tasks. Tasks in a typical cluster include both integrated combinations of content areas—such as reading, writing, and social studies— and specific content activities—such as those exclusive to math or science. Each student receives some activities for each of the content areas assessed, but the activities tap different aspects of the content. Thus, one student might have the outcome "reading to be informed" as the reading component and economics as the social studies component, while another student might have "reading for literary experience" and geography as part of social studies.

Examples of Assessment Activities

An example of an integrated activity is a fifth grade task on snowy regions. It includes a passage about the characteristics of such regions, a narrative that dramatizes the importance of snow to a village in China, questions about the readings and how they are related, map activities, and writing activities. Some questions are scored to yield evidence of both reading proficiency and understanding of social studies concepts. For example, to answer the question "If Yu-ling lived where you do, would her feelings about snow be the same as they are in the story? Explain your answer," students not only need to use information from the story but also information about geography and their own communities—that is, social studies information.

In one cluster of activities, students choose a story from three or four possibilities and answer generic questions on the story selected. The questions are carefully crafted so students can give rich answers after reading any of the stories. For example, students might be asked to pick a character and tell how that character is similar to someone they know or have read about, or they might be asked to produce a story map or summary. Both questions could be applied to many different stories. The writing prompt administered with this type of literature-choice task asks students to write a story, poem, or play about a topic of their choice to be included in an anthology for the class.

Some of the reading questions also are scored to provide information about language usage. This approach to scoring is a result of the Maryland State Board of Education requirement that separate scores be reported for language usage and for writing. In order to gather enough information to provide a reliable score without using multiple-choice items, the committee of teachers and supervisors guiding the assessment development decided to use some of the longer written responses to reading questions as evidence of students' ability to use language in context. Some questions contain a cue telling students to "check the spelling, capitalization, punctuation, and grammar" of their written responses. These items are scored twice, each time by different scorers using separate scoring guides for reading and language usage. Thus, the items are scored for both reading and writing, but each is treated as a separate domain.

The following is an example of an activity based on Lynne Cherry's *The Great Kapok Tree* that is scored for reading and language usage:

> At the end of the story, the man did not cut down the tree. Pretend you are the man. Write a note to your boss explaining why you won't cut down the tree. Use information from the story in your explanation. Because your note will be read by your boss, be sure it is clear and complete. Also, check for correct spelling, grammar, punctuation, and capitalization.

The scoring guides for this sort of item are carefully designed to ensure that the aspects of writing do not contaminate or influence the reading score, and vice versa. If a student has written the correct answer to a reading question but the answer is poorly constructed (incomplete sentences, incorrect grammar, and so on) the student can receive full credit for the reading response but would not get a high score in aspects of writing. The teachers scoring for reading become adept at reading invented spelling and looking past the mechanics of the writing for evidence of making and extending the meaning of what was read.

In addition to tapping the cognitive outcomes ("Reading for literary experience," and so on), the assessment includes items that tap students' attitudes and the metacognitive strategies they use for constructing meaning in both reading and writing. The following is an example:

When you read a story such as *The Great Kapok Tree*, you may come to a part that you don't understand. Put a check mark in front of each thing below that tells what you might do. You may choose as many as you want. If you do something that is not listed, write it on the line next to the word "other."

Sometimes I:

_____ keep reading and then come back to that part.

_____ skip over the part that is confusing.

_____ ask someone about the part that is confusing.

_____ try to sound out new words.

_____ use a dictionary.

_____ other: _____

The assessment taps writing proficiency through the use of long activities (90 minutes) that allow for the use of the steps in the writing process: prewriting, drafting, peer response, revision, and editing. Some of the prompts require students to gather information from a passage used for reading assessment; these prompts can be scored for reading as well as writing. As with the items scored for language usage and reading, there are separate scoring guides for these reading-related writing prompts, and scoring is completed by different scorers for reading and writing. The following is an example of an extended writing prompt scored for reading as well as writing. It is administered after reading activities based on *The Great Kapok Tree* and a magazine article on rain forests.

Pretend you are a member of the Save the Environment Club at your school. The club has been reading and discussing how important the rain forests are to our environment. The principal has asked you to present a talk at the next parents' meeting informing the parents about why everyone should be concerned with what is happening to the rain forests. So that you will remember to include important details, your principal has asked you to write out your talk first. Use information from your reading to help prepare the talk.

All the items on the assessment are open-ended. Some of the reading items give students a choice of drawing a picture or writing in response to a question. We are finding that students do an excellent job of using drawing to show how they have constructed and extended the meaning of what they read. Some items ask students to organize information using whatever method they choose: flow chart or web, outline, diagram, or other relevant means. (Figure 3 gives an example of one such response.) These items are scored using the same scoring guides that are applied to the written responses for evidence of constructing, extending, and examining meaning. They provide alternative response formats and lessen the emphasis on students' writing fluency. They also reflect the types of activities that students do in response to reading in their classrooms and in the world outside of school.

Building Background for the Assessment Tasks

All tasks begin with preassessment activities designed to activate prior knowledge or fill in gaps in background experience. The tasks do not assess prior knowledge but do try to activate it. While the choice of topics for assessment activities is guided by efforts to avoid areas that would provide either an advantage or disadvantage for students from specific cultural or socioeconomic backgrounds, there is no way to ensure that all students have comparable background information related to assessment tasks. The preassessment activities can at least provide some leveling of background knowledge by focusing students' ideas and providing passage-relevant information to all students. Many of the preassessment activities involve coopera-

Figure 3
Flexibility of Response Formats

In the chart on page 64, check the box for the story you read. In the story you read, identify four story elements: main character(s), setting, problem, and resolution. You can do this by creating a story map, writing a summary, or drawing a picture. If you draw a picture, be sure to label each story element.

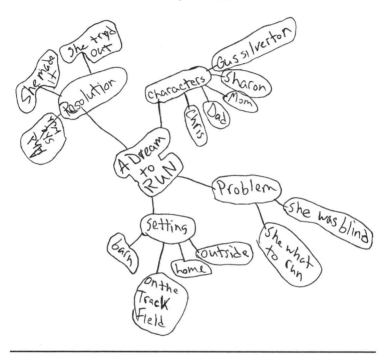

tive or collaborative work in small groups; sharing with peers helps provide motivation for engaging in the assessment tasks. Here is an example of a preassessment activity:

The teacher says, "Does anyone know the term *rain forest*? Write on your paper several words you think might describe a rain forest." Allow one minute for this activity. The teacher then says, "Now turn to your partner and share your list." Allow another two minutes for this activity. Now the teacher says, "Let's share some of the words or phrases that you associate with a rain forest." List students' responses on the chalkboard. Allow no more than three minutes for this activity.

Reading items are developed employing the taxonomy used for the 1992 National Assessment of Educational Progress (NAEP), which was based on Langer (1989, 1990). The taxonomy includes four general types of reading activities: (1) a global understanding or general idea of the text; (2) an interpretation of the text through connections and extensions; (3) a personal response to the text that explicitly relates background knowledge and experiences to the text; and (4) a critical stance and a consideration of how the text was crafted. In the first year of the assessment, items were written to tap a single type of response. For example, a question on the theme of a story was intended to tap global understanding of the passage. However, as we recognized that proficient readers spontaneously move through several types of interaction when responding to text, we decided to develop items that allowed students to consider the text from several perspectives, as in the following example:

> Your teacher plans to use the story The Great Kapok Tree and the article "Paradise Lost" with her class next year. Because she wants to be sure her students understand the importance of rain forests, she asks you to help decide which one of these selections the class should read first. She also wants to know the reasons for your choice. To be sure she doesn't forget, she asks you to write down your answer and to use information from both the story and the article to support your advice.

To answer this question thoroughly, students need to consider what each text is about in general, specific ideas in the texts, how the texts are written, and their own personal responses to the texts.

How Is the Assessment Scored?

Scoring has provided us with insight into the characteristics of good items. Small groups of teachers and supervisors, including members of the coordinating committee, were asked to review and revise the scoring guides and choose anchor papers for each question that demonstrated responses at each of the five proficiency levels. These became the training materials for those teachers who were hired to score the assessment during the summer.

As mentioned earlier, in addition to items scored for both reading and writing, some items are also scored for reading and social studies or reading and science. Some of these items have separate scoring guides, but where evidence of proficiency is the same for both reading and the content area, one scoring guide is used for both areas. As we look at students' performance across items on all the content areas, we are beginning to see more and more overlap in the characteristics of good responses: extensions of ideas through inferences and connections; thoroughness; adequate, clear support for answers; and complexity in perceptions. The double scoring of certain items emphasizes for teachers and students the interrelatedness of reading and other content areas.

The analysis of assessment results for 1991 led us to revise our scoring guides so they would be more congruent with what we observed and hoped to report. We began to see the need for a general scoring guide that could be applied to all reading questions for all grade levels (see Figure 4). The guide can be applied partially to questions that evoke limited responses. For example, a question might only be worth three points,

Figure 4
Generic Rubric for Reading Activities

Note: The scoring criteria are applied as cued for or required by the activity. Not every activity cues for all the possible behaviors described in the generic rubric. Thus, the scoring guide for specific activities can stop at different points. For some activities, the scale will shift downwards by one point. It is possible in some instances for this rubric to be applied across more than one activity in a task, in which case the scorer would determine which score point description generally characterizes the responses being considered.

0 = No evidence of construction of meaning.

1 = Some evidence of construction of meaning, building some understanding of the text. Presence of defensible, and possibly some indefensible, information.

2 = A superficial understanding of the text, with evidence of meaning construction. One or two relevant but unsupported inferences.

3 = A developed understanding of the text with evidence of connections, extensions, or examinations of the meaning. Connections among the reader's ideas and the text itself are implied. Extensions and examinations are related to the text but explicit references to the text in support of inferences are not present. When more than one stance is possible, the response may remain limited to one stance.

4 = A developed understanding of the text with evidence of connections, extensions, and examinations of meaning. Connections among the reader's ideas and the text itself are explicit. Extensions and examinations are accompanied by explicit references to the text in support of inferences. When possible, the response indicates more than one stance or perspective on the text; however, only one stance is substantially supported by references to the text.

5 = A developed understanding of the text with evidence of connections, extensions, examinations of meaning and defense of interpretations. Connections among the reader's ideas and the text itself are explicit. Extensions and examinations are accompanied by explicit references to the text in support of inferences. When possible, the response indicates more than two stances, all substantially supported by references to the text.

6 = A complex, developed understanding of the text with evidence of connections, extensions, examinations of meaning, and defense of interpretations. Connections among the reader's ideas and the text itself are explicit. Extensions and examinations are accompanied by explicit references to the text in support of inferences. Responses indicate as many stances as possible based on the activity, all substantially supported by references to the text. These responses reflect careful thought and thoroughness.

Codes : A, blank—there is no response.
B, the writer's response is off task or off topic. It does not address the question that was asked.
C, unscorable—the writer's response cannot be read (e.g., it is illegible, incomprehensible)
D, copied from test text.

so the guide would be applied up to the three-point level. These generic guides are also more useful for classroom teachers than the earlier guides that differed with each question.

How Is the MSPAP Evolving?

A coordinating committee of selected reading and language arts supervisors developed the outcomes statement, design, models, and specifications for the first assessment that was administered in May 1991. For the 1992 assessment, classroom teachers, including representatives from special education and vocational education, joined the committee to work on the revision and expansion of the assessment. The actual assessment activities were developed by teachers from all 24 school districts in the state. Each district was invited to send three reading teachers, one for each grade level assessed, to one of four regional assessment-development workshops. Three teachers were sent for each of the other content areas addressed by the assessment.

Teachers working on the development of items were given sample tasks, directions about what types of questions work for tapping the outcomes to be measured, and characteristics of performance assessments. For example, as part of the training, teachers distinguish between questions that require students to use information from the text and those that can be answered solely on the basis of background knowledge. Similarly, although it is desirable to know whether students liked or would recommend a story, question that generate answers such as "Yes," "No," or "My friends don't like to read about animals" do not provide evidence of constructing meaning, an outcome evaluated in the reading assessment. By asking students to explain their opinions using information from the text they read, an item can provide evidence of whether students have understood or interpreted what they read.

Teachers were given sets of possible passages organized around themes to help them develop the assessment tasks. These included stories, poems, articles, trade books, and directions. At times, the teachers supplied additional, richer passages from their own resources. As a guideline for generating tasks, the teachers were asked to think about the ideas and characteristics in the passages that they would want to consider or discuss if they were going to talk about them with someone.

After items were drafted by the representative group of teachers, they were reviewed by separate committees, also consisting of teachers and reading or language arts supervisors from local systems. These committees were responsible for checking possible item and passage bias, determining whether items could be scored reliably, confirming that there were sufficient items to measure each content area, and reviewing the overall range of thinking activities and performance characteristics of the tasks. Items identified as problematic were then revised by a smaller group of available, highly capable teachers from the original pool of item writers. This group also represented the range of communities in the state.

In addition to developing assessment tasks, teachers have other significant roles in the MSPAP. They work on developing scoring guides, select anchor papers for the scoring process, and score items. When the preliminary data for the 1991 assessment were released, teachers played a significant role in the press conference explaining the connections between the assessment and what they were doing in their classrooms.

What Were Our Major Challenges?

We found that the task developers sometimes had difficulty avoiding the use of the very literal questions they were accustomed to encountering in published materials. An additional challenge was avoiding multiple questions that tapped the same information from the text. Finally, writing questions that provided clear support for students' performances and could be scored for evidence of reading outcomes sometimes proved a greater challenge than expected. Questions had to be worded carefully to provide cues, elicit rich responses, and help students understand what was expected without constraining creativity. For example, directing students to "use information from the story to explain your answer" let them know that a text-based response was required.

The total time for the development of the first assessment after the outcomes had been articulated was less than one year. Developing the MSPAP on this "fast track" was difficult (committee members jokingly said we were building an airplane while it was already in flight), but this problem appears similar to those faced by new assessment efforts in other states. There were two choices: to keep the old, norm-referenced instruments as the major assessment tools while development proceeded slowly, or to pull out all the stops and move forward with a new performance assessment. The latter promised more support for dramatic and earlier school improvement by showing existing gaps in school performance.

Is the Program a Success?

As of the time of writing, there is not yet enough evidence to determine whether the assessment has had a positive effect on the performance of schools. The

1992 MSPAP data are being used as a baseline to determine future progress. However, there are signs that the assessment is promoting teachers' growth. The processes of item development and scoring are viewed by teachers as valuable professional-development activities that provide them with an opportunity to examine issues, beliefs, and practices related to reading. The following are comments from teachers written after the first development sessions: "This workshop was intellectually stimulating. I learned how to evaluate my questions much more critically. I hope to be able to share some of my knowledge with others in my county" and "I thoroughly enjoyed this experience. I feel much more secure in my ability to teach and to prepare my students not only for this test, but for employing a higher level of thinking in their total development." These responses suggest that even the assessment-development process has had a positive impact on instruction.

The scoring workshops also gave teachers insight. They came to recognize what types of questions evoked thoughtful, thorough, and creative responses. They also realized how important it is for students to be able to justify their inferences and evaluations and how infrequently they do so, both on the assessment and in their classrooms.

The format of the assessment, with longer texts and open-ended questions, is having an effect on instructional activities. The student observation sheet in Figure 1 was developed by teachers after they learned about the design of the assessment. For some teachers, the MSPAP reinforced the importance of students developing their own responses to reading. Discussion led by students is one approach that allows students to generate and revise their understanding of what they read. The use of response logs is another approach that supports students' performance on the assessment—or, from a different perspective, it is an activity that is now promoted by the assessment. Letters and calls from teachers and principals indicate that the assessment format has provided support for teachers already using these approaches and has led others to try them.

Where Do We Hope to Go Next?

As we have worked on developing tasks for the assessment and analyzing students' responses to them, we have become aware of a need to increase the richness of the tasks so students can demonstrate complex thinking spontaneously. We continue to find questions on the early drafts of the assessment that we recognize as shallow or silly when we take a second, third, or fourth look at them. But we are improving. We continually ask ourselves questions about what really is an authentic task for third, fifth, and eighth graders.

We are finding that our items are more likely to evoke rich responses and engage students' interest when we integrate reading assessment tasks with tasks from other content areas. In addition, the authenticity and cohesiveness of the reading assessment tasks are enhanced as a result of integration with other subjects. We would like to increase that integration in the future, making the connections among different content activities smoother. Focusing on solving real-life problems could make future assessment tasks more authentic and engaging. This type of focus could also help teachers who are developing the assessment design tasks that are rich, relevant, and interrelated. We want to keep moving our assessment toward the goal of allowing students to show us how well they can use reading as a tool for life, both in the classroom and in the world outside school.

References

Langer, J.A. (1989). *The process of understanding literature* (Tech. Rep. No. 2.1). Albany, NY: State University of New York, Center for the Learning and Teaching of Literature.

Langer, J.A. (1990). The process of understanding: Reading for literary and informative purposes. *Research in the Teaching of English*, 24(3), 229-257.

Karen K. Wixson

COMMENTARY ON   *The Maryland School Performance Assessment Program*: A New View of Assessment

THE MARYLAND SCHOOL PERFORMANCE ASSESSMENT PROGRAM (MSPAP) is a statewide assessment designed to determine the effectiveness of public school education in Maryland. This type of measure is often referred to as a "high-stakes" assessment, because it serves as a means of holding teachers, administrators, and school boards accountable for student achievement. The consequences of high-stakes assessment often go well beyond those intended by their originators. For example, an assessment may pose questions to determine students' knowledge about different skills and strategies such as the way texts are organized or what constitutes a good summary. In a high-stakes environment, an unintended consequence of such questions may be what we referred to in Michigan as "silly coaching"— that is, instruction that may raise test scores because students are better able to answer certain questions but which is unlikely to promote learning that transfers to authentic reading and writing situations.

The possibility of unintended consequences highlights the importance of examining other areas of concern in addition to the test itself when evaluating new test-development efforts. These areas include the outcomes on which the assessment is based, the process of test development, the assessment tasks, test validation, the scoring and reporting of test data, and related professional-development opportunities. A brief discussion of each of these areas, both generally and in the context of the MSPAP, follows.

Outcomes

Assessment removed from the context of well-developed student outcomes has little meaning. Yet for years, high-stakes tests have been developed in the absence of clearly stated outcomes or with outcomes that do not reflect current theory and research within a given subject area. It is also important to recognize that even within a current theoretical perspective, outcomes may vary in ways that lead to major differences in assessment. For example, student outcomes developed within the context of a constructivist view of reading may or may not attend to areas such as use of technology or appreciation of English language and literature within society. Assessments of these outcomes will, of necessity, differ as a function of the inclusion or exclusion of outcomes in these areas.

The reading portion of the MSPAP is based on five reading outcomes. From the information provided, the assessment appears to address all five directly. These outcomes reflect current views of reading but do not extend to other related areas such as self-assessment or appreciation of the cultural diversity embodied in various texts and linguistic communities. It is also important to note that there are separate outcomes for reading, writing, and language usage, rather than a set of integrated outcomes for literacy or language arts. Separate outcomes are likely to result in separate areas of instruction. This tendency may be mitigated, however, by the fact that the MSPAP assesses these areas in an integrated fashion along with science and social studies. A single assessment that yields scores in these separate areas is certainly more likely to promote integrated instruction than would separate assessments.

Test-Development Process

The test-development process is important in high-stakes assessments that are designed to improve instructional practice. As we learned in our efforts to develop new reading assessments in Michigan and Illinois (Peters et al., 1992), the process can elicit a variety of responses ranging from ownership among the consumers of the assessment to alienation of those for whom it is intended.

The MSPAP appears to have an excellent test-development process. Large numbers of Local Educational Agency (LEA) personnel were involved in both development and scoring of assessment tasks. These types of collaborative efforts build support for the assessment, and serve as a means of professional development for those involved. There is also a recognition among the test developers that the process is one of continuous revision and refinement and that there is a need to provide for ongoing development activities. This is absolutely essential if an assessment program is to keep pace with rapid developments both in the subject areas and in the field of assessment itself.

Assessment Tasks

The nature of the assessment tasks is extremely important in high-stakes tests because the tasks are likely to serve as models for instruction designed to improve student performance. This puts a tremendous burden on the assessment tasks to be generalizable to the broader domain of achievement. As noted by Greeno (1989), performance is highly task-dependent; research in learning and cognition emphasizing the context-specific nature of thinking suggests that there will be limited generalizability from task to task. The task-specific nature of student performance also raises questions of fairness for those who may have different educational backgrounds. Until there is some type of assessment of our educational institutions, we can never be certain that all students have had the opportunity to engage in the types of activities included on newer performance-based assessments.

From the information provided, it appears that the reading tasks in the MSPAP are consistent with what is considered to be good instructional practice. It is less clear, however, how well the collection of tasks represents the domain of reading. Of great concern is the possibility that individual student scores will be based on performance on a small subset of items. Such scores require evidence of the generalizability of tasks to the larger domains of reading and writing, and of their fairness with regard to students of differing cultural and linguistic backgrounds.

Scoring and Reporting

Methods of scoring and reporting are important to consider because stakeholders attend carefully to "what counts." If the intention is to promote certain instructional practices through the use of particular tasks, then those tasks must carry weight in the final scoring and be reflected in reports of the results. For example, a task calling for a personal response to literature might be included in an assessment as a guide to instruction but left unscored and unreported. This could result in a lack of instructional attention to this task on the part of the test consumer. Conversely, it is also important not to overspecify test results in ways that suggest outcome-based instruction can be fragmented.

It should also be understood that the richer the tasks, the more difficult they may be to score equitably.

As noted by Linn, Baker, and Dunbar (1991), questions of fairness loom as large for performance assessment as they do for traditional assessment, and it is a mistake to assume that shifting from fixed-response standardized tests to performance-based assessments obviates concerns about biases against racial and ethnic minorities.

The MSPAP is noteworthy in its attempt to promote integrated instruction through the double scoring of items in more than one curricular area. Although it appears that not all the reporting decisions have been made, one area of concern is the possibility of obtaining individual scores based on "noncomparable" sets of items. Because students across the state will respond to different sets of texts and tasks, their scores cannot be compared. Furthermore, as noted previously, the highly task-dependent nature of performance would make it difficult to generalize from a limited set of assessment tasks to the broader domain of achievement.

Test Validation

Linn, Baker, and Dunbar (1991) suggest the need to adopt a broader view of validity in evaluating performance assessment than has been used to evaluate traditional assessment. Among the criteria suggested are generalizability, fairness, and consequences. Specifically, generalization from the specific assessment tasks to the broader domain of achievement needs to be justified. Furthermore, it cannot simply be assumed that more authentic, performance-based tasks are more equitable for students with different cultural and linguistic backgrounds. We must have evidence of this.

High priority also needs to be given to collecting evidence about the intended and unintended effects of assessments on the ways teachers and students spend their time and think about the goals of education. It should not be assumed that new assessments are immune to the factors that have led to the corruption of old tests. Evidence is needed that performance assessment has the intended positive effects without having undesirable effects at the same time.

Little evidence regarding these validation criteria have been presented relative to the MSPAP. The time and resources necessary to undertake the types of validation studies needed to meet these criteria are among the more serious issues associated with new performance-based assessments. The need for change must be tempered with the recognition that innovation must proceed slowly, or these assessments will face an entirely new, and perhaps more difficult, set of problems than those faced by more traditional assessment programs. Interpretation of evidence of the consequences of this assessment may be premature at this stage of the development process. However, plans to collect these data and the collection of baseline data are not unreasonable expectations for the future.

Professional Development

The effectiveness of high-stakes assessment is directly related to the provision of extensive opportunities for professional development. These are needed to assist LEAS in implementing practices consistent with the outcomes being assessed. Without this, the assessment can become a weapon to be used against teachers and students, rather than a support for effective instruction and learning.

Although there is an indication that Maryland districts have formed consortia to assist with professional-development activities, it is unclear if the state has taken an active role in this area. If the burden is left to the districts, this can promote inequities in learning experiences related to the activities on the assessment.

This area must be addressed at the state level on an intensive, long-term basis if the assessment is to have the intended effect on teaching and learning.

Summary

In summary, the MSPAP is a good example of the newer performance-based assessments being developed at the state level. The notable features of this assessment are the test-development process and the integrated nature of the assessment tasks. Since it is a high-stakes assessment, however, greater attention needs to be given to how the results will be reported, to state-level professional development activities, and to obtaining evidence of the validity of the assessment with regard to the areas of generalizability, fairness, and consequences. Despite these problems, the MSPAP should be recognized as an important next step in the progression toward instructionally valid large-scale assessments.

References

Greeno, J.G. (1989). A perspective on thinking. *American Psychologist*, 44(2), 134-141.

Peters, C.W., Wixson, K.K., Valencia, S.W., & Pearson, P.D. (1992). Changing statewide reading assessment: A case study of Michigan and Illinois. In B.R. Gifford (Ed.), *Policy perspectives on educational testing* (pp. 295-385). Norwell, MA: Kluwer.

Linn, R.L., Baker, E.L., & Dunbar, S.B. (1991). Complex, performance-based assessment: Expectations and validation criteria. *Educational Researcher*, 20(8), 15-21.

PART FIVE

AUTHENTIC READING ASSESSMENT, PRESENT AND FUTURE

CHAPTER 11

Sheila W. Valencia
Elfrieda H. Hiebert
Peter P. Afflerbach

REALIZING THE POSSIBILITIES OF AUTHENTIC ASSESSMENT: CURRENT TRENDS AND FUTURE ISSUES

THE PROJECTS DESCRIBED IN THIS VOLUME clearly demonstrate the complexity of developing and implementing new forms of reading assessment. From the projects oriented toward individual children and classrooms presented in Part Two to the more structured classroom-based assessments that might inform district policy in Part Three to the large-scale assessments in Part Four, all the efforts discussed represent a commitment to change. Although each project confronted a unique set of needs, constraints, and issues, the projects in each part share some similarities; those similarities are representative of the issues faced by other assessment projects at the classroom, district, and state/provincial levels.

The type of classroom-based project represented in the second section takes advantage of the renewed attention on assessment to examine instruction and learning without concern for reporting outside the classroom or for the high-stakes consequences often attached to assessment. This set of circumstances leaves participants in these projects free to experiment with assessment in a fairly unconstrained and exploratory way. The focus is on improving teaching and learning, and assessment is the vehicle that directs those efforts.

The classroom-based assessments exemplified by the cases in the third section attempt to address some aspects of accountability and reporting. These projects try to balance the systematic information needed for accountability with the flexibility and sensitivity necessary to meet individual students' needs in classroom contexts. In many ways projects of this type are the most difficult and complex to implement. Rather than being encouraged to explore and adapt a new assessment concept in their classrooms or simply to administer an on-demand task, the teachers involved in these projects are asked to use some prespecified assessments that are not necessarily part of their regular repertoires. For example, although teachers may be experienced in taking notes on students' oral reading or home reading, the need to share running records or home reading logs may require a change in classroom routines and teachers' record-keeping strategies.

Finally, large-scale assessments such as those described in the fourth section have to contend with the development and implementation of authentic, on-demand tasks that can be administered to thousands of students and scored and reported accurately, effectively, and efficiently. Interestingly, all three projects described in Part Four acknowledge the importance of classroom-based information and suggest that in the future it be used along with large-scale–test results. Although the projects reported in this section are not yet high stakes, there is little doubt that they will soon have powerful consequences associated with them. Assessments such as these are attempting to ensure the trustworthiness needed for high-stakes decisions, while at the same time trying to implement more authentic reading assessments and use multiple indicators of students' abilities.

Looking across the nine cases and responses, the differences do become clear—various audiences, uses, constraints, and expectations serve to circumscribe each of the assessments. However, it becomes equally clear that there are important common trends in authentic reading assessment across the projects. In this chapter we look across the projects and commentaries, and at our own investigations of other assessment efforts, to present a summary of current trends in reading assessment and the issues educators will face as the new generation of assessment grows and matures.

Current Trends

In our overview in Chapter 1, we noted that the authentic assessment movement has highlighted changes in three fundamental aspects of assessment: (1) the nature of the assessment tasks and contexts, (2) the active engagement of teachers and students in the assessment process, and (3) the needs of various assessment audiences (policymakers, administrators, and classroom teachers, for example). The case studies in this volume differ in their emphases and forms, but these three features are addressed in one way or another in all of them. The progress that the new generation of assessments has made can be seen in relation to these three aspects.

Assessment Tasks and Contexts

All the new reading assessments include activities intended to be more relevant and meaningful—more authentic—for students. The use of longer, more naturally occurring texts is now standard in reading tests and on-demand tasks. In some cases, students are even asked to read and respond to multiple texts on the same topic. The questions students answer and the tasks they are asked to complete are, for the most part, more complex, realistic, and appropriate for the text and the students (Mitchell, 1992). Reading and writing are generally integrated.

In classroom-based efforts such as portfolios, the reading texts and tasks are assumed to have the same improved characteristics because they come directly from actual classrooms where high-quality literacy interactions occur. Although this is a logical assumption, it is not always well founded. For example, the selections that students summarize may not be high-quality texts; the questions they answer may require only superficial, fill-in-the-blank types of responses. Embedding assessment in the classroom doesn't guarantee high-quality literacy texts and tasks.

The context of assessment has also changed from the solitary, one-hour, booklet-and-answer-sheet setting to a more natural and realistic context in which students work over a longer period, often in collaboration with peers. The assessment is often embedded in the classroom context, either by drawing assessment information directly from the classroom or by making the assessment task resemble actual classroom activities. Even when the assessments are more like the on-demand tasks of district tools or state/provincial assessments, students are often engaged in some social interaction or discussion about the tasks with peers or with teachers that simulates typical classroom situations.

Most new assessment efforts emphasize the link among curriculum, instruction, and assessment (Calfee & Hiebert, 1991). Instead of simply hoping that the assessment will overlap with the curriculum—as has happened in the past—assessments are being designed to tap specific outcomes or goals. This beginning with outcomes rather than the "test" has caused many provinces, states, districts, and classroom teachers to reexamine their literacy goals for children. By all reports, this process of identifying critical goals is central to the process of developing authentic assessments.

Engagement of Teachers and Students

One of the most prevalent trends in authentic assessment is the recognition that if assessments are to have a positive effect on teaching and learning, then teachers and students must have a role in developing, interpreting, and using them. Perhaps this is best manifested in the numerous portfolio projects underway. Portfolios seem to have enormous appeal to teachers, students, and parents, most likely because they encourage active participation in the assessment process and provide tangible and understandable evidence (Valencia, 1990). In addition, portfolios have the advantage of encouraging self-reflection and examination of growth over time, aspects of learning rarely captured in standardized tests or even in the newer once-a-year performance tasks.

Another trend that promotes involvement is having teachers develop and score some of the new assessments. The past model in which test companies assumed sole responsibility for these aspects of assessment has been replaced with local or statewide discussion of goals, development of tasks consistent with good instructional practice by teams of teachers, classroom administration, and scoring of students' work. Along with this model has come the understanding that assessment development is a long-term professional-development process that requires a deep understanding of literacy learning and instruction. Because authentic assessment encourages higher levels of literacy learning and because its implementation is integrated with sound classroom practice, it has a more profound and complicated impact on instruction. It becomes more difficult simply to coach students for the assessments or to add another week of instruction on particular topics so students will do well on the test. There is an understanding that helping teachers and students prepare for authentic assessment requires a reexamination of instruction, a process of continual work requiring constant support.

Needs and Interests of Various Audiences

A major trend in new assessment projects is the attempt to explicitly and systematically address and reduce the tensions among different assessment audiences. Most of the new large-scale and districtwide assessment projects advocate the use of classroom-based assessment alongside other measures. The phrase "multiple indicators" captures a goal of many of these projects: to combine on-demand performance assessments and classroom-based assessments. Even when on-demand tasks are to be administered to large numbers of students, the recommendation is to supplement the resulting data on achievement with classroom-based information to yield a more accurate picture for all audiences (Resnick & Resnick, 1992). However, although multiple indicators may be the espoused goal of many, few projects have initiated attempts to realize this goal. All these projects highlight the value of teacher involvement in the development and evaluation of new assessments. One implication is that the classroom-assessment link can be strengthened by relying on teachers' knowledge of students, curriculum, and instruction in designing the assessments. Similar connections are fostered when teachers examine, use, and score students' work. Whether teachers are working alongside students on portfolios, examining students' work with a group of colleagues, or scoring large-scale assessments, they are gaining first-hand understanding of how classroom curriculum and instruction are linked to the focus of the assessment and to student performance.

Future Issues

The authors of the commentaries, and even the chapter authors themselves, raise unresolved issues and concerns for the future of authentic reading assessment. In some cases, the issues are simply a reflection of the short period this movement has been with us. We need time to examine the intended and unintended effects, study implementation issues, and determine the feasibility of new assessments in terms of time and money. Some of these issues cannot be studied until assessments are in place for a significant period of time. This is particularly true for portfolio assessment, which must be well established in a classroom before its effectiveness as an assessment tool can be determined. All anecdotal evidence thus far suggests that this process may well take several years.

In other cases, the issues raised suggest that we need to collect data immediately, before assessments are put into place and before they are ascribed high stakes. Issues such as the content and nature of the

assessment, fairness, quality, and psychometric characteristics need to be addressed immediately. Although
considerable strides have been made in the areas of
tasks and contexts, engagement of teachers and students, and needs of different audiences, these areas
still pose certain challenges. We highlight some of
these issues for future consideration.

Assessment Tasks and Contexts

As the cases in this book demonstrate, there
have been major changes in the content and format of
assessment tasks and strategies. While these are
important steps, it would be a mistake to assume that
simply having students read longer texts, provide written answers to questions, or collect work in folders constitutes better and more authentic assessment. For
example, it is easy to imagine that reading and analyzing a Shakespearean sonnet or an O. Henry short story
could be an authentic and cognitively complex task or,
conversely, that reading a lengthy piece on the Ice Age
and writing down the five most important facts could be
quite inauthentic and cognitively limited. Similarly, we
have seen "portfolios" containing nothing but fill-in-
the-blank–type worksheets, work copied from the chalkboard, handwriting exercises, and tests that would not
qualify as more authentic or "better" than traditional
standardized tests. We need to *ensure* that future assessments capture high-level literacy outcomes and not
simply assume that new or longer is better (Shavelson,
Baxter, & Pine, 1992).

Judging the quality of new assessments also
raises the issue of whose notion of authenticity is valued. Some educators are concerned that authenticity
has been equated with functional literacy or something
akin to the "life skills" curriculum popular in the 1960s.
They are concerned that the term might signal an anti-

intellectual or anti-academic definition of worthwhile learning and tasks. For example, some might judge reading about bicycle safety and creating a poster as more authentic than conducting research and writing a paper on the Wright brothers' first airplane. But the questions "What is authentic?" and "Who is to judge authenticity?" must be asked.

Similarly, questions of the value, relevance, and authenticity of the assessments are inextricably linked to the value, relevance, and authenticity of the outcomes or goals of the curriculum. Are all curricula equally strong? Should goals selected by students or teachers be the basis for assessment, or should all students have a core of common goals? Of course, if outcomes or goals are absent, vague, or superficial, the link among assessment, curriculum, and instruction is lost and the validity of the assessment becomes suspect. In other words, it would be difficult to know what the assessment should assess and if it is doing so effectively. The point here is twofold: first, if new assessments are intended to tap higher level literacies, then we must examine the quality of both the assessments themselves and the outcomes they purport to assess; second, if classroom-based assessments such as portfolios and teacher self-studies are based on the unique curriculum of each classroom, then it becomes difficult, if not impossible, to look across classrooms. Furthermore, the work inside portfolios is in many ways as much of an assessment of the teacher and the instructional activities provided for a particular child than it is of that child's full range of abilities. If students have been encouraged to write spontaneous responses to texts, for example, their portfolio entries may show little growth when measured against a rubric for summaries. We need to confront these issues as we try to use artifacts from a variety of classrooms for assessment.

Another issue related to the quality of the tasks emerges because most on-demand assessments include fewer, albeit it more complex, tasks on which students can demonstrate their abilities. Many of the new assessment tasks take several days to complete. There may be multiple texts and student-written responses, but these are usually centered around a single topic or problem. It is unlikely that a student will respond to more than one task. This raises concern about whether the assessment task is representative of other literacy tasks we would expect students to be able to do. Furthermore, differences in purpose, texts, and student background may render tasks more unique than representative, making interpretation of overall reading ability difficult. We simply would not know if a student's performance on a particular task would generalize to his or her capabilities in other important aspects of literacy (Haertel, 1992; Linn, Baker, & Dunbar, 1991).

These issues of representativeness and generalizability are less problematic when matrix sampling is used. This means that many different tasks are developed and administered. Each student might complete only one or two tasks, but over all the students in the school or district, all the tasks are sampled. Under these conditions, it is possible to sample a larger portion of the types of tasks we want students to be able to do, and it is possible to get a general idea of how groups of students perform across them. Although some U.S. states use this procedure, others feel pressure to report individual student scores. In places where legislators have written a requirement for individual student scores into law, those working on authentic assessment efforts obviously have no alternative but to report these scores. When individual scores are reported, issues of representativeness and generalizability are critical. Since reporting of individual scores seems to be a trend even when additional performance indicators are encouraged, we need to establish procedures for determining if assessment tasks adequately represent individuals' development of the critical literacy abilities we value. We then need to establish guidelines for reporting and using assessment results effectively (Haertel, 1992; Linn, Baker, & Dunbar, 1991).

Engagement of Teachers and Students

The involvement of teachers and students in authentic assessment projects is gratifying. Their voices are being acknowledged and heard in ways they never were before. Up to this point, however, many of the assessment projects have been voluntary and exploratory. There have been few mandates and requirements of those not interested in or opposed to these new ideas. Many projects are still in the pilot stage; compliance is optional and stakes are low. This is a luxury enjoyed by a new idea. It is unlikely to last much longer.

The success of new assessment efforts will be determined in large part by the ways in which we help teachers learn about them and about the content and theory behind high-level literacy instruction. Every new project has acknowledged the need for long-term professional development, yet most of the rhetoric and funding is earmarked for the assessment itself. Those who have been intimately involved in new efforts have stressed that authentic assessment is as much an instructional issue as an assessment issue. This is especially critical when we examine classroom-based efforts such as portfolios. Authentic assessment requires the ongoing involvement of teachers, not simply the administration of a test or set of tasks. If we are going to succeed, attention and support must be given to instructional improvement as well as to assessment development.

Issues of equity and fairness also must be addressed (Garcia & Pearson, 1991). Classroom-based assessments are particularly sensitive to these issues because the only indicators of what a student can do are those generated in the classroom. One could imagine a student who has received marginal instruction and opportunities to learn and whose portfolio indicates no evidence of critical reading, extended writing, or personal ownership of literacy. One assumption might be that the student has not developed these abilities; another might be that he or she hasn't been provided with the classroom experiences to learn and demonstrate them; still another might be that he or she possesses all these abilities and more, but that classroom activities haven't given him or her reason to demonstrate them. The same child might have been evaluated differently had he or she been in a different classroom or if a different teacher had evaluated the work (Gipps, 1993).

Fairness and equity issues also play out in task difficulty and scoring of on-demand tasks. We've noted that one problem of many authentic assessments is the limited number of tasks to which a student responds. For students reading far below grade placement, this problem is compounded because they may not be able to respond to a significant portion of the assessment, if at all. Task difficulty is more than the reading level of the text—it is a complex combination of the text, the questions, the response mode, interest, background knowledge, and other factors. Open-ended written responses are becoming the norm, but relying solely on writing may well put some students at a disadvantage. Furthermore, unbiased answer keys must be developed and scorers must be trained to reliably evaluate answers of students from diverse backgrounds. These issues have critical implications for the fairness and equity of authentic assessment.

Needs and Interests of Various Audiences

As noted, many district and large-scale assessment programs now acknowledge the importance of using multiple indicators of students' achievement and are promoting assessment systems that use classroom information in combination with other, more standard authentic assessment. This approach marks an important change in philosophy but it has not yet been adequately tested in practice. We don't know how information from different classrooms, districts, and provinces or states can be used to create this new model of multiple indicators. There might be particular types of assessment that are more useful for assessing particular aspects of literacy or several assessments that provide complementary information about the same outcomes. What will happen when results from different types of assessment yield different, perhaps conflicting, results? Will one be given more credibility than another? Will certain types of evidence be granted high visibility while others are viewed simply as optional extras?

Experience indicates that high-stakes assessments will exert the greatest influence on instruction. Some argue that the nature of portfolios and other classroom-based assessments makes them most useful for instruction but also most problematic for high-stakes decisions. Others argue that the constraints that would have to be placed on classroom assessments to give them credibility would undermine their effectiveness. These are important considerations. Decisions about such issues will ultimately give voice to or silence new efforts. They will also determine the impact various assessments will have on teachers and children.

Summary

We are at a crossroads in assessment. Few would argue for the status quo. We now have the momentum and support of policymakers, researchers, administrators, teachers, and parents to make a change. We need to take advantage of the interest in authentic assessment to explore every way possible to improve and expand our vision of literacy assessment. It has taken decades and millions of dollars to create the assessment system we now have. It would be naive to believe that we could create an effective new system in just a few years. We need to move slowly and cautiously into these new arenas, but we must move. The alternative is to remain in an assessment environment that has not worked very well for any of us—least of all for students.

These case studies and commentaries demonstrate the knowledge, creativity, and commitment of many in our field who are struggling to make a difference. As their colleagues, we need to be their strongest supporters and their most ardent critics. Together we can create better assessments and better instructional opportunities for all students.

References

Calfee, R., & Hiebert, E.H. (1991). Classroom assessment of reading. In R. Barr, M.L. Kamil, P.B. Mosenthal, & P.D. Pearson (Eds.), *Handbook of reading research: Volume II* (pp. 281-309). White Plains, NY: Longman.

Garcia, G.E., & Pearson, P.D. (1991). The role of assessment in a diverse society. In E.H. Hiebert (Ed.), *Literacy for a diverse society: Perspectives, practices, and policies* (pp. 253-278). New York: Teachers College Press.

Gipps, C. (1993, April). *Emerging models of teacher assessment in the classroom.* Paper presented at the annual meeting of the American Educational Research Association, Atlanta, GA.

Haertel, E. (1992). Performance assessment. In M.C. Alkin (Ed.), *Encyclopedia of educational research* (6th ed.). Washington, DC: American Educational Research Association.

Linn, R.L., Baker, E.L., & Dunbar, S.B. (1991). Complex, performance-based assessment: Expectations and validation criteria. *Educational Researcher, 20,* 15-21.

Mitchell, R. (1992). *Testing for learning: How new approaches to evaluation can improve American schools.* New York: Free Press.

Resnick, L.B., & Resnick, D.L. (1992). Assessing the thinking curriculum: New tools for educational reform. In B.R. Gifford & M.C. O'Connor (Eds.), *Future assessments: Changing views of aptitude, achievement, and instruction* (pp. 37-75). Boston, MA: Kluwer.

Shavelson, R.J., Baxter, G.P., & Pine, J. (1992). Performance assessments: Political rhetoric and measurement reality. *Educational Researcher, 21,* 22-27.

Valencia, S.W. (1990). A portfolio approach to classroom reading assessment: The whys, whats, and hows. *The Reading Teacher, 43,* 338-340.

Author Index

Note: An "f" following a page number indicates that the reference may be found in a figure; an "n" that it may be found in a note.

Scott, J.A., 70
Searfoss, L.W., 184
Seda, I., 127, 133
Shavelson, R.J., 11, 21, 251, 254, 293, 300
Shepard, L.A., 7, 21
Shulman, L.S., 92, 97
Slater, W.H., 97
Slavin, R.E., 16, 21
Smith, J.K., 21
Smith, M.L., 7, 21, 106, 125
Spandel, V., 129, 130, 132
Speidel, G.E., 125
Stake, R., 50, 51, 62
Stallman, A.C., 7, 21
Stauffer, R., 178, 184
Stevenson, H.W., 45
Stewart, J.P., 109, 125
Strickland, D.S., 156
Sunstein, B., 31, 39

T

Taylor, B.M., 66, 70
Taylor, D., 38, 40
Tester, H., 17, 19
Tharp, R.G., 125
Thomas, A., 17, 19
Tibbetts, K., 112, 126
Tierney, R.J., 92, 93, 97, 138, 156
Tunnell, M.O., 104, 125
Turbill, J., 50, 62, 66, 70
Turner, J.C., 125

V

Valencia, S.W., 7, 14, 20, 21, 70, 105, 125, 130, 133, 138, 148, 156, 157, 165, 168, 184, 185, 190, 192, 219, 227, 247, 248, 254, 283, 290, 300
Vogel, M., 31, 40

W

Watson, D., 170, 177, 184
Weaver, P.A., 97
Weiler, K., 39
Whang, G., 40
Wiggins, G., 73, 88
Wilkinson, I.A.G., 70
Williams, D., 62
Wilson, P., 125
Winograd, P., 17, 19, 65, 70
Winters, L., 92, 97
Wise, A.E., 7, 20
Wixson, K.K., 185, 190, 192, 227, 254, 283
Wolf, D.P., 130, 131, 133, 139, 156, 157, 166
Wolf, K.P., 70, 160, 166
Woodward, H., 55, 62
Wurster, S.R., 17, 19

Y-Z

Yumori, W., 112, 125, 126
Zakaluk, B.L., 172, 184
Zancanella, D., 31, 40
Zessoules, R., 167, 184

SUBJECT INDEX

Note: An "f" following a page number indicates that the reference may be found in a figure.

trasted, 49; goals of, 1-2 (*see also* Outcomes, assessment-related); "high-stakes," 277, 287; importance of, 1; instruction and, 3, 10, 47, 64, 67, 86, 95-96, 136, 144, 154, 167, 185, 187-88, 191, 195, 238, 245, 248, 249, 252, 253, 272, 274, 278, 279, 290-92, 294, 296-97 (*see also* Assessment, curriculum and); of language arts progress, 58f, 59f, 197-227, 256-58, 263-64, 265, 278; literature-based, 168-69, 233 (*see also* MAP); of mathematics skills, 200, 224, 241, 258, 262; norm-referenced, 242; on-demand, 12-13, 204, 216, 223, 226, 291, 295, 297; outcome-oriented, 194-95 (*see also* Outcomes, assessment-related); performance-based, 11, 63, 220, 223, 225, 244, 245, 247, 248, 250-51, 253, 280-83; portfolio (*see* Student portfolios, assessment of); project approach to, 8; in reading (*see* Reading assessment); reflection and, 181; of science comprehension, 11, 200, 258, 262, 269, 278; "situated," 186; of social studies knowledge, 200, 258, 262, 263, 269, 278; state and 71-72, 89, 90, 93-94, 127, 193, 195, 196, 247, 273, 286, 295 (*see also* ASAP); California, assessment techniques in; MSPAP); student discussion during, 205; tacit knowledge and, 53-54; teacher-based (*see* Student portfolios, assessment of); traditional forms of, 44-45 (*see also* Standardized tests); U.S. and (*see* National Assessment of Educational Progress); in writing skills, 3, 6, 11, 12, 15, 71-72, 199-203f, 205-207, 210-12, 215, 241, 248, 256, 262-66, 269, 278,

280. *See also* Evaluation; Preassessment activities
AUDIOTAPES: MAP use of, 173-74
AUSTRALIA: literacy assessment in, 46-70
AUTHENTIC (term): vs. *alternative* (term), 11
AUTHENTIC ASSESSMENT(S): administration of (*see* Procedures, assessment); challenges of, 14-19; in classroom, 23-25, 99-102 (*see also* Student portfolios, assessment of; MAP; Responsive evaluation); of collaborative efforts, 8, 16-17; defined, 11; evaluation of, 18; goals of, 8-10; limitations on, 42; nature of, 6, 8, 10, 15, 18; of reading skills (*see* Authentic reading assessment); shortcomings of, 44; state role in, 18, 24 (*see also* Assessment, state and). *See also* Assessment; Authentic reading assessment
AUTHENTICITY (term): 293-94. *See also* *Authentic* (term)
AUTHENTIC READING ASSESSMENT: 2-4; in classroom, 287, 289, 291-92, 296, 298 (*see also* Authentic assessment, in classroom); future of, 292-99; large-scale, 193-96, 286-88, 291, 292, 298 (*see also* ASAP; California, assessment techniques in; MSPAP); state of the art in, 287-92, 299. *See also* Assessment; Authentic assessment
AUTHORS: student analysis of, 261f
AUTOBIOGRAPHY: as assessment medium, 207f, 233

B

BASAL READERS: 95, 108, 135; as MAP resource, 172

HARRIS, KAREN: 32

HAWAII: portfolio assessment in. *See* KEEP

HEADNOTES: ASAP rubric, 238, 239f

HISPANICS: of Arizona school system, 229-30

HISTORY: assessment of student knowledge of, 200

I-J

IDEAS: development of student, 58f

ILLEGIBILITY: 270f; as ASAP problem, 239

ILLINOIS: assessment techniques in, 279

ILLUSTRATIONS: as clues to unfamiliar words, 174, 232f; MAP standards for book, 172. *See also* Drawings, student

INFERENCES: reader, 261v, 269, 270f, 274

INFORMATION: reading for, 203f. *See also* Writing, informative

INSTRUCTION: assessment and, 3, 10, 47, 64, 67, 86, 95-96, 136, 144, 154, 167, 185, 187-88, 191, 195, 238, 245, 248, 249, 252, 253, 272, 274, 278, 279, 290-92, 294, 296-97; curriculum and, 290, 292, 294; "learner-centered," 43; literacy-portfolio influence on, 77; standardized tests and, 7, 99; tacit knowledge and, 54. *See also* Memorization; Seatwork; Teachers; Tests; Worksheets

INTENTS: and activities contrasted, 51

INTEREST SURVEYS: 8

INTERNATIONAL READING ASSOCIATION: and language arts guidelines, 10

INTERVIEWS: as authentic-assessment technique, 8, 58f, 60, 76, 79, 138

INTUITION: influence on assessment/evaluation of, 53-54

INVENTORIES: reading, 6, 178, 179

JOURNALS: double-entry, 208

K

KAMEHAMEHA (Haw.) ELEMENTARY EDUCATION PROGRAM: *See* KEEP

KEARNS, JANE: 35

KEEP (Kamehameha [Haw.] Elementary Education Program): 100, 103-26; commentary on, 127-33; problems of, 112-15, 118, 121, 128

KINDERGARTEN: assessment in, 109

KING, MARTIN LUTHER, JR.: 231

KNOWLEDGE: comprehension and, 223; nature of, 186; prior, 252, 257f, 266, 271; reading for, 203f (*see also* Writing, informative); tacit, 53, 54

L

"LAMENT, THE" (Chekhov): 232

LANGUAGE (means of expression): assessment of student command of, 58f, 59f, 197-227, 256-58, 263-65, 278; and communcation, 197, 219; episodic approach to teaching, 57-61, 65-66; learning and, 219; understanding of, 107f, 111f, 116, 117, 118f, 119. *See also* Sounds; Speaking; Words

LANGUAGE: (tongue): assessment mitigated by considerations, of, 229-30, 280. *See also* English; Spanish

LANGUAGE ARTS: California assessment of skill in, 197-227; guidelines for English, 10; literature-based approach to, 197-98; Native Hawaiians and (*see* KEEP); standards for, 69; state criteria for, 249. *See also* Listening; Reading; Speaking; Writing

PEERS. See Students, collaboration among; Teachers, collaboration among

PICTURES. *See* Drawings, student; Illustrations

PLAYS: student-written, 13, 263. *See also* Drama

POEMS: as ASAP resource, 233, 244; as assessment medium, 204; as MSPAP resource, 260, 272; as portfolio element, 36, 37, 151f; student analysis of, 293; student-written, 263

POLICYMAKERS, EDUCATIONAL: 222, 227; and assessment, 15-16, 288, 299; and KEEP results, 120; and standardized tests, 100; and student scores, 295. *See also* School boards

PORTFOLIOS: multidiscipline, 74; parent, 34 (*see also* Parents, and student portfolios); student (*see* Student portfolios); teacher, 29, 35-36, 41, 74 (*see also* Literacy portfolios, collaborative)

POSTERS: student-produced, 231, 236, 242f, 294

PRAGMATICS: 170

PREASSESSMENT ACTIVITIES: MSPAP-related, 266-69

PREDICTIONS: reading-based, 257. *See also* Inferences, reader

PREREADING: as ASAP element, 233-35, 242f, 244, 248

PRESENTATIONS: student, 13

PREWRITING: 265

PRIMARY LANGUAGE RECORD, THE: 17

PRINCIPALS, SCHOOL: and KEEP results, 120, 121; and MSPAP, 275; and student portfolios, 159

PROCEDURES, ASSESSMENT: 11-14

PROGRAM ACTIVITIES: 51

PROGRAM INTENTS: 51

PROJECTS, STUDENT: assessment of, 13

PROMOTION, GRADE: out of literacy-portfolio environment, 85

PROMPTS: reading/writing, 174, 200, 201, 204-206, 208-11, 222, 263, 265-66

PULLOUT PROGRAMS: 28

PUNCTUATION: ASAP focus on, 239f; as MSPAP concern, 264

Q

QUESTIONNAIRES: as portfolio element, 141, 143

QUESTIONS: answered via prior knowledge, 271; drawings as answer to, 266; encouragement of student, 58f; multiple-choice, 273; outcome-driven, 273; reading log–related, 142; student, 58f, 59f; true/false, 233

QUIZZES: comprehension, 6

R

RACE: and ASAP reading selections, 244; as assessment factor, 281

RANKING: as assessment technique, 233

READABILITY: as MAP consideration, 172

READING: assessment of (*see* Reading assessment); at-home, 100, 142, 180, 287; comprehension of, 105, 107-110f, 113, 115-19, 142 (*see also* Language, understanding of; Reading, for meaning); constructive, 219, 278; defined, 202; as dynamic, 190; enjoyment of, 58f; for meaning, 235, 258, 270f (*see also* Reading, comprehension of); nature of, 180-81, 219; oral (*see* Reading aloud); purposes of, 203f; silent, 171, 174, 189 (*see also* Sustained silent reading); sub-grade, 297; transactive, 219; voluntary, 105, 107f, 117, 118f, 119, 191; writing integrated with, 76,

SCRIBE: student as workshop, 59f

SEATWORK: dampening effect of, 86

SEEDING: as scoring technique, 238

SELF-EVALUATION: 37; goals proceeding from, 36-37; student, 14, 25, 27, 30-31, 36, 38, 41, 69, 139, 141, 149; teacher, 24

SELF-EVALUATION SLIPS: 151f

SEMANTIC MAPS: 228

SEMANTICS: 170

SENTENCES: ASAP focus on, 239f; completion of, 233, 264; comprehension of, 177, 179, 187; sequencing of, 236. *See also* Punctuation

SEQUENCING: as assessment technique, 233

SEX (gender): as ASAP reading-selection factor, 244

SHORT STORIES: as ASAP resource, 232; as MSPAP resource, 255; student analysis of, 293

SILENT READING. *See* Reading, silent

SLOS. *See* Student learning objectives

SOCIAL STUDIES: assessment of student knowledge of, 200, 258, 262, 263, 269, 278

SOUNDS: letters and, 111f, 232f

SPANISH: as Arizona tongue, 229-30

SPEAKING: assessment of, 182, 197, 248; as portfolio-relevant skill, 74. *See also* Language (means of expression)

SPECIAL EDUCATION STUDENTS: 229; ASAP and, 249; MSPAP and, 271

SPELLING: ASAP focus on, 239f; invented, 111f, 264; as MSPAP concern, 264

SSR. *See* Sustained silent reading

STANDARDIZED TESTS: 6-7, 15, 17, 86, 105-106, 108, 114, 119, 136, 161, 194, 223, 226, 248, 290, 293; abandonment of, 103, 195; as ASAP element, 229; and ASAP scoring contrasted, 241; in Australia,

48; evaluation of, 18; fairness of, 281; instruction and, 7, 99; KEEP incorporation of, 121; reading-related, 16; in Rhode Island, 73; shortcomings of, 7-8, 9, 106, 134, 135, 161, 185, 224, 249; strengths of, 224-25; teachers pro, 112; tyranny of, 99-100; writing-related, 11

STORIES: 169; as assessment medium, 204, 207f; MAP, 171-76f, 188, 189; as MSPAP resource, 260, 263, 267f, 272 (see also *Great Kapok Tree, The* [Cherry]; as portfolio element, 151f; retelling of, 80, 81, 141, 143, 150, 151f, 174, 176f, 177, 179, 187; student-written, 263 (*see also* Anthologies, of student writings). *See also* Characters; Fiction; Short stories

STONE FOX (Gardiner): 207-10

STORY MAPS: 76, 80, 263, 267f

STRATS PAC, MAP: 171, 178-82

STUDENT LEARNING OBJECTIVES (SLOS): 135-37, 139, 144, 152

STUDENT PORTFOLIOS: 223, 259, 290, 297; art-oriented, 149; ASAP-related, 240, 248, 249, 252-53; assessment of, 12, 13, 14, 17, 292-94, 296, 298 (*see also* Literacy portfolios, assessment of); literacy-oriented (*see* Literacy portfolios); reading-oriented (*see* Literacy portfolios); writing-oriented (*see* Literacy portfolios). *See also* Literacy portfolios

STUDENTS: after-school lives of, 26, 31-33 (*see also* Parents); collaboration among, 16-17, 59f, 79, 194, 205, 209, 212, 220, 222, 226, 265, 289-90 (*see also* Anthologies, of student writings; Conferences, student/student; Student writing, collaborative); ESL (English as a second language),

THESAURUS: as student resource, 111f

THINK-ALOUD PROTOCOLS: 8

TRANSCRIPTS: MAP use of, 171, 174, 179

TRIANGULATION: of evaluation-related evidence, 51

TYPEFACE: MAP standards for, 172

U-V

UNDERSTANDING: influence on assessment/evaluation of unconscious, 53-54

USAGE. *See* Language, understanding of

VALUES: influence on assessment/evaluation of personal, 54, 57, 59

VERMONT: assessment procedures in, 127, 188

VIDEOTAPES: class-produced, 13

VOCABULARY: 105, 107f, 111f, 116-19; MAP requirements re, 172; test-oriented, 169. *See also* Words

VOCATIONAL EDUCATION: MSPAP and, 271

W

WASHINGTON (state): portfolio assessment in. *See* Bellevue (Wash.) Literacy Assessment Project

WATSON, DOROTHY: 169

WEBS (diagrams): student use of, 266

WHOLE LANGUAGE THEORY: 47, 48, 50, 55, 64, 103-105, 112, 117, 119, 128, 131, 168, 169, 178

WINNIPEG, MAN.: assessment techniques in. *See* MAP

WOMEN: and mathematics, 224

WORD PROBLEMS: 75

WORDS: and meaning, 202; understanding of, 10, 105, 107f, 111f, 116-19, 173, 177, 179, 232f, 265. *See also* Capitalization; Grammar; Sentences; Spelling; Vocabulary

WORKSHEETS: 66, 95; dampening effect of, 86; as portfolio element, 151f, 293; teachers under pressure to use, 99

WORKSHOP(S): classroom as, 57, 59f, 226-27; KEEP-related, 104; MAP-related, 171; MSPAP-scoring, 274; writers', 107f, 112

WRITING: aesthetic, 203f; constructive, 219; expressive, 203f, 207f; informative, 203f, 207f, 258, 262 (*see also* Reports, informative); nature of, 219; observational, 207f; personal, 203f; persuasive, 203f, 207f, 233; process approach to, 104, 105, 117, 118f, 119; purposes of, 203f; student (*see* Student writing); transactive, 219. *See also* Authors; Books; Narration; Prewriting; Reading, writing integrated with; Revision

WRITING CONFERENCE SLIPS: 151f

WRITING FOLDERS: 8, 149

WRITING LOGS: 212